Suck Your Stomach In and Put Some Color On

Suck Your Stomach In and Put Some Color On

What Southern Mamas Tell Their Daughters That the Rest of Y'all Should Know Too

Shellie Rushing Tomlinson

Berkley Books, New York

BERKLEY BOOKS
Published by the Penguin Group
Penguin Group (USA) Inc.
375 Hudson Street, New York, New York 10014, USA
Penguin Group (Canada), 90 Eglinton Avenue East, Suite 700, Toronto, Ontario M4P 2Y3, Canada (a division of Pearson Penguin Canada Inc.) • Penguin Books Ltd., 80 Strand, London WC2R 0RL, England • Penguin Group Ireland, 25 St. Stephen's Green, Dublin 2, Ireland (a division of Penguin Books Ltd.) • Penguin Group (Australia), 250 Camberwell Road, Camberwell, Victoria 3124, Australia (a division of Pearson Australia Group Pty. Ltd.) • Penguin Books India Pvt. Ltd., 11 Community Centre, Panchsheel Park, New Delhi—110 017, India • Penguin Group (NZ), 67 Apollo Drive, Rosedale, Auckland 0632, New Zealand (a division of Pearson New Zealand Ltd.) • Penguin Books (South Africa) (Pty.) Ltd., 24 Sturdee Avenue, Rosebank, Johannesburg 2196, South Africa

Penguin Books Ltd., Registered Offices: 80 Strand, London WC2R 0RL, England

Family photos courtesy of the author's personal collection.
Cover photo by Veer.
Cover design by Sawsan Chalabi.
Text design by Tiffany Estreicher.

PUBLISHING HISTORY
Berkley trade paperback edition / May 2007

Library of Congress Cataloging-in-Publication Data

Tomlinson, Shellie Rushing.
Suck your stomach in and put some color on : what southern mamas tell their daughters that the rest of y'all should know too / Shellie Rushing Tomlinson.—Berkley trade paperback ed.
p. cm.
ISBN 978-0-425-22134-1 (pbk.)
1. Southern States—Social life and customs. 2. Louisiana—Social life and customs. 3. Mothers and daughters—Southern States. 4. Tomlinson, Shellie Rushing—Childhood and youth. 5. Tomlinson, Shellie Rushing—Family. 6. Cookery, American—Southern style. I. Title.
F209.6.T66 2008
975—dc22 2008000287

PRINTED IN THE UNITED STATES OF AMERICA

20 19 18

To all the wonderful Southern women who share my DNA (Duly Noted Abnormalities), whether by blood, by choice, or both—I love you more.

Contents

Acknowledgments

Heartfelt thanks to everyone who has played a part in seeing *Suck Your Stomach In and Put Some Color On* published. To my husband, Phil, who loves me despite the fact that I can remember the words to an age-old tune about a woman whose husband thinks he's a chicken, but I can't seem to remember to buy milk when I go to the store for—what else—milk. To Papa, Mama, Cyndie, Rhonda, Jessica, Patrick, Phillip, and Carey for being graceful when I tell more than I should, more often than you prefer. To my extended family and friends who know I'm always looking for material and talk to me anyway. To Rhonda Perry for all of the the da, da, das. To my agent, Michael Psaltis, for taking an interest in my ramblings and beating the drum for me. To my editor, Denise Silvestro, for seeing something in the proposal and for walking this newbie through the publishing process with kindness and respect. To Mike Blakeney and John Frantom for helping me get *All Things Southern* to the radio and TV each week. To the radio stations who carry my segments. To Ed Murphy and KNOE TV8 for bringing me into the family. To Kathy Spurlock for inviting me to join the *News-Star* fold. To all the porchers who listen, watch, or read *All Things Southern* and to the fine Southern Mamas who contributed their witty and wise words to this project. I only wish I could have included every letter and e-mail I collected. Many worthy submissions fell prey to space constraints. All of you are helping me follow my dreams and I love you for it, but my greatest passion and gratitude is reserved for my Lord and Savior. Thank you, Jesus.

Cynthia Darlene

Rhonda Arlene

Shellie Charlene

1

Dry It Up

What Southern Mamas Tell Their Daughters About Life, Faith, and Education (with Main-Dish Recipes Southerners Refuse to Live Without)

My mother's teenage marriage ended badly. Forty years later her second one continues to thrive. When Mama's prince and my papa—the only daddy I've ever known—brought us to live on his farm in northeast Louisiana, she was a young twenty-two-year-old with three little girls: Cynthia Darlene, Rhonda Arlene, and Shellie Charlene (that's me)—ages five, three, and two.

You did see those middle names, didn't you? That was before people fell for the whole "natural childbirth" thing. Back then, heavy meds and semiconscious deliveries were all the rage. I blame the drugs for the whole Darlene, Arlene, and Charlene thing. Either that, or Mama was hoping we'd become a famous country music act like the Mandrell Sisters. Unfortunately, my sisters were one singing sibling short of a trio (that'd be me, again). Come to think of it, Barbara and Louise were also one sis short on harmony, and her name rhymes with ours! Sorry, Irlene, but that has got to be a sign. I'm not sure what it means, but give me some time and I'll get back to you. We Southerners pride ourselves on being able to tie everything to a sign.

I don't know that for certain—the part about Irlene not being able to sing—that's just what my sisters used to say to harass me back when the highlight of our Saturday nights in the country was watching *Barbara Mandrell and the Mandrell Sisters.*

"See, Shellie!" one of them would say. "Barbara and Louise both do solos, but you don't see 'em giving Irlene one. They just flash the camera to her banging on the drums every now and again."

I said it then and I'll say it now: whatever! I loved Irlene. She seemed so happy just to be a part of it all, much as I would've enjoyed being a part of our family sing-alongs around the piano, but no—everyone always seemed to tire of singing about the time I'd join in. Coincidence? I think not. I'd like my family to know that I have managed to survive without any emotional scars from those painful experiences. Sometimes I go for months without even thinking about it.

My Southern Mama always said I could get glad in the same pants I got mad in.

Peggy Corbett
Tuba City, Arizona

It must have been quite an adjustment for Mama to leave her parents, siblings, and friends in the busy city of Natchez, Mississippi, and move to the end of a dirt road in rural Louisiana. It would be years before we'd get a phone at our little house back on Bull Run, and Mama's long-awaited mail from her family in Mississippi was delivered to her mother-in-law's house a few miles closer to the highway.

My sisters and I were intrigued by our new papa's mother, Ola Mae Rushing. Grandma Rushing was a unique individual who'd led a very interesting life. Grandma didn't have

My parents the day Papa married "us."

much formal education to speak of but she was sharp—sharp as a tack folks said. Grandma was pleased when I learned to read, but when I fell head over heels in love with the magic of words, a bond formed between the two of us unlike anything the rest of the family shared. Nothing pleased her more than finding me reading a book, and I must've made her plenty happy because I read 'em as fast as I could get 'em checked out of the bookmobile that lumbered down our country roads once a month.

I was just a little thing when Grandma surprised me with a very special gift. I'll never forget opening up the box that held a brand-new typewriter and hearing her tell me to write down my own words. In the ensuing months and years, Grandma eagerly read every word I pecked out with my two skinny forefingers. Grandma Rushing went to her grave at ninety-four, still believing I'd be a famous writer. Our dream—hers and mine—remains unrealized, but it's okay. Her gift to me was her belief in me. I wish every child could be given such a priceless treasure.

Ghost Stories and Double Beds

My sisters and I met Grandma Rushing in her twilight years, long after she'd arrived in the Louisiana Delta as a newlywed from the hills of Kentucky to set up housekeeping in a tent with dirt floors. Some of her ways were different, in a "Grandma, why do you leave your gum on the bedpost at night and chew it again the next morning?" sort of way.

Grandma Rushing birthed ten kids of her own and raised another couple that weren't hers but should have been. She was home alone when she went into labor with her last child. In the stoic spirit of her Southern heritage, Grandma buttoned up her bottom lip and anchored the dress tail of her youngest child (who would one day become my papa) under the heavy bedpost. She smeared honey on his fingers and gave him a feather to keep him busy so she could get busy. Grandma birthed the baby, cut the cord, and returned to her daily chores. This daunting piece of family trivia came back to me years later when I was having my own birthing experience.

I was in the early stages of labor with my son, my second child, when my doctor—who had been with me for the marathon event of my daughter's birth—mentioned a plan "to speed things up a little." It sounded like a good idea, but something about his next intention bothered me.

My mom always recited this little poem:

When a job is once begun
Never stop until it's done.
Whether it be great or small,
Do it well or not at all.

Billie Francis Naff
Banks, Missouri

"If you'll hold still, Shellie, I'm just gonna rip your membrane. It might sting a bit." It didn't sound appealing, but short of jumping up and leaving the table without waiting to be excused, what was a well-raised Southern girl to do? I thought of Grandma Rushing and did my best to hold still. (FYI: By "sting" doctors mean blackout level pain.) Grandma, God rest her soul, would not have been impressed with my performance.

During my grade school years, I would get off the school bus at Grandma's house several times a week. My job was to stay overnight and keep her company. Several years earlier, Grandma's husband, Claude, had come in from the fields for lunch and surprised everyone by trading in his overalls for angel wings. While Grandma warmed his plate, Papaw Claude sat down on the couch to close his eyes and rest. He never got back up.

My mama said, "If you let anyone look at me after I'm dead, I will haunt you for the rest of your life."

Crystal L. Costello,
West Monroe, Louisiana

Grandma didn't mind being alone during the day, but she hated staying by herself at night. This fear made it even harder for me to understand one of her stranger little habits: My beloved grandmother would tell me spooky stories late at night that scared the bejesus out of me! Then we would go to bed and *she* would go to sleep.

Grandma Rushing was a heavy lady. I remember lying beside her on a double bed, trying in vain to stay on my side instead of rolling into the middle. Sometimes, when all was quiet in the house, she'd bolt halfway up in the pitch-black room and say, "Is that you, Claude?" Thankfully, my dead grandfather never answered, but the memory still gives me goose bumps.

Mama used to fuss at Papa, wondering why his mother would want to scare a little kid like that. He'd wink at me and laugh. I took that to mean it was okay to be old and a little short of center. It's a Southern thing. We like eccentric people. Heck, we're even fond of crazy. Here's a little tip you'd all do well to remember: Someone once said, "Every family tree produces a few nuts. Look around; if you don't see one, it could be you."

Mama may not have understood the reasons behind a lot of her mother-in-law's ways, but she never failed to show Grandma Rushing the proper respect. By her example she ingrained in us girls one of our most valued Southern traditions: Your elders deserve respect, period. No ifs, ands, or buts.

> Mama said, "As you get older, ask people about their family members and listen to their response! And always tell them, 'Tell your mama I said hi.' "
>
> Tommye Tonneson
> West Monroe, Louisiana

Of course, Mama was just a young girl herself back then, doing her best to figure out the wife and mother thing. Along with her other new chores, Mama was expected to both feed the chickens and wring their necks, to work a garden and freeze the produce. Unfortunately, her talents at the time lay more along the lines of playing the piano. She had a great deal of learning to do. I didn't realize this back then, but by the time I was old enough to notice, I saw only a competent farmhand, bean-truck driver, cook, and housewife. When she admonished us to "do a good job or you'll have to lick your calf over," it sounded like she'd been licking calves her whole life.

Keep On Keeping On...

I suppose Mama hated to hear us girls whine more than anything. Moping wasn't allowed at our house. We learned to count our blessings right along with our fingers and toes. Whatever the circumstances might be, we were expected to "dry it up." From the looks of things, it's a concept that bears repeating. These days, a girl can't turn on the TV or radio without hearing someone whining about something. Everyone can't be disenfranchised at the same time, folks. Do the math. Someone has got to be doing the disenfranchising. I swanee, I thought for the longest time everyone was just put out 'cause they couldn't get their own Burger King or something, but I get it now. Everyone's a victim, right? Wrong. I'll tell you like Southern Mamas tell their daughters: "Pick your lip up, girl. If you keep it run out there like that, you're liable to trip on it."

> Mama said, "Dry it up or I'll give you something to cry about!"
>
> Gerry Binkley
> Jacksonville, Florida

I grew up thinking everyone knew how to dry it up, but the older I get, the more I realize how many people missed the message. For instance, several years ago I read about a Cincinnati Bengals fan who had the gall to sue the management for not fielding a competitive football team. How ridiculous is that! We Saints fans have set a much better example. Season after humiliating season we have stood by our team. Suing them never entered our mind. We just put grocery bags over our heads and forged on. I don't want to brag, but we finally made it to the playoffs in 2007. Sometimes it takes a little time, but a stiff upper lip will eventually prevail. It's the Southern way and it makes our mamas proud.

In the tradition of my Mason-Dixon ancestors, I'm used to doing things the hard way. I was born with both of my feet turned in. By the time I was old enough to walk, they had me in corrective shoes with heavy metal braces joining my ankles and knees. Mama said when I learned to walk anyway, in record time, she figured nothing was gonna slow me down.

My mom always told me, "Don't cry over spilled milk. Feed the cow and milk her again." In many situations in life, I remember this and it gives me the determination to rise up out of discouragement and overcome.

Lou Buffkin
Daughter of Julia Waddell Buffkin
Tabor City, North Carolina

I was also born with a sunken place in my chest where my breastbone wasn't fully formed, thus leaving my heart partially unprotected. During my early childhood, the doctors warned Mama to do everything she could to make sure I didn't take a blow to my chest. They were afraid my heart might stop.

My older sisters weren't so concerned. When Mama wasn't around, Cyndie and Rhonda would tell me I was deformed just to get me worked up. But that was okay. I'd find Mama and tell her they had hit me in the chest. My tormentors would get a whoopin' and I'd get even. That's another Southern trait, although we well-brought-up Southern ladies don't like to think of it as revenge. We prefer to think of ourselves as being resourceful.

Dreaming of a Beige Christmas

Mama's "get over it" philosophy ran through our lives, shaped our thinking, and became the yardstick my sisters and I used to measure everyone we met. We weren't dry behind the ears good (that's Southern speak for yard young'uns), when we listened to Bing crooning on our black-and-white TV about a white Christmas and decided he was a whiner. Being the realistic daughters of the Deep South that we were, we'd long since given up dreaming about a white Christmas. A mushy beige Christmas was 'bout the best we could hope for.

I do recall a handful of times when the planets lined up, hell froze over, and the weatherman tried to sell us on the remote possibility of a white Christmas. It was the original snow job. He tried, bless his heart, but you didn't have to be the brightest bulb on the tree to see that he didn't really believe it either. Maybe it was the way he crossed his fingers on one hand and pointed to the weather map with the other.

Speaking of the white stuff, I've had people who weren't from around here write to me asking, "You mean it never snows down there?" I tell 'em, "Of course it snows, silly! It just doesn't stick... and it looks more like sleet."

I don't tell y'all these things so you'll feel sorry for us. Our mamas taught us to keep on keeping on and that attitude was formed in us the very first time we built a snowman out of muddy slush and watched it melt by midmorning. Yankees might have a white Christmas fall right out of the sky, but here in the South we have to create Christmas. And we do just that, with a gazillion little white lights.

We put lights everywhere, and I do mean everywhere! Yes, it's true... We have even, on occasion, lit up our Christmas sweaters. Sure it's more work our way, but that suits us just fine, because

One of the sayings my sisters and I used to hear all too often from my mother if we were acting better than someone else went something like this: "Don't spit too high but what it will fall back down on your own nose."

Rita Ainsworth
Oak Grove, Louisiana

once we're done, we don't go around pining for a white Christmas, we just plug it in.

Attitude Adjustments

Like most Southern girls, my sisters and I learned to dry it up the hard way. Our mamas call 'em *attitude adjustments.* The whole idea can be boiled down to two big Southern tenets. Rule number one: Don't wait for your circumstances to change to be happy. Or, as we like to say around here, "Sister girl, you can get glad in the same pants you get mad in." Rule number two: The world doesn't owe you a living. I realize you won't hear that kind of talk from any of the Washington Party Boys. That's 'cause they all want your vote, sugar. Someone's gotta tell you how the cow eats the cabbage. The sooner you take some responsibility for where you are and figure out a plan for where you want to go, the better off you'll be.

Mama always said, "If you're making an ugly or funny face and the clock strikes the hour, your face will look that way forever."

Pat Prater
Munford, Texas

By the time we were teenagers, Mama was all about helping us learn to manage our moods. If we girls were pouting about something, we needed an attitude adjustment. I hated having my attitude adjusted. It was never pleasant and Mama was always in charge of the adjusting.

This is around the same time Mama became obsessed with crowds and the importance of not following them. (To this day I do my best to look the other way when a crowd forms.) I have never personally known anyone who jumped off a bridge, but Mama seems to have met more than her fair share of such people. She has always shown an unusual interest in bridge jumpers. "If your friends jumped off the bridge, would you?" she'd ask. Of course, my sisters and I always needed more information. "How high was the bridge?" "Who all was going?" "What are they wearing?" "What are they going to say about the kids who don't jump?" As badly as we hated the idea of being left out, we knew better than to express these concerns to Mama. There was only one correct answer, "No, ma'am." Anything more and we'd be looking at another attitude adjustment.

I've often been asked why I talk about Mama so much on my radio and television segments. Besides the obvious reason—Southern Mamas on the whole are a flat-out wealth of material—the older I get the more I realize the most important life lessons I ever learned came at Mama's knee, or at the end of her switch. In case you haven't noticed, life is hard and with it comes endless opportunities to have your attitude adjusted. Here's a piece of hard-earned advice: It's much less painful if you're the one who does the adjusting.

When faced with a decision about having a hysterectomy at an early age, I went straight to my mother for counsel. (Southern Mamas have a direct line to God, don't you know?) When I shared with her how I'd always wanted more children (I already had two boys), Mama said, "Don't mourn what you don't have and thank God for what you do."

Nancy Huey
Choudrant, Louisiana

Mama Teaches Us About Faith

Mama came by her no-nonsense ways honestly. She was the daughter of a Southern Baptist preacher who took her daddy's faith in God and made it her

My grandparents, Reverend and Mrs. Marvin Stone, head to church.

own. I wish y'all could've known my Papaw Stone—he was my hero. He's been trading gospel stories with the Apostle Paul for years now, but I still miss him something awful. Papaw loved to preach and he loved to laugh. He spent most of his time doing one or the other, if not both. I remember listening to him from the pews of Riverside Baptist Church in Natchez, Mississippi.

One Sunday morning Papaw was hard at it when he jumped a rabbit called "women's lib." That was back when ladies were burning their unmentionables in public. Papaw wasn't very politically correct. He was just about to get that rabbit penned up when a woman shot up out of her pew, let out a big old "humph!" and started for the door. Papaw got that familiar twinkle in his eye and called out to her retreating back, "That's all right, ma'am . . . I can hit a moving target as well as I can a sitting one."

Over the dinner table later, we cousins watched as Grandma Stone chewed on him hard about what subjects he should and should not get into from the pulpit. He just grinned at her and winked at us . . . That was Papaw for ya.

I realize preachers aren't always known for their sense of humor, but Papaw Stone was an exception. One of his favorite pranks was the hot coffee scam. His eyes would start twinkling anytime circumstances presented him with an unsuspecting couple. While Grandma Stone went to slice the pound cake, or whatever treat she had on hand, Papaw would set his joke up by bringing a steaming hot cup of coffee to their female guest. Once served, he'd excuse himself to go back to the kitchen.

Moments later Papaw would return with his own cup and the gentleman's cup, walking very slowly. "Careful now," he'd say, as he crossed the room with the cups balancing carefully in their saucers, "I'm afraid I filled 'er up a little high." Then, just as the man would reach for his coffee Papaw would "trip" and send those empty cups straight into the man's lap. Here's a fact: scalding hot coffee will make a grown man dance, be it real or imagined.

As big a ham as he was, there was one thing Papaw didn't joke about and that was God's word. He believed every jot and title and preached it from cover to cover. Mama took to her daddy's teachings and when we girls came along she set about handing her faith and his familiar lessons down to the next generation.

I heard and saw in my Southern Mama the type of faith

that stands the tests of time. I remember her saying, "God wouldn't like that." To my young ears, it sounded like she was recounting a personal conversation. My image of God was formed during those years. I saw Him as stern but loving, equally ready to hug or discipline. The picture continues to serve me well today.

> Mother taught me to be honest and law-abiding because, "You're going to be dead a long time."
>
> Patsy Myers Herrington
> Lake Providence, Louisiana

Mama expected her daughters to serve God. Anything less was unthinkable. To accomplish these goals, and like most of her Bible Belt neighbors, she spit-shined us and took us to Melbourne Baptist Church every single solitary time the doors were open. We grew up in the second pew from the front, left-hand side.

I was an adult before I learned to appreciate the type of Southern raising I had in that church pew. Because of Mama's dogged determination, I can honestly say I can't remember a time when I wasn't aware of God. I didn't have to find my faith. I grew up convinced that God was never more than a prayer away.

Of course, best as I could figure, He was on Mama's side. I hope that doesn't sound sacrilegious. I know God doesn't take sides, but back then we girls were pretty sure He and Mama were in cahoots. She was constantly reminding us that God knew what we were doing. I won't say she outright told us He was tattling, but it was definitely implied. As a matter of fact, we were so convinced of this divine collaboration that Mama could

> My Southern Mama said, "Always remember, Mom and God are watching you."
>
> Debbie Wilson
> Magee, Mississippi

often get us to incriminate ourselves with one simple line, "Isn't there something you want to tell me?"

We girls gave up a lot of goods on ourselves before we got old enough to realize that Mama often knew nothing of our crimes. The woman was simply fishing. By this time we had become know-it-all teenagers. We were positively giddy with the realization that we really weren't under twenty-four-hour surveillance after all. Mama adjusted just as fast to this little setback, quickly adding another Southern Mama principle. She freely admitted that a girl could fool some of the people all of the time and all of the people some of the time—but let her never expect to fool her Heavenly Father any of the time. Mama knew the Final Tally principle was a hard one to ignore.

The subject of fooling the fallible reminds me of a little story about Mama Ruth and Aunt Eddie, two old belles in our community. They weren't kin to me, that's just what everybody called 'em. One fine Sunday morning, Mama Ruth and Aunt Eddie were headed to the Lord's house with Mama Ruth's daughter and grandson. They were running late too. As Mama Ruth pulled in and parked the car, she reminded the group to hurry, and everyone unloaded quickly—well, almost everyone. Aunt Eddie was moving at a snail's pace. The family waited in the boiling sun while Aunt Eddie emerged slowly from the car.

"I swanee, Eddie," Mama Ruth grumbled. "You're moving slower than molasses this morning."

Aunt Eddie ignored her. Now, Aunt Eddie was well up in years when this happened, but her pace had nothing to do with her age and everything to do with the new dress she was wearing. Aunt Eddie was determined to see that both of them got maximum exposure. Once inside, Aunt Eddie eagerly took the lead and paraded the group clear to the front. The preacher had barely begun his sermon when he made a crucial mistake. "For our closing hymn," he said, "we will stand and sing, 'Stand Up, Stand Up for Jesus,' but first let us consider—" Unfortunately, Aunt Eddie was always fast at considering. She sprung up like she'd been shot from a cannon!

"Sit down!" Mama Ruth whispered, jerking on Eddie's dress-tail. "Not now!"

They were making quite a scene when Aunt Eddie whispered even louder, "The man said to stand up for Jesus and that's exactly what I'm doing."

As the preacher tried to decide what to do, the rest of the congregation looked around at one another and began to rise to their feet one by one. The pianist took that as her cue and tore into the closing hymn and the preacher said, "Well, praise the Lord!"

Later, over a big lunch of fried chicken with all the fixin's, Mama Ruth chastised Eddie for showing off her dress and pretending like she was standing up for Jesus.

"You're just jealous," Aunt Eddie said. "Besides, if I'd had a new hat to go with my dress, I think I could've started a revival!"

Can I Have a Witness?

Seeing as how our lives revolved around the church, getting a new preacher at Melbourne Baptist Church was a big deal to me and my sisters—especially if he had kids. Unless, heaven forbid, they were girly-girls (girly-girl was a derogatory name my sisters and I gave girls who weren't as rough around the edges as we were). The appearance of girly-girls in our community placed an incredible hardship on us because we were still expected to entertain them.

I remember once when the Good Lord showed us His favor and sent us the Reverend Paul Carter to guide our flock. Reverend Carter had not one, but three boys: Ricky, Randy, and Reggie—who almost lined up in ages with Cyndie, Rhonda, and Shellie. When Ricky, Randy, and Reggie were in trouble, their mother called them Richard, Randall, and Reginald. And if she called those names at the same time our mama yelled for Cynthia Darlene, Rhonda Arlene, and Shellie Charlene, you could bet the farm there'd been a discovery and someone was fixin' to pay the piper.

To our new buddies' shame, their mother liked to slick their hair back for church, way back, so it made a little mound on top. Being the oldest, and a new teenager, Ricky hated this look the most. Enter Cousin Steve, well known for his ability to wart the horns off a billy goat. Steve took one look at Ricky and named him "Pompadour." Ricky backed his ears; he didn't need a reason to whoop Steve. They hadn't hit it off; but Pompadour? While none of us kids knew what Pompadour meant, it flat-out didn't sound good to our young Southern ears. The situation was crystal clear: Cousin Steve was calling Ricky out in front of God and everybody and he kept it up throughout the service, whispering "Pompadour" from the pew behind us.

At the final amen, we kids quickly adjourned to the parking lot to see just how Ricky would kill Steve. However, Cousin Steve, whether intimidated by the murderous Ricky or just eager to continue the sport, was quicker. He locked himself in our car, cracked the window, and continued his taunting, "Oh, Pompadour!"

> My Southern Mama taught me to "pick your battles and make 'em count!"
>
> Terri Hall
> Marshall, Virginia

We'll never know what Ricky would've done next for that's when we heard "Richard Paul Carter! What's going on here?" Steve grinned and time stood still before Ricky finally turned and walked away, thus proving once and for all that nothing makes it easier to resist temptation than a proper upbringing—unless it's witnesses.

How to Tell If You Are or Were a Girly-Girl

For educational purposes only, I've borrowed a phrase from Mr. Foxworthy to help y'all see where you fit in. (Don't sue me, Jeff. Mama says imitation is the highest form of flattery.)

- If you wore shoes anywhere other than church between the months of May and September... You could have been a girly-girl.
- If you enjoyed fishing but were never able to bait your own hook... You could have been a girly-girl.
- If you never learned to make a spitball that would stick on its target... You could have been a girly-girl.
- If you have ever voluntarily worn a dress to school, if you were the teacher's pet instead of her personal challenge, if you preferred hopscotch on the sidewalk at recess rather than football with the boys... You could have been a girly-girl.
- If you've never gone swimming in a ditch after a big rain, if you've never pinched a live lizard behind his neck so you could clamp him on your ear like an earring, if you've never been scolded for making unladylike noises with your palm cupped under your armpit, and if you don't know that minnows will never turn into fish, not ever, no matter how long you keep them... You could have been a girly-girl.

- If you've never swung from your knees on a tree limb, if you don't know that green tree frogs will stick almost anywhere, if you've never pulled on your hair to straighten out the ringlets your mama put there...You could have been a girly-girl.
- If you've never worn abandoned locust skins as jewelry, if you weren't willing to give mouth-to-muzzle resuscitation to the family pet, if you didn't feel obligated to accept every "double-dog dare" thrown your way, and if your idea of dressing up never included cowboy boots, your dad's work shoes, or Indian feathers...You could have been a girly-girl.

Simply put, if your mama wasn't always reminding you of the things little ladies did and did not do...You could have been—and probably were—a girly-girl.

School Bells Ring, Are You Listening?

My sisters and I had a thirty-mile bus trip to school both ways and we knew exactly what was expected of us once we disembarked from the big yellow beast: *Get good grades and don't sass the teachers.* Respecting those in authority was equally as important as the high marks. I meant to respect my teachers; it's just that I also liked to entertain my classmates, a dilemma that often left me between the proverbial rock and a hard place.

I was, at best, a frustrated entertainer. My heart's desire was to be a country-western singer like Loretta Lynn. There were some immediate problems. To begin with, I had a speech impediment; if you heard me speak today you might think I still do. But back then, you couldn't understand a word I said. My older sister Cyndie was my official interpreter for the first decade of my life. And now that I can speak for myself, I'd like the record to show I did not say a lot of the things she interpreted.

My Southern Mama said, "When you educate a man, you educate one person. When you educate a woman, you educate a family."

Liz Fischer
Palm Harbor, Florida

My sisters gave me a hard time at home, but then I went to school and my embarrassment quadrupled. When I was in the second grade, a speech therapist would come to the door of our class once a week and call for the speech kids. All the kids in my class would turn around and chant, "Speech kids, speech kids." While this man did everything he could to help me learn to roll my R's, I kindly plotted his death.

To further complicate my future career plans as an entertainer, I couldn't carry a tune in a bucket. Faced with my lack of singing talent, I turned into one of those people who always have a story to tell, an idea that worked out a lot better for the late Jerry Clower (for you culturally challenged non-Southerners, he was the first and best country comedian and a Mississippi legend).

My desire to entertain kept me in trouble. I remember being in Mrs. Gilly's fifth grade at Tallulah Academy when Ray Stevens's "The Streak"—that song about a fella running nekkid through the supermarket—became popular. Of course I memorized the words. And of course, when Mrs. Gilly left the room I saw my chance to perform. I was standing on the top of my desk well into my routine when my previously laughing audience suddenly fell silent. I didn't have to turn around. I could feel Mrs. Gilly's breath on my neck. My parents, my principal, and my teacher banded together and encouraged me to give up entertaining and concentrate on getting an education.

Life had come calling for my parents at a very young age, and as a result, neither of them have a college education; it's something they both regret. My sisters and I may have felt education was a tiresome duty, but we knew our parents considered it a privilege we dare not waste. We girls also knew that if we got in trouble at school, we were the ones who needed to be worried—not the teachers.

My mom told me to take auto mechanics in school (which I did). She said I should know how to fix my car. Then I should act stupid so a man would fix it for me, but at least I'd know if he were doing it right because, after all, "It's not ladylike to work on a car."

Pam Drummond
Fullerton, California

Of course, it has often been said that experience is the best teacher. I would have to concur. There were many times during those years when fate would play into Mama's hands and we kids would learn priceless lessons all on our own.

I remember a day when my extended family was congregated up at my grandma's house in Natchez, Mississippi. While the adults drank black coffee and caught up with one another's lives, my cousins and I were outside playing Cowboys and Indians. The middle gang (me, Lisa, and Rhonda) were the cowboys. The older gang (Cyndie, Steve, and Rod) were the Indians. At some point, the Indians decided they needed more realism. They slipped in Grandma's house to look for war paint, but the only thing they could find was a tube of white stuff in Papaw's side of the medicine chest. They had wanted color, but it did appear to be the right consistency and it even had a little nozzle on it they could use like a paintbrush. Beggars can't be choosers. They borrowed the tube and painted themselves up nicely.

The battle was waging hard and heavy between us cowboys and the highly decorated Indians when Grandma Stone happened to catch a glimpse of their war paint from the kitchen window. She came outside and called us all over. After a brief inspection of the fierce Indians, Grandma smiled. Then she started laughing until tears began rolling down her cheeks. Once she'd composed herself, she explained that their choice of war paint was more commonly known as hemorrhoid cream and the Indians should wash their faces immediately.

> When something was wrong, my Southern Mama would deal with it by saying, "Oh, nobody will know it in a hundred years."
>
> Jean Ormand
> Jackson, Mississippi

Being the youngest, we cowboys were confused as to the nature of the problem. Cyndie and Rod weren't much clearer, but they could tell it wasn't a good thing. Indian Steve was the first to figure it out. After Grandma went inside, he explained to his fellow natives the connection between the previously used applicator and their chosen site of application.

That day we kids learned that knowledge was better than assumption, but experience trumps 'em both. Or in the words of the late, great Southerner Mark Twain, "A man who carries a cat by the tail learns something he can learn no other way."

It's My Turn

Years passed quickly on Bull Run Road and I grew up ready to take both the knowledge and the experiences I'd gained from my Southern upbringing and pass them on to the next generation. My Southern Mama taught me that into every life a little rain must fall, but if you have a good umbrella and a tube of red lipstick, you can get through anything. It's a little life lesson I like to think I've passed down to my own daughter.

Recently we Southerners found ourselves the object of the whole world's focus, thanks to those twin babes Rita and Katrina. If times hadn't been so difficult we might have relished the world's attention; we do love drama. As it was, we felt sorta overscrutinized. Still, as the responsible hostess of *All Things Southern*, I feel impressed upon to share with the rest of the country the long-standing and effective coping mechanisms of the Southern female. When trouble comes calling, our mamas taught us to pray—then we laugh, shop, and eat. Eating is not only allowed, but encouraged during each stage.

It was September 2005 and Hurricane Rita was approaching land and outfoxing the experts as to her likely destination, when my busy, young, executive daughter began evacuating Houston with her busy, young, executive boyfriend from nearby Katy, Texas. They embarked on I-45 with a million of their closest friends, turning a four-hour trip to Dallas into a twenty-two-hour nightmare. It took my family's combined coping resources and the Job-like patience of her boyfriend, Patrick, to get Jessica Ann through it.

I was Dallas bound myself that day, traveling I-20 with Mama and Aunt Judy when Jessica's first emergency call came in. Mama and Aunt Judy made like the Lennon Sisters and commenced to singing hymns, while I started praying. Justifiably frightened about spending the night on the interstate in the storm's path, Jessica called repeatedly. Shouldn't they turn around? She implored over the phone, looking for the answer she wanted to hear. She wanted advice but she'd morphed back into her childhood days when the very sight of a wasp could render her nonnegotiable. I felt they should continue north. Our impasse produced dramatic pleas over the cell phone. "Why, Mama?" Jessica Ann wailed into the phone. "Why do you want me to die on the interstate?!"

Granted, it was funnier twenty-four hours later in my sister's living room in Dallas than it was in real time, but Jessica Ann is Southern through and through. She knows it can be necessary to skip steps to survive! Her sweet Patrick (who is now her beloved husband) likes to tell us how she lifted her head at one point to announce in true Scarlett O'Hara fashion, "If we ever get out of this, I am so going shopping." Friends, it has been noted that humor is remembering tragedy when things are tranquil. Here in the Deep South we're hoping we've all had enough material to last a lifetime.

My mom, Mossie Howard Good, was talking about someone who had been going through a hard time and was feeling sorry for himself. She told me, "It's okay to fall down, Betty, just don't waller."

Betty Hannah
Gallion, Alabama

Southern Staples and Main-Dish Recipes

A look into the wit and wisdom of our Southern Mamas on life, faith, and education wouldn't be complete without checking out our stove tops. As surely as we build our lives on their early teachings, we build our meals around the staples they taught us to cook and the main dishes that we can't and won't live without. Oh, sure, we might modify 'em somewhat—a little less salt meat (cured pork) here, a little more extra virgin olive oil there—but give 'em up? Never! A Southern girl knows that you can't get a real power lunch at the sushi bar. I hope you enjoy the following staples and classics I've learned from my Southern Mama, and a few others I've added to the "wouldn't live without" category. Of course, we have to start with the Holy Trinity of Southern Cooking. For in a Southern kitchen, that's where most everything begins.

~ The Holy Trinity of Southern Cooking ~

My mama taught me to cook with the trinity, although she didn't refer to it by that name. I was grown and married the first time I heard the expression. It was in the home of a mature Southern belle, Arabelle Hamilton of Lake Providence, Louisiana, who shared with me the much-anticipated, all-important advice her mother left her with on her wedding night: "Honey, when you're late with supper, or just plain tired, remember to have the Holy Trinity of Southern Cooking (onions, celery, and bell pepper) sautéing in a dab of butter or bacon grease on the stove when your man comes home. It'll put him in a good mood and you can feed him anything."

onions
celery
bell pepper
butter or bacon grease

You might notice that I didn't tell you how much to use of each. This isn't culinary school, sugar. Dice up some veggies and drop 'em in the butter. We have bigger fish to fry, so to speak…

~ Stuffed Bell Peppers ~

SERVES 6

Mama taught us girls to stuff a pepper with a "use what you've got" attitude born of living miles from a grocery store. For instance, if you don't have salsa on hand, try a can of diced tomatoes. The art of substitution is country cooking at its best.

6 large green bell peppers
1 pound ground beef, cooked and drained
1 medium onion, chopped
1 cup rice, cooked
1 16-ounce jar of your favorite salsa
½ teaspoon garlic powder
1 teaspoon Tony Chachere's Original Creole Seasoning (or your favorite season-all)
salt and pepper to taste
6–8 ounces cheddar cheese, shredded

Preheat oven to 350 degrees.

Begin by cooking the bell peppers for five minutes in six cups of boiling water. Drain, remove the tops and seeds, and set aside.

Combine the ground beef with onion, rice, and salsa. Season with garlic powder, Tony Chachere's, salt, and pepper.

Stand peppers upright on an ungreased baking dish and stuff them with beef and rice mixture. Cover with foil and bake for 35 minutes. Remove the foil, top with cheese, and bake another 10 to 15 minutes, or until the cheese is bubbly.

~ Mama's Smothered Chicken ~

SERVES 6–8

This dish provides the heart of a great comfort meal and brings back memories of putting my feet under Mama's table at home. Smothered chicken is kind of like being smothered by your mama's love—we Southerners don't think you can get too much of either!

1 medium fryer, cut into serving pieces
salt and pepper to taste
4 tablespoons butter
¼ cup flour
juice of ½ lemon
2 tablespoons Worcestershire sauce
1½ cups water

Season fryer well with salt and pepper. (I like to let it stand a while like that in the refrigerator. If you have the time, let it stay in there for an hour or so.)

Preheat oven to 500 degrees.

Place your chicken in a 9 × 13-inch baking dish and dot it with butter, then sprinkle with flour. Turn the oven down to 350 and bake the chicken until it begins to brown. At that point add the lemon juice, Worcestershire sauce, and water. Cover tightly with foil and bake another hour and a half or so, or until you can poke it with a fork and watch that delicious meat just fall off the bone. (Remember to baste it occasionally by taking the juices from the bottom and driping 'em over the top.)

Serve this chicken to your hungry bunch and watch it disappear right before your eyes.

~ Ranch Style Chicken ~

SERVES 6–8

Yes, there are potato chips in this recipe, Doritos even. We do that sort of thing down here. We might be a proud people, but we're nothing if not resourceful. (If it makes you feel better, you can always hide the bag.)

1 cooked chicken, skinned, deboned, and chopped
1 can cream of mushroom soup
1 onion, chopped and sautéed in butter
1 can cream of chicken soup
1 can diced tomatoes with green chiles
½ teaspoon chili powder
⅓ cup chicken broth
8 ounces Velveeta cheese, grated
½ cup water
½ teaspoon garlic powder
8 ounces mild cheddar cheese, grated
1 14-ounce bag of Doritos

Preheat oven to 350 degrees.

Mix all your ingredients together except for the cheddar cheese and Doritos. Put Doritos in a greased 9 × 13-inch baking dish and top with the chicken mixture. You're almost done! Sprinkle cheddar cheese on top and bake for 25 to 30 minutes.

Here's a little prayer we country folks have been known to tack on to the blessing before we eat a meal this good: "Amen, Brother Ben, back your ears and dive in."

~ Pork Roast Barbecue ~

SERVES 8–10

Barbecue reigns in most any form here in the South, and which state does it best is a controversial can of worms I'm not about to open. The first rule of pulled pork is that it's best slow cooked on the grill, but I've adapted my recipe to the oven and you're gonna have to try it to believe how good it is. Cook this one all day and fill your house with the tempting smells of slow-cooked barbecue. When it comes time to eat, you won't be disappointed!

18 ounces hickory-flavored barbecue sauce

6 ounces hot barbecue sauce or more if desired

⅓–¼ cup white vinegar

1 3–4 pound fresh pork shoulder roast

Preheat oven to 225 degrees.

Take a cast-iron skillet and two long pieces of foil, approximately two feet each. Place first sheet of foil in skillet with the ends hanging over the sides. Lay the second piece across the skillet crosswise, again with the ends extended. (You're making a pocket for the roast.)

Combine barbecue sauces and vinegar. Place your roast in the center of the foil packet. Pour sauce mixture over top.

Wrap the roast tightly in foil and bake for eight to nine hours. Remove from oven. Carefully open packet and slide foil from under the roast, leaving the roast and juices in the skillet. Using a fork, pull the roast into pieces. Add a little more barbecue sauce to keep the pork from drying out and return to oven for another hour or so.

Serve on hot buns. Some folks like to put coleslaw right on the sandwich, but my bunch likes it on the side.

~ Crawfish Rotini ~

SERVES 6

The truth is we can put away some mudbugs down here in the Delta! Let me show y'all how to do my Crawfish Rotini. (Don't mind the noise. That's just me singing one of my favorite songs, "You Get a Line and I'll Get A Pole, Honey.")

4 tablespoons butter
1 medium onion, chopped
2 stalks of celery, chopped
½ green pepper, chopped
1 can cream of mushroom soup
1 can diced tomatoes and chilies (or just diced tomatoes if you can't find one with chilies)
1 pound crawfish tails, peeled and cleaned
salt and pepper to taste
dash of All Things Southern Hot Sauce (or another hot sauce)
dash of Slap Ya Mama Cajun seasoning (or your favorite season-all)
1 pound plain macaroni, cooked and drained
1 pound Velveeta cheese

Preheat oven to 350 degrees.

In butter, sauté the onion, celery, and pepper until onions are translucent. Add mushroom soup and tomatoes. Add the crawfish tails and season well with salt and pepper, a dash of hot sauce, and a shake of a good, spicy season-all.

In a separate bowl, combine the warm macaroni and Velveeta cheese, stirring until the cheese melts. Add the crawfish mixture and place in a large greased casserole dish and bake for 35 to 40 minutes.

Have mercy! Let's eat... All together now while we set the table: "You get a line and I'll get a pole, honey. You get a line and I'll get a pole, babe. You get a line and I'll get a pole, we'll go fishing in the crawdad hole... Honey, baby, mine."

~ Shellie's Strapping Burgers ~

8 BURGERS

Fire up the grill and put on a bunch of my Strapping Burgers, but be warned: There's nothing timid about these babies. You'll want to check your diets at the screen door!

2 pounds ground beef
salt and pepper to taste
2 tablespoons dried parsley
1 teaspoon garlic powder
1 tablespoon soy sauce
1 tablespoon steak sauce
dash of All Things Southern Hot Sauce (or whatever poor substitute you can find ☺)
8–10 slices of bacon, fried and crumbled
2 2½-ounce jars of mushroom pieces
1½ cups grated Monterey Jack cheese

Season the ground beef with salt and pepper and mix in dried parsley, garlic powder, soy sauce, steak sauce, and hot sauce. Pat the seasoned meat into sixteen very thin patties.

Top eight of the patties with the bacon, mushroom pieces, and cheese. Put a second thin patty on top of each and press down on the edges to seal.

Throw 'em on a hot grill until they're at the readiness you enjoy. Have mercy, that's good eating, Southern style!

2

Hickey, My Hind End! Give That Boy a Pacifier

What Southern Mamas Tell Their Daughters About Sex, Dating, and Coming of Age (with Tempting Dips and Appetizers That Leave You Wanting More)

I've been married for over twenty-five years, and with both my son and daughter recently married, I wouldn't be surprised if I was a grandma soon. But, even now, as I attempt to opine on the subject of S-E-X, the echo of my Southern upbringing causes me to proceed carefully and almost apologetically. Everyone talks about sex now; no one talked about sex when I was a young girl, although they did spell it when absolutely necessary. Down South we call it "bedroom talk" and it remains impolite conversation for mixed company. Don't get me wrong. We enjoy our fair share. I'm just saying that we'd be more comfortable if Victoria still had a few secrets.

What Happens When It Is Your Time

I was ten, eleven maybe, when Mama became obsessed with time. It was a big topic of conversation between her and my oldest sister Cyndie. Was it Cyndie's time? Did Cyndie need anything from town for her time? Mama's new preoccupation was oh-so-mysterious and yet full of promising opportunities. All Cyndie had to do was nod and Mama would return from town with Cyndie's own little brown bag from the drugstore! "How cool is this?" I thought. And if Cyndie was being particularly mean to me and Rhonda (it should be noted that if Cyndie was awake she was mean on some level), Mama would tell us that it was Cyndie's *time* and Rhonda and I would understand *when our time came.* Color me confused.

I was the eldest of six, with two younger sisters. My mother always told me, "Don't you dare ruin your reputation. You better think of your little sisters coming along behind you!"

Sandra E. Hopper Dill-Little
Gaffney, South Carolina

On one hand, the whole thing was kind of creepy sounding, as if our own dear mama was anticipating our early demise. On the other hand, I liked the idea of "my time coming," as it seemed to come with built-in excuses for what Mama would have usually called poor behavior.

Unfortunately, my time came earlier than Mama expected and before she had taken the time to fill in the gaps in my limited understanding. What's worse, she wasn't even home when it went down. Sure enough! I was going to die, just as I had suspected! I took the alarming news to Cyndie, who handed me some helpful feminine hygiene products and shoved me in the hall bathroom. Then, from the other side of the door, my sister supplied me with less information than a *New York Times* reporter gets in the White House briefing room and told me when I figured it out she would open the door. Welcome to puberty. Enjoy your stay.

Fast Girls

With the onset of "my time," the last of my Southern Mama's three little girls was on her way to womanhood. It's entirely possible that Mama hasn't slept a full night since. The risk of sexually transmitted diseases or potential emotional problems resulting from promiscuous behavior wasn't my Southern Mama's primary concern. No, ma'am. The overriding issue back on Bull Run Road was premarital sex in and of itself. "Sex without the benefit of marriage" was a clear no-no. The Good Book said anyone who wasn't married was supposed to abstain. Those who didn't abstain were referred to as "fast" girls. It was years before I realized these girls weren't so much quick on their feet as they were quick to get off 'em.

My mama would only say that "nice girls don't do that." She never said what "that" was.

Betty Halley
Mer Rouge, Louisiana

To avoid the many dangers the opposite sex presented, Mama taught my sisters and me to dress like little ladies and "just say no" years before Mrs. Reagan adopted the phrase. This teaching was underscored by bovine metaphors like "no one would buy a cow when he could get the milk for free." While the cow analogy probably made more sense to my older sisters, it was the type of riddle that contributed to my early confusion on speedy women. At the same time, it was typical of the veiled references

Mama's advice on dating: "Never let any boy touch you anywhere for any reason."

Mary
Texas

that surrounded Certain Subjects whenever my mama and the other adult women in my community felt compelled to speak on these topics. In case you aren't from around here, let me elaborate. "Certain Subjects" is a euphemism for sex and childbirth and should be discussed in a low voice.

The women of my childhood detested coarse conversation as much as coarse behavior. Unmarried girls didn't get, you know—that word. They got "in trouble." As a little girl, I lived in fear of crossing the line between The Trouble Mama was always saying my sisters and I were in, and The Trouble that made people lower their voices. By the way, married ladies didn't get—you know—that way either; they carried children and they expected children, but no one ever said they were... well, you know what I mean.

Mama on Marketing and Moving Vehicles

As we grew up, Mama's lessons on sex became much clearer in the privacy of our own home, but they were still couched in ladylike language. In her constant efforts to guard our innocence, a task complicated by the bra-burning antics of the rest of the country, she instructed us girls "not to advertise things that weren't on sale." Or, as generations of Southern girls have been taught, "It's fine to dress so they know you're a woman, as long as they can still tell you're a lady."

Mama said, "Sex is for man and wife only. Never let a boy any lower than your neckline and any higher than your dress tail."

Billie Rachell
Downsville, Louisiana

Have I mentioned that this

was in the swinging seventies? From what my sisters and I could see, there was an S-E-X revolution going on and no one seemed all that concerned about sales and marketing. The operative word appeared to be *free.*

While my sisters and I considered many of Mama's ideas on modesty to be much too old-fashioned at the time, I now long for the days when a trip to the mall didn't include the display of more unbecoming body parts than a national plumbers' convention.

Speaking of plumbers, I really must digress for a moment. If you're of a certain age, you might need the smelling salts on this one, but here goes.

> When referring to the way I dressed, my mom always said, "Leave something to the imagination."
>
> Rebecca Flora
> Tampa, Florida

High-fashion experts are now telling us that that area back there—and I'm trying to do this as delicately as possible—that line where the Good Lord split us... they're saying it's "the new cleavage." I swanee! I heard it on the news and I almost fainted.

I don't see how much lower they can go. As it is, they're wearing two individual pant legs. If my Southern Mama had caught my sisters and me in something like that, she would've given us a few quick wedgies before she took us to the bedroom for a heart-to-heart. Which brings us back to the plumbers, God love 'em; you do realize that we owe the poor things an apology! It appears that they've been on the cutting edge of fashion this whole time. But enough of this, I should quit while I'm ahead. If you'll pardon the pun, there are already way too many behinds.

The older we got, the more detail Mama went into on The Troubled girls we'd heard so much about when we were younger. It became clear to me that The Trouble could be traced to parked cars. If and when we were granted permission to occupy a vehicle with a boy, said vehicle best be kept moving.

Included in Mama's breakdown on the dangers of parked cars was the clarification of some other warnings I had long needed help deciphering. "Necking" for instance. I had yet to "neck" with a member of the opposite sex and I didn't understand the threat that the close proximity of necks could produce. Similarly, I knew that sitting in a boy's lap was serious enough to warrant consideration as an addendum to the Ten Commandments, but I had never figured out why it could lead to The Trouble. When Mama's delicate explanation failed to produce a clear picture for me, my older sister Cyndie was more than happy to elaborate, jumping in to provide an unparalleled education and images I would have preferred to erase. It was just as well. Mama was through with innuendoes. The perils of parked cars could no longer be avoided.

> Mama said you can always tell if a young lady is having sex because it makes her hips wide.
>
> Linda Nelson
> Monroe, Louisiana

With this in mind, my Southern Mama began taking great pains to lay out the many dangers surrounding the opposite sex. For whatever reason, she began speaking in military terms, explaining that kissing was the "upper persuasion of lower invasion." (No, I'm not making that up. You don't have to make up that sort of thing when you have a Southern Mama.) While this may have just been Mama's subconscious way of making the opposite sex sound like the enemy, even she had to concede that unless she wanted three old maids on her hands, our opponents would have to be recast as necessary evils.

Mr. Right, the Game Show

Somewhere amid all those evil-minded boys Mama had been warning us about was Mr. Right, and it was our job to find him, an activity that had all the makings of a good game show. If one were observant, there were certain clues to lead you to the prize. I'll be happy to review Mama's rules in case any of y'all are out there looking for yourself, or trying to help your own daughters stage a successful hunt.

Mama always said, "Boys are like streetcars. There will be another one by in the next fifteen minutes."

Evelyne Edmonson
Pine Bluff, Arkansas

Door Number One: Mr. Right will come from a good family. Good families don't necessarily mean wealthy ones, either, although money is a big plus and it never hurts to start at the top. It's just that Southern Mamas are realists. They teach their girls to reach for the stars but they realize strictly confining the search to a wealthy suitor can seriously wreck their baby's odds. For this reason they're generally satisfied if the boy comes from clean-living, hardworking people who know how to get themselves to the Lord's house on Sunday. Mr. Right might be hard to peg, Honey, but here in the South, good families are easy to spot. A reputation for working and churchgoing get high marks for all those in the family tree. Serving time does not.

My mother always told me, "It's just as easy to fall in love with a rich man as it is with a poor one."

Debra Elmore
Walnut Creek, California

Door Number Two: Quality contestants are neat and

clean. They look adults in the eye and say, "Yes, ma'am" and "No, ma'am." No bona-fide contender would dream of offending his crush's mother by being disrespectful. This is serious. A potential Mr. Right can prove himself to be Mr. Wrong with one careless "uh-huh," "yes," or "what?"

My mother and I were discussing what a certain divorced man was doing—putting his girlfriend's daughter before his own. Mother said, "I call that salting the calf to get the cow!"

Gloria Chapman
Mer Rouge, Louisiana

Never lie down with someone who has more problems than you do: When you get up, their problems will be yours.

Elizabeth Powell Crowe
Huntsville, Alabama

Door Number Three: We may have been in the middle of the Mr. Right Game Show but Mama's message wasn't veering much from the days when she first introduced us to the great battle of the sexes: The contestants may vary in size and shape, but they are all similar in one regard. It's up to the female not to encourage the males' lewd ideas because these single-minded contestants "are all after one thing," and they are quick to tell a girl anything to "have their way." I recall this being somewhat confusing because Mama also liked to say, "Mr. Right will not try to get a girl to do anything a girl doesn't want to do." If you're fuzzy on this one, take heart. As conflicting as the two ideas seem to be, your confusion will be cleared up quickly once you get in the game. It doesn't take the sharpest tool in the shed to see that this last qualification trips up many a good candidate.

Door Number Four: Mr. Right will be good to his mama.

This particular bit seemed a little self-serving to me too, but Mama assured us it was a crucial part of the evaluation, and personal experience has taught me that she was right on the money. If your man can't say a nice word about his mama, Sugar, you best run for the hills.

"See how he treats his mama. If he's good to her, he'll be good to you." It worked. I have a wonderful husband who loves me and his mama!

K. Towns
Marion, Louisiana

Perhaps the most surprising rule lay behind Door Number Five: Mama said Mr. Right was looking for us too! This was quite a revelation and it lent itself to another round of teachings on what we should and shouldn't do to make sure he found us. For instance, one should run slow enough to allow oneself to get caught by Mr. Right—without looking too easy or "forward" as Mama liked to say. This can be a delicate part of the dance, even for us Southern girls. But there are ways to avoid being considered forward. Our mamas agree that one big no-no is calling the object of your affection rather than waiting for him to call you. Calling boys sends all the wrong signals. You could be on "proceed with caution" and he'll be hearing "all systems go."

Mama always told my sister and me that nice girls don't call boys; they wait on boys to call first. Our response, "But if I don't call him, I won't get to talk to him" always brought out her favorite line: "Get over it. You're gonna be faced with that the rest of your life."

Jodi Meeks
Monroe, Louisiana

Tarring Your Reputation and Your Hide

Having girls old enough to fraternize with the enemy kept Mama in a state of perpetual anxiety. She was almost as concerned with our public fraternizing as she was with our private sessions. She was forever reminding us that "people would talk." Perhaps her concerns about what they would talk about can best be explained through a little piece of news I pulled off the World Wide Web. Then again, it may not, but I've been dying to tell y'all about this, and it does seem a perfect time to bring it up.

Mama warned us against PDA's, public displays of affection, with these words, "When someone sees that they think, 'If they're doing that in public, I can't imagine what they're doing in private!'"

Dana Fortenberry Gillett
Rayville, Louisiana

I recently read about a hot new tourist attraction. It's a hill in a small village in Romania. I understand the natives have long considered their hill to be a mystical spot that helps women conceive children. I'd rather not spell it out, but they believe that very spot is necessary to achieve success. Are you with me, yet? Come on, Sugar, they've even planted extra bushes and trees to conceal the, uh, family planning. The article implied the whole world is flocking to their little hill! I feel the heavy responsibility to speak for a legion of Southern Mamas when I say, "Heaven help us all, I sure hope none of you Southern girls plan to flock over there."

My mom always told my sisters and me, "Not to go kissing behind the garden gate—love might be blind but the neighbors ain't."

Angie McCranie
Natchez, Mississippi

I had hoped everyone got the sort of teaching Mama gave my sisters and me on PDAs—public displays of affection—but this is so alarming, I feel compelled to review the rules: Nice girls do not drape themselves on boys in public. Draping is excessive or inappropriate touching and our Southern Mamas have a strong distaste for such behavior. It causes them to say things like, "IfIeverseeyoudrapingyourselfoveraboyinfrontof-GodandeverybodythewaythatSmithgirlwasalloverBobbyMac,I sweartomysoul,girl,I'llslapyouNEKKIDrightthere." Southern Mamas often forego breathing to make a point.

I've never seen anyone "slapped nekkid" but I've heard about it all my life. Sometimes after a person threatens to slap you nekkid, they'll tag on the phrase "and hide your clothes," which brings us right back to the discussion at hand: PDAs.

If you should ever hear such harsh words from your own sweet mama's lips, threatening a show of disciplinary force that is so extreme it will remove your clothes from across a crowded room (or hill), please remember, she has your best interest at heart. She knows the object of your affections might well enjoy being draped by you in public, as evidenced by that silly grin on his face, but everyone else will think you are "experienced."

I was raised by my Southern Mawmaw who said, "Boys don't mind having fun with easy girls, but when they decide to get married, they look for a girl they can respect and one who'll be respected by their family and friends."

Donna Hicks
Temple, Texas

Mama taught us that experience is good in the job market, Sugar, but not if you're trying to snag Mr. Right. Even if your sweetie values your prior experience—and he won't, but work with me here—when his mama and her people get through tearing you down, that boy will drop you like a bad habit and you'll be right back at Door Number One. You can recover from being too forward and still win Mr. Right, the Game Show. Showing too much experience with draping is another matter entirely. Can you say "game over"?

It's Hard to Date in Lockdown

By the time my sisters and I were old enough to date, we had more than a decade of Mama's teachings on the opposite sex echoing through our heads, all of them woven in and around the concept of mutual respect. Aretha may have sung about it, Rodney may have whined about it, but Mama could spell it frontward and backward three times fast because "boys won't respect you if you don't respect yourself."

> If you let a guy kiss you on the first date, he'll think you're cheap.
>
> Jean Ormond
> Jackson, Mississippi

Mama had laid this groundwork years before in conversations with her friends while we played childhood games nearby. "No self-respecting daughter of mine will ever run out to get in a car because a boy honks a horn!" she'd exclaim to her friends as they sipped coffee. "Why, if he can't come to the door and ask for her, and meet her daddy and me, he might as well not stop at this house." By the time we were old enough to be expecting company, we knew full well we best share the rules with our dates before they ever made it to the house.

And while we're on the subject of dating, my sisters and I weren't raised at San Quentin, like many of our dates claimed—our parents weren't that lenient. Before we left the house (on a preapproved excursion to a preapproved location with a preapproved date), Mama would give us the once-over: Too much makeup—back to the bedroom to try again. Too much skin—back to the bedroom and don't bother coming back out again. (For more detail on these and other fashion faux pas, see chapter 7, "Spit-Shined in Public.")

> My mom said, "If you waller with the pigs, you'll get mud on your face."
>
> Karen White
> Coppell, Texas

Once we passed inspection we could leave with a reminder of our curfew—eleven o'clock—and that meant being in bed with your teeth brushed and your makeup off, not parking in the driveway. If we were late, Mama would be standing on her head.

Have I mentioned this special skill? Like many of her counterparts, my Southern Mama was and remains a world-class head-stander. Many things prompt Mama to stand on her head, but not knowing where her girls are will do it every time. Mama spent a lot of time on her head when we were teenagers.

I wish I had a dollar for every time I heard her say, "Where in tarnation have you been? I've been standing on my head for hours!" We girls couldn't figure out how she did it. I know that, personally, I would've been too light-headed to put us through twenty questions if I'd been on my head for hours, but not Mama. She could spend an evening on her head and conduct an investigation the FBI could only dream about.

Along with the looming possibility of cross-examination, we girls always left our house toting that heavy Southern responsibility to "remember who you are" and "don't forget your raising," seeing as how "your actions reflect on this family, whether you like it or not." Unlike the heavily veiled references of my early childhood, these warnings were anything but vague. By now, we knew exactly where the line was. If and when we crossed it, pleading ignorance was a dead-in-the-water defense.

For instance, one of Mama's dating peeves concerned what we used to call passion marks, or hickeys. To a Southern Mama, seeing a hickey on a girl's neck is akin to having the word *easy* tattooed on her forehead. "I better not ever see a hickey on one of my daughters!" Mama said more than once. "Why, that is so trashy. If he needs something to suck on, I'll get the boy a pacifier." Justifiably mortified at the idea of Mama giving one of my dates a binkie, I was quick to remove my neck anytime such a situation began to develop. As I remember, not everyone did....

Mama said, "Sit with your legs together. You're not taking pictures."

Ann Cowen
Chapel Hill, North Carolina

One summer Papa's niece Penny came for a visit. My mother's little brother, Rod, was living with us at the time, helping Papa out on the farm. We were teenagers by then, and my sisters and I knew full well not to come home with hickeys on our necks. Not being raised under our roof, Rod and Penny had missed the memo. One evening the two of them spent some time getting better acquainted. When my mama saw that passion mark on Penny's neck, she lit into them like who would've thought it. "Rodney Ryle Stone," she said. "You better hope and pray I don't tell your daddy!" The Reverend Billy Graham would have been proud; Penny and Rod were prayer warriors for at least a good week. Oh, and a special note to those who like to stereotype us Southerners: Penny and Rod aren't even remotely related. So if you were thinking kissing cousins and all of that, sorry, wrong again.

Dead Rabbits and Southern APBs

Poor Mama, her little girls had grown up. Our social opportunities were expanding under her nose and beyond her reach. The possibility of us necking was but one of the worries keeping her up at night. Not much time passed between Rod and Penny's necking incident and the summer my friend Reba began to suspect she had a bun in the oven. Naturally, she began to panic since she'd had supper without saying grace. (Yes, you do. Think about it. You don't have to speak Southern to figure that one out. Reba was worried she was in the family way without the benefit of marriage.)

Reba knew she needed to go to the doctor and find out, but a checkup here in our small town was out of the question. The rabbit wouldn't have died before her dear mama did. In other words, the doc's receptionist would've been on the phone before the door hit Reba's backside to casually mention that "the Smith girl just left."

"Oh," her friend would've said. "Is she sick?"

"Not yet..." Running Mouth would've replied. And Reba's mama would've found out lickety-split and put the Southern Mama's version of an APB out on her head. This All Points Bulletin is translated on Southern streets as "you better give your heart to Jesus, girl, because your butt is mine."

> When someone was trying to get information my grandma didn't want to give (this would've been considered gossip), she would say, "Don't pick me. I ain't no banjo!"
>
> Jackie Smith
> Columbia, South Carolina

Reba decided to see a doctor in the next town. "Come in

Here's something I always told my twin daughters: "When a single woman is pregnant and doesn't want to be, she has no good options left. It doesn't matter if she's fourteen or forty. She can have an abortion and live with that; give the baby up for adoption and always wonder; or try to raise the child alone." It's rough advice but it made an impression.

Liz Fisher
Palm Harbor, Florida

tomorrow," they told her over the phone, "and bring your first-morning specimen." Bright and early the next morning Reba dutifully placed one of her mama's quart-size canning jars chockfull of her first-morning specimen on the receptionist's desk. The look on the lady's face told my friend that this was possibly one of those times when "a little dab will do ya."

In the end, Reba got the news she was dreading and her mama still managed to find out in record time. Maybe she put a trace on that missing fruit jar. Who knows? Southern women will present you with canned tomatoes while reminding you in the same breath that they "want that jar back!" Regardless, once the dust cleared, Reba discovered the silver lining in every Southern girl's cloud: Her mama was beside her all the way. Fact is, you'll have an easier time separating us from our Mason jars than coming between us and our daughters, but I wouldn't try either. It gets ugly both ways.

Guarding the Assets

Although I had to watch my two older sisters enter the dating game first, the extra time just served to give me more opportunities to figure out all this S-E-X. Mama had done a thorough job with her responsibilities. I understood that boys were only after one thing and that one thing should be guarded at all costs. I was in my early teens and thus too young to date in Mama's eyes, but I was getting mighty interested in this dangerous new world. The scrawny, immature boys in my class acted too silly to be considered a threat, but the upperclassmen were another matter—yes indeed, there were a couple specimens there that seemed to be well worth the risk.

My mom always told me to keep a quarter in my shoe when I left the house. If I got in trouble and lost my purse, I'd always be able to call home. Every time I started out the door, she'd say, "Gail, do you have your quarter?"

Gail Bedillion
Dallas, Texas

I was going to school in Tallulah, Louisiana, at the time, and the rules at Tallulah Academy were very clear: Students in grades ten through twelve could leave campus and go uptown for lunch; for everyone else, the campus was closed. One day a senior asked me, a ninth-grader, to go to lunch with him. Surely I couldn't be blamed for being so mature!

Joe K. and I had a splendid time eating burgers with our fellow young adults at the Wagon Wheel but trouble was on the horizon. Afterward, we were walking back through the school parking lot when I heard the gravelly voice of our principal, Coach Racer Holstead. "Shellie Rushing... Is that you? When did you get to be a soph-o-mo?" Uh-oh, game over!

Within minutes, Coach Holstead was staring at me from the other side of his desk while I begged for mercy, trying to trade on the goodwill he had for my older sisters. Coach weighed his paddle in his hands while I pleaded. "Rushing," he said (Coach never used your first name), "if I don't give you a licking, everybody at this school will think they can get away with this. I'll have fifth-graders going to lunch."

"Yes, sir," I said, trying to look as remorseful as possible.

Suddenly, Coach took his paddle and began to slap it hard

against his bare hand. I looked up at him in surprise. "Well," he said. "You gonna sit there—or you gonna holla?"

I hollered to the heavens from pretend pain while Coach swatted his own hand, and when I finally got to leave his office, I made sure I was seen rubbing my seat of education. Coach, if you're listening, I realize that by sharing our little secret all those football players you coached over the years are gonna know you really do have a heart. But, really, Coach, I have a feeling they knew it all the time.

Southern Dips and Appetizers

It would be a few more years and a lot more advice from Mama before we girls found our Mr. Rights. We'll continue that discussion in the love and marriage chapter. Right now, I'd like to share a few tempting recipes, for as surely as dips and appetizers are meant to prepare you for the meal to come, our mamas' teachings on Certain Subjects were heavy on the wisdom of the old adage "Leave 'em wanting more." Here are a few of our favorite recipes to get your meal started off right and keep your guests hanging around anticipating even better things to come.

~ Louisiana Caviar ~

SERVES 6–8

There are folks who would say we're not very cultured in the South. I respectfully suggest the term is relative. Some of those folks wouldn't recognize the proud traditions of our Southern culture if they bit 'em on their stirring hand. For instance, here's our version of that highbrow aphrodisiac known as caviar. But, do be careful about consuming large quantities in mixed company. It's guaranteed to increase your blood flow just like its fancy cousin.

1 large jar hot picante sauce
2 cans black-eyed peas, drained
1 can hominy or sweet corn, drained
4 green onions, white part only, chopped
1 white onion, diced
½ bell pepper, diced
2 fresh tomatoes, diced
½ cup fresh cilantro, finely chopped
5 jalapeño peppers, seeded and chopped
2 tablespoons ground cumin
2 tablespoons cracked black pepper
1 tablespoon salt
1 tablespoon sugar
dash of All Things Southern Hot Sauce

Mix all ingredients together and refrigerate for about 24 hours. This allows the flavors to get to know one another. Serve with crispy tortilla chips. If you have a family of cheese lovers, you might want to sprinkle some sharp cheese across it first. We do.

~ Jezebel Sauce ~

SERVES 6–8

Folks say this hot little sauce got its name from that infamous bad woman in the Old Testament. The horseradish is what makes it dangerous, but the mixture of jellies and cream cheese will wiggle right into your heart. If you want to heat things up, this one's for you.

1 18-ounce jar of pineapple preserves (I use apricot)
1 18-ounce jar of apple jelly
1 small can dry mustard
1 small jar of horseradish (Don't use the whole jar; just taste test until your eyes burn and you croak for water.)
cracked pepper to taste

Combine all ingredients; blend well. Put in jelly jar and refrigerate. Serve over cream cheese with Wheat Thins or your choice of cracker for dipping. Keeps well!

~ Mexi-Corn Dippers ~

SERVES 6–8

This little dip starts with jalapeño peppers and ends with cayenne, but the sour cream and mayonnaise will help keep the lid on the heat. On the other hand, if you want things to get rowdy, ratchet up those peppers, and enjoy yourselves!

1 jalapeño pepper, chopped
3 green onions, chopped
3 cans Mexi-corn, drained
1 can diced green chilies, drained
1 cup sour cream
1 cup mayonnaise
1 teaspoon cumin
1 teaspoon garlic powder
1 teaspoon chili powder
dash of cayenne pepper

Combine jalapeño pepper and green onions and set 'em aside. Now, blend Mexi-corn with green chilies, sour cream, and mayonnaise. Stir in the onion and pepper mixture and season with the cumin, garlic powder, chili powder, and cayenne! Chill and serve with chips. (We like Fritos Scoops!)

~ Sweet and Spicy Pecans ~

SERVES 6–8

These pecans remind me of the Southern women I know and love—they're sweet and spicy. They're a nice treat to serve with a cup of coffee. However, I speak from experience when I say just don't make 'em too far in advance if they're for a special occasion, or they'll never make it to the big event.

3 egg whites
¼ cup water
2 cups granulated sugar (I use Splenda)
2 tablespoons ground cinnamon
1 teaspoon ground nutmeg
½ teaspoon ground cloves
½ teaspoon salt
½ teaspoon ground cayenne pepper, or black pepper to taste
1¼ pounds pecan halves

Preheat oven to 325 degrees. Meanwhile, in a large bowl, whisk together the egg whites and water. Stir in sugar, cinnamon, nutmeg, cloves, salt, and cayenne pepper. Blend well. Fold in pecan halves, tossing to coat thoroughly. Spread pecans out on a baking sheet, one layer deep. That's very important. Bake about twenty minutes stirring every ten minutes. Spread on wax paper to cool before serving. Yum!

~ Overstuffed Jalapeño Bites ~

SERVES 6–8

Here's a great recipe for the fire-breathers among us. It's ridiculously simple but the combined flavor of the cream cheese and bacon make it irresistible. Just be careful to use gloves around those fresh jalapeño seeds or you'll be caught playing with fire, and I don't mean the opposite sex.

1 8-ounce tub whipped cream cheese
1 teaspoon Tony Chachere's Original Creole Seasoning (or other season-all)
dash All Things Southern Hot Sauce
12 fresh jalapeño peppers, halved lengthwise and seeded
12 slices bacon, cut in half

Preheat oven to 400 degrees.

Now, for the stuffing, combine cream cheese, Tony Chachere's, and hot sauce. Once it's stirred up well, stuff the jalapeño boats with it.

Finish by wrapping a half slice of bacon around each stuffed pepper. Place 'em on a single layer on a baking sheet and bake 'em for 45 to 50 minutes or until the bacon is brown and crisp! Have mercy! That's good eating…

~ Homemade Pimiento Cheese ~

SERVES 6–8

If you've only experienced the store-bought variety, you might think you don't like this Southern delicacy. That would be a shame. Spread some of my Southern Mama's Pimiento Cheese on a piece of bread and treat yourself to the real stuff.

1 pound sharp cheddar cheese, grated
¼ cup mayonnaise
¼ cup buttermilk
¼ onion, diced
1 2-ounce can pimientos, diced and drained, juice reserved
½ teaspoon cayenne pepper

Combine cheese, mayonnaise, and buttermilk. Stir in onion and pimientos. (Be sure to save the pimiento juice. You'll need it to help work with the cheese.) Okay, season with cayenne pepper and that's it! This cheese spread will keep in the refrigerator for several days. You can enjoy it on fresh bread, or stuffed in the hollow of a celery stick—but you'll enjoy it 'cause you're eating Southern now.

~ Fried Dill Pickles ~

SERVES 6–8

Southern girls know how to dress up to get a man's attention. It's a talent we use in the kitchen as well. Here's an easy way to take a dill pickle from the doldrums to the delightful. Sometimes I substitute sliced jalapeño peppers for the pickles. Either way, they're habit forming.

1 cup milk
1 egg, beaten
3½ cups flour
salt and pepper to taste
1 quart sliced dill pickles, drained
vegetable oil, for frying

Combine milk and egg in a bowl. Put the flour in a plastic bag and add salt and pepper. Dip pickles in egg mixture and then shake in flour. Once the pickles are well coated, deep fry them in oil until they turn golden brown and float on the surface. Enjoy!

3

Once You Get Your Hooks In

What Southern Mamas Tell Their Daughters About Love and Marriage (with Casserole Recipes to Hold It All Together)

There comes a day in a young Southern girl's life when she comes face-to-face with the realization that, contrary to a good bit of earlier evidence, there's actually a heart beating in her mother's chest and—this is always a shocker—a romantic one at that. Suddenly, the same woman who has spent your formative years sermonizing on the inherent threat of the opposite sex and the clear and present danger it poses to your reputation, morphs into an advice columnist. She is now eager to dispense advice on how to reel in the man of your dreams.

> Once I got older, Mama told me, "Never date anyone you wouldn't consider marrying. You never know when you'll fall in love."
>
> Lissa Spears
> Natchez, Mississippi

Where once she taught you to be suspicious of all boys, she is now sharing secret feminine wiles. Granted, you will think her wiles are silly. My sisters and I did. I suspect laughing at our mamas' wiles has been the standard reaction of generations of females that came before us. For instance, I remember my Southern Mama telling us to keep our elbows nice and soft because it is one of the first things a boy notices. She said this with a straight face too, which left ample room for me to wonder if she was: a) naïve, b) seriously deceived, or c) merely projecting her own desire for us to have soft elbows onto our prospective beaus. You see, it had been my misfortune to develop at an early age. Mama could have possibly sold that line to my flat-chested classmates, but I was quite sure the boys in my class didn't even know I had elbows. Clearly, a third eye would've gotten me less attention.

When mother wanted to teach me to flirt, she said, "Roll your eyes."

Mary Louise Nackley
Roanoke, Virginia

I noticed this heightened interest in my chest the most during P.E., also known as Physical Education or Painful Endurance. This is a class that kids were once required to pass yearly in order to prove they could withstand various degrees of humiliation. We were running laps that fateful day and by "we" I mean the female students. When my group ran by the boys at the trampoline station a voice called out with a voice that haunts me to this day, "Hey, guys, look a here! Shellie Rushing's top half is running twice as fast as the bottom."

While the memory of that event haunted me and cast considerable doubt on Mama's Elbow Theory, the facts couldn't be denied. Mama had a new willingness to help sharpen our hunting skills. While this can be a disconcerting phenomenon for Southern girls, it need not be cause for alarm. Now that I've given birth to a female child of my

My great soothsayer was my late grandmother Chi-Chi. She always told me, "Never trust a man who wears more jewelry than you do."

Linda Cox
Tillar, Arkansas

very own, I realize my poor mama hadn't developed a split personality; she was simply following well-honed Southern Mama instincts. It is first and foremost our duty to instill the fear of God and premarital sex in our daughters. Only then do we consider them ready to choose a mate—with our help, of course.

Someone for Everyone

By and large, Southern Mamas hold to the theory that there is "someone for everyone." My dear mother was no exception. If someone broke my heart, he simply wasn't the right one, end of story. She wouldn't put up with us mooning over some boy. A Southern girl is taught to hold the opinion that she is better off without anyone who doesn't appreciate her considerable charms. There are plenty of fish in the sea and all that.

If backed into a corner, Southern Mamas will grudgingly admit that the theory of Someone for Everyone can grow old if the someone in question has been looking long, but this is all the more reason a girl should keep her hook baited. Should you find yourself in such a position, retaining a sense of humor will be a tremendous asset. My cousin Paula sets a good example here. The girl's been fishing for a while. Her mother, God love her, continues to encourage Paula to hang in there, but it really isn't necessary. Paula is far from pining away. She has a full life; it just doesn't include Mr. Right—yet.

If I wanted to date someone who was interested in another girl, my mama would look at me and say, "There's many a slip between the cup and the lip, honey." In other words, "Don't give up yet, it ain't over 'til the wedding ring is on the finger!"

Cynthia Wolfe
Columbus, Georgia

I saw Paula for the first time in a long time the other day. She was her usual witty self; the girl could always keep me in stitches. When I commented on how badly I had missed her wicked sense of humor, her mother rolled her eyes.

"Well, you're in luck. She's been in a foul mood all day," Aunt Diane said. "You know her birthday is coming up. She's touching thirty and feeling sort of anxious about not finding Mr. Right."

Paula rolled her eyes. "Mama," she said, "go ahead and tell the truth. I'm not touching thirty; I'm beating the heck out of it." Paula and I laughed. Aunt Diane didn't. A few minutes later, Aunt Diane tried again.

"Seriously, Paula, Honey, I wish you wouldn't be so discouraged. You'll find someone that appreciates you. Remember what I've always said, 'There is someone for everyone, one man for one woman, just like the Good Lord intended.' You'll see, Sugar, it's a wonderful arrangement."

"Relax, Mama," Paula said. "You sold me on that idea a long time ago. I don't want to change it; I just want to get in on it."

You go, Paula. Not only has the girl managed to keep a sense of humor about the whole thing, she has also displayed a willingness to switch baits if necessary. Recently, after ten years in the business world, Paula decided to shake her life up a little. She's now training to become a flight attendant.

My mama always says, "Every old shoe has a mate." I find myself thinking of that quite often when I see mismatched-looking couples.

Lisa Taylor
West Monroe, Louisiana

Paula tells me it's not as easy as you think to get accepted into flight attendant school. She had to fill out a questionnaire a mile long and then she was called in for an interview.

A businesslike, no-nonsense woman ushered Paula into her office, and after a barrage of questions, the lady looked at Paula quite seriously and asked, "And why do you want to be a flight attendant?"

Paula thought about that a minute. All she could hear was her mother's voice in her head telling her that it pays to tell the truth. "Well, ma'am," she said, "to be completely open with you, I thought it would be a great chance to meet men."

That answer surprised the lady. "I appreciate your honesty," she told Paula, "but you can meet men anywhere."

"Yes'm," Paula said, and then added with her characteristic wit, "but, with all due respect, ma'am, they're not strapped down."

Paula said she was surprised when she got the job because the interviewer didn't seem pleased with that answer. She just frowned and noted something on Paula's application without comment. Aunt Diane, however, was practically beaming with approval at Paula's story.

> Mom had a little rhyme, "Don't get married until you're twenty—times are hard and days are plenty."
>
> Edie Walker
> Blackly, Oregon

High Noon at the OK Corral

Southern Mamas appreciate the sort of aggressiveness Paula displayed during her job interview. Whether you're searching for Mr. Right, or building a business from scratch, Southern Mamas believe in putting a shoulder to your dreams and feet to your prayers. If you want it, go after it. Things may not always work out the way you hope, but let it never be because you didn't try. Forgive me if that doesn't fit with the stereotypical idea of the fragile Southern belle who spends her days resting on the couch and fanning herself between fainting spells, but I don't know that mythical breed. The Southern female of my experience is more likely to gear up for battle than retreat to the sofa.

I remember once during high school when bad blood between my friend Cynthia and another girl built until they picked a time and place to address their issues—think high noon at the OK Corral. The final straw had come when Cynthia got a note from her arch enemy that read, "Your butt is a turnip patch and I'm fixin' to do the picking!" Everyone who was anyone congregated at the convenience store parking lot that afternoon to see the fur fly. There was name calling, hair pulling, and punches—and that was just the kids trying to get a front-row seat. I was with Cynthia later that afternoon when she told her mama about the altercation. Her mother wasn't at all pleased things had gotten physical, but anyone could see how proud she was that Cynthia had faced her problems head-on. Southern girls are taught to confront issues, not run from them.

Which reminds me. Do y'all remember the Runaway Bride from Georgia who got all the media attention a couple summers ago? It's okay if you don't. We can still use the poor thing for an example. As lathered up as the professional journalists were about that story, they completely missed the obvious. I couldn't help but notice in all the interviews conducted during the bride's disappearance that it was her jilted groom, her loving stepdad, and her future father-

Mama said, "Never put your husband in a situation where he has to choose between you and his mother."

Marilyn Corley
Vicksburg, Mississippi

in-law standing front and center with supportive quotes. You didn't see her Southern Mama there, did you? And neither hide nor hair of future mother-in-law, right? Allow me. I believe I can help the experts with this one.

Every little Southern girl grows up dreaming of a great big wedding just like the one Jennifer ran from. We do love drama, and twenty-eight attendants and six hundred guests practically sings "center of attention." Unfortunately, the bride in the center of it all seemed not to have realized what the more mature Southern women around her would have been all to aware of: You only get one wedding in your lifetime—your daughter's. I'm just sayin', Jennifer's flight was her dear mama's slight. While the men were making happy faces to the camera, Georgia Mom was dabbing her eyes with the dining room tablecloth, knee deep in a room full of wedding presents, painfully aware her child hadn't been able to handle the pressure.

Her Southern Mama would have also known the rules about returning all those wedding gifts. They must go back, whether the event is cancelled or postponed—unless the second date falls within the two-month clause. But, here's the clincher: Georgia Mom would have also been painfully aware that her still unmarried daughter was over thirty. This might not be an issue anymore in some places, but down here we're still honest enough to admit that there comes a time when the bloom begins falling off the rose.

My mother had a bad experience with her first husband. So her advice to me was, "Before you accept a proposal, find out if he is really single, can hold a job, and whether or not his mother is dead. Then you'll get a husband who is devoted only to you, provides security, and you can avoid mother-in-law problems."

Dr. Kathie T. Erwin
Memphis, Tennessee

And while I am supposing (and I'll be the first to admit this is mere speculation), one can only guess at the disposition of the publicly embarrassed mother of the groom. Many customs of wedding planning, like being careful not to alienate your future mother-in-law, also apply to calling it off. Setting her darling son up as a murder suspect would fall under the "doesn't bode well for the future in-law relationship" category.

No, siree, you can bet your bottom dollar neither of these women appreciated the way Jennifer handled her wedding stress. Here's the hard truth: Rarely does a Southern girl look back on her wedding preparations with fondness. The wedding day, perhaps, but the many details that lead up to putting on that proper Southern ceremony can tempt anyone into being a runaway bride.

Wedding Bells and Prison Records

I speak from experience. It was the summer of 1981. I was about to become a married lady, or perhaps a convicted felon. It was touch and go for a while. The problem was one of conflicting goals. My obsessed opponent and I both had our priorities. I wanted to sleep later, work on my tan, read bride magazines, and go four-wheeler riding on the levee with my sweetie—perfectly reasonable behavior from my perspective.

My mom used to tell me, "Never is a long, long time so be careful when you say 'never.'" After the death of my first husband I had said I'd never remarry. I used to also say that I'd never live in Louisiana. I should tell you that I'm remarried and living in Louisiana.

Donna L. Johnson
Lake Providence, Louisiana

My Southern Mama, on the other hand, was completely irrational. She droned on and on about silly little details like alterations, thank-you notes, flowers, and guest lists. And she asked the most boring questions, such as, "Did you get your blood work done?" and "Have y'all gone to get the marriage license, yet?" *Puleease.* Did I mention that I was a mere child? I was eighteen years old and fresh out of high school. All I wanted was to marry my honey and drive back and forth to college in a nearby town. Papa had given his permission, even if he had added that I was barely "dry behind the ears." I didn't much like hearing that, but, looking back on it now, I suppose he was right.

Mama may have stood on my last immature nerve that whole summer, but I now realize that one of us needed to be paying attention. Southern weddings are highly orchestrated events, preceded by an appropriate number of showers, coffees, and teas. A Southern girl's wedding season is not a sprint. It's a Dixie marathon, and it's not recommended for the faint of heart.

The first leg of this bridal marathon is generally the "Coffee," a formal affair similar to the "Tea," with the most notable difference being the Coffee is an A.M. event and the Tea is held in the afternoon. Coffees are come-and-go meet-and-greets traditionally held on Saturday mornings, almost always between ten and twelve. It's totally acceptable for them to be held at the Country Club or otherwise dignified forum, but they're most often given at a private residence that's been spit-shined to a fare-thee-well.

I once commented to my mother about a "lady" we both knew, saying that she "had married that man for his money!" Mother very quietly said to me, "If she married him for his money, she'll earn every penny."

Lola Dillon
Armona, California

She may have still been pulling weeds from her flower beds at the crack of dawn, but the lady of the house now appears serene and unflustered, projecting a confidence that suggests her baseboards are always spotless, her windows forever sparkling. This charming hostess is either a very close friend of the mother of the bride or a member of the mother's church family, but it's traditionally her ties to the mother of the bride, rather than the bride herself, that has summoned her to action. She is joined by a number of other hostesses with similar commitments to the bride's family. It's very likely their own Coffees were given by either the mother, aunt, or grandmother of the bride. Today's term is *paying it forward*, but Southern women have been doing it for generations. Note to newcomers: If you're invited to a Coffee, there is almost no acceptable reason not to attend short of death, and maybe childbirth (but if that child is sleeping through the night you'd best suck your stomach in and show up).

Many Southern women actually enjoy Coffees and Teas. They attend with no ulterior motive other than to see everyone and catch up on the latest, especially as the bridal season tends to coincide with spring, when everyone is eager to get out and about. Others put in their time at these events year after year solely to get their shower cards punched before their daughter's or granddaughter's time comes. No, there are no actual cards, but trust me on this "they" know whether or not you're there. "They" always know. It's not uncommon to hear someone voice concern over another's absence as in, "You know I don't believe I've seen Linda this morning. I do hope everything's okay..." The experienced belle is adept at judging the speaker's sincerity. Here's a clue for the novice: If her voice trails up and her eyebrows lift ever so slightly, it's highly probable that she's implying Linda, Poor Thing, was too lazy to make the effort.

It occurs to me you could be getting the impression the Southern Coffee is merely a frivolous opportunity for a hen party. Good heavens, I hope not. Such an assumption would be a travesty. These events actually serve an important societal function. It's where young Southern girls learn the art of small talk and experienced women keep their skills honed. The Coffee is held throughout several rooms of the house, often including the porches and patios, all of them holding beautiful tables dripping with flowers, crystal, and silver, and laden with food and drink. The fluidity of the setting allows the Southern female to practice maneuvering among people of all ages. She learns how to join an intimate twosome, interact, and move on—without appearing either pushy or aloof.

As the situation dictates, the young belle will remember to show respect to the aged, concern for the ill, and admiration for another female's lovely appearance, without once forgetting to ask about anyone's mama. This all happens within the course of thirty or so minutes, for once she has nibbled and chatted her way around the house, making sure she has seen and been seen, she is allowed to make a gracious exit.

My mama had this advice, "The first time, marry for love. The second time, marry for money." On a simliar note, I heard this one from a middle-aged woman from North Carolina, (not my mama but a Southern Mama nonetheless): "You can marry more money in a minute than you can make in a lifetime."

Courtney Fingar
Washington, D.C.

Showers are slightly more intimate and generally much more fun as the informal setting has been known to allow for more extended interaction. This can be good and it can be bad, depending on the guest list. Take Sue Ellen Binder and Georgia Hathcock, please. The two of them are forevermore sniping at each other. They absolutely can't get along. For the most part, they try to avoid each other, but this is a small town.

Yesterday they both showed up at a shower for a mutual friend. It wasn't pleasant. They sat on opposite sides of the room but every now and again they'd meet at the refreshment table. (Unlike at Coffees, shower food is generally confined to a certain room or area of the hostess's house.) During one of those little meetings, Georgia sidled up just as a few of us began talking about the winter pounds that have crept up here and there. It wasn't a conversation anyone wanted to have with Georgia. The woman still looks good and she knows it, and she likes everyone else to know it, but then again she has never given birth, a fact most of the girls like to remind each other of behind her shapely back.

Georgia walked up about the time Sue Ellen was talking about buying some new spring clothes for a few upcoming events. "Shopping is just not any fun these days," she moaned. "The clothes are ugly and nothing fits—I'm afraid I've put on a little bit of extra weight."

Georgia raised her eyebrows ever so slightly, but Sue Ellen saw it. That's when I backed up just a little, out of experience, don't you know.

"I saw that, Georgia Hathcock," Sue Ellen said. "I'd like you to know that in the first place, you are flat-out rude. I may have gained five or six pounds, but at least I can lose 'em. You on the other hand, will never change." And with that, she stormed off.

The ensuing silence was brief. "Come on, y'all. Don't look at me like that," Georgia said to the silent little group left standing there with their jaws hanging open. "I'm just saying, the poor thing may have gained five pounds in the first place—but you can't tell me she didn't gain another five or ten in the second one."

While there may be a bit of guest stress at these get-togethers, it doesn't compare to the strain on the poor bride-to-be. Along with the stress of making out the guest lists for all of these parties, which can be a walk through a mine field all by itself, the young bride-to-be is simultaneously juggling 967 wedding details as she attempts to carry off the wedding of her dreams without breaking the family farm. Fortunately, there are cocktail parties scattered throughout the season, events distinguished by the allowance of men and music. Said men are notoriously clueless to any undercurrents between anyone, and therefore unconsciously efficient at relieving the mounting pressure.

The Blushing Bride

Yes, the wedding season can be a notoriously stormy time for mother and daughter, and as previously noted, my mother and I were no exception. The two of us mixed like oil and water. We fought like cats and dogs. We collaborated like Democrats and Republicans. I could elaborate, but I think you're with me.

The short version is that I did manage to become a blushing bride that summer, and one without a police record. And may I add that *blushing* is an appropriate word. Those tying-the-knot preparations brought on a strange new reality, requiring me to rethink everything I thought I knew about the Southern women in my world. It was as if I had unconsciously entered—cue the horror music, *dunt-dunt-dunt-dunnnn*—the twilight zone. The slightest hint of this developing new trend had begun when Phil and I announced our engagement. It only built in intensity as the big day drew nearer.

For the Southern women in my life (my own dear mother

included!) began to openly discuss the pleasures of that off-limits activity they had previously distanced themselves from and cautioned me to avoid! Hold the phone. Stop the presses. Prepare for takeoff. However you'd like to say it, people, I was about to receive blatant permission to have legal marital relations.

> I'm a Southern Mama and I've told all of my children to remember this one thing: Whatever bad habit your sweetheart has before you marry—it'll multiply by a hundred afterward. Now if you can live with that, then you should have a happy marriage.
>
> Brenda Vicars
> Alabama

To be clear: I was going to have S-E-X. I knew it. They knew it and—IT WAS OKAY. Wait, scratch that. It wasn't just okay, it was all good. This is where it got truly strange. Not only were they approving of the idea, they were actively encouraging it.

Those mature belles snickered like hormonal schoolgirls during my lingerie shower. The naughtier the nightie, the heartier they laughed. Frankly, it was all too weird. I was finding it much harder to flip the switch. I avoided making eye contact with these women, these warriors who had once guarded my innocence like soldiers at Fort Knox and who were now gleefully predicting my frilly little garments wouldn't stay on long enough for the lace to itch.

> My aunt Margaret refused to tell me what happened on a honeymoon, but she took the opportunity to deliver a sermonette on honeymoon etiquette: "Be as pleasant as possible and remember to exclaim over special treats."
>
> Janet Fitzgerald
> Reedsport, Oregon

One of my aunts, who will remain nameless in this anecdote, took it upon herself to tell me what to expect. She spoke in code, but the gist of her information was very clear.

She explained that there would be a certain amount of pain involved, but it was a good kind of pain. Excuse me?

Days later, I was leaving my wedding reception with my brand-new husband and trying my best to ignore the knowing smiles plastered on everyone's face. I knew we'd be leaving them behind, and yet, somehow it seemed they were all going with us.

Holding on to the Prize

My and Mama's summer of discontent wasn't the last time we clashed, but it did signal the worst of our mother-daughter conflict and the beginning of a totally new relationship. Now that my sisters and I had joined the ranks of married women, Mama quickly turned the page. Time was of the essence. We were ready for a brand-new chapter in the continuing-education course that is a Southern girl's lifelong privilege. Mama was now intent on teaching her daughters how to make sure the knot stayed tied.

Mama's advice was heavy on two particular points: You need to keep a fire going in both the bedroom and the kitchen. Southern Mamas across the board believe if a girl tends to these blazes, she won't have to worry about her Sweet Thang volunteering with anyone else's department.

> Mama said, "Anyone can get married but it takes hard work to stay married."
>
> Andrea Leslie
> Dallas, Texas

Speaking of being all fired up, not long ago my friend Paulette e-mailed me what was supposed to be a serious news article. She'd found it online and it was being heralded as a brand-spanking-new scientific theory.

We have a long-standing tradition in our family, based on advice from my grandmother Margaret from Augusta, Georgia. It was given by her mother, Senie Matilda, on her wedding day in 1941.

In that time, at least in our family, girls were given absolutely no advice or information on sex as they entered marriage. As Margaret changed her clothes to leave for the honeymoon, Senie Matilda came into the room to help her daughter finish up.

"Well, you're a married woman now," Senie Matilda said to her daughter. "And so I'll give you the same advice my mother gave me on my wedding day."

Margaret held her breath, anxious for any information on what lay ahead.

"Keep a pillow between ya," said Senie Matilda.

And that was it. Was the pillow meant to go between her knees—between my grandparents as a buffer? The world will never know.

As my grandmother repeated the story to us before she passed, she always followed it with, "And I've been married for years, had four children, and I still don't know what she meant."

As her granddaughters grew and married, the one sure way to stop the flow of tears on our wedding days was for a mother, aunt, or grandmother to discreetly sidle up to us at some point during the day and whisper, "Now remember. Keep a pillow between ya!"

Rebecca Murphy,
North Augusta, South Carolina

In a nutshell, the article reported that, after much study, a team of researches had concluded that, and I'm quoting here: "Hungry men find larger women more attractive." The findings, published in the *British Journal of Psychology* stated hungry men are more tolerant and, therefore, more accepting of plump women. Imagine that.

I hit Reply and told Paulette I was filing this great big news flash under, "No, duh!"

You'll have to forgive me if the eureka moment seems a tad anticlimactic. Southern girls are taught that hungry men will tolerate a lot of things if you've got something good cooking on the stove. It may be universally understood that the way to a man's heart is through his stomach, but Southern Mamas have long been known to build on that theory with this one: It's also the way around whatever pickle you may find yourself in.

My Southern Grandma raised me. She told me, "It's what he can't get at home that looks good over the fence."

Kay Bradley Hirt
Piqua, Ohio

Our mamas have been teaching this concept since the day Eve said, "Hey, Adam, you hunky husband, I need to tell you about a little something I did earlier that's gonna cost us big. But first, are you hungry, Precious? I was just about to get an apple pie out of the oven." Okay, so I've taken liberties with the storytelling here, but I'm talking about women who were raised in the Bible Belt, people. We know about these things. And yet, Paulette, my fellow belle whose elevator has been known to get stuck on the lower floors, was still convinced the news release held great promise.

"I think it's pretty cool," she said later that afternoon when she dropped by. "Think about it, Shellie. No more worrying about whether Jerry Don and Phil think we're getting fat. We'll just starve 'em into thinking we're still hot."

Sometimes you have to shake Paulette to get the wheels turning again. "What about that last line in the article?" I asked her.

"What part's that?"

"The part where Professor Swarmi says the subjects revert to their original tastes in women once they've eaten."

Paulette never hesitated. "Whatever," she said. "You can't trust a man named Swarmi." I was about to point out she'd already bought most of Swarmi's theory when the girl had a eureka! moment of her own. "Besides, men always fall asleep after they eat! So we starve 'em until they think we're hot, they go to sleep, they wake up hungry and voilà—we're still hot!" Paulette, she might not make the rules, but she sure can play the game.

Fire Insurance

As previously noted, our mamas teach us that keeping the home fires burning extends beyond the kitchen and into the bedroom. While most young married couples find it ridiculously easy to generate the necessary heat in this area in the early days of their marriage, Southern Mamas are realists. This is why they sell their daughters a little fire insurance by teaching them that it will become necessary to tend this hearth even when one is feeling less than "fiery." A belle

On the subject of the marriage bed, Mama told me she didn't see what all the fuss was about. She said she just did what came naturally and it seemed to work out just fine.

Carolyn Henderson
Greenville, Mississippi

should willingly commit to her wifely duty and let her feelings catch up. In the interest of being delicate, I'll simply say Southern Mamas believe this type of effort will benefit from Newton's first law of motion: An object in motion tends to stay in motion. You figure it out.

When I got married, my mother gave me this advice: "Never worry about an unmade bed or getting a made-up bed messy. If you care more about a made bed than your husband's affections, he'll take them someplace else."

Beth Adams
Dallas, Georgia

As serious as my Southern Mama was about managing the heat, she made it clear that neither a kitchen fire nor a bedroom fire, nor a combination of the two, would be able to save a marriage that wasn't built on respect. Mama taught my sisters and me that a strong marriage is the result of both parties honoring their commitment and valuing their spouse. It's generally acknowledged that a successful marriage is a two-way street. My Southern Mama improved on that idea somewhat by modeling a marriage that looked more like a one-way street with each of them taking turns at the wheel.

I watched my parents' very successful marriage thrive on love and respect. Through my mother's example I learned the more you respect your husband the more he'll respect you and take care of you. If you are selfish and think only of yourself, then so will he!

Kimberly Siddons
Lenoir, North Carolina

My sisters and I have watched Mama walk this "Love and Honor" talk for years. We learned as very little girls that when Papa came in from a hard day in the fields, he was king. Mama not only had his supper cooked, but she served his plate and kept it full of seconds until his appetite was sated. She was never ashamed to do things for him that he was capable of doing for himself. Quite the contrary, it was obvious she enjoyed tending to him.

Trust me. I know that sounds antiquated. When my sisters and I became know-it-all teenagers, we bristled at it too, but if Mama sensed our disapproval, she didn't care. She was quick to tell us girls it was part of a wife's responsibilities to wait on her husband. If we cringed when she said it, so be it. Her man had worked a long, hard day in the fields and she was going to see to it he was rested and refreshed before it was time for him to go at it again.

It must be noted here that Mama's gospel of mutual respect was lived as clearly as it was preached. Papa may have been king, but he loved his queen and treated her as such. Mama would have nothing less. Her loving care wasn't demanded nor taken for granted. It was appreciated.

Mama was teaching us by example that love may lead to marriage but mutual respect will be the glue that holds it all together. Of course, my sisters and I didn't grasp such a deep message at the time. All we knew as little girls was that their love for each other made us feel safe. If we thought that love was threatened, our whole world felt threatened.

Mama took the Bible's warning to "not let the sun go down on your wrath" and taught me not to go to bed angry. She said, "Stand behind the door and pop out and do something funny to break the anger."

Pat Bland
Denton, Texas

Once, back on Bull Run Road, Mama got so mad at Papa she resorted to flight, roaring out of the driveway in our old brown Dodge. She was just planning on driving around and cooling her jets, but we didn't know that. When Papa took off after her, we girls held hands and sang hymns. Hey, we were church kids; it was all we knew. The two of 'em have since admitted to feeling more than a little guilty when they returned smack in the middle of "Amazing Grace."

These days, few people my age live like my parents. Like most of my friends, sometimes I "serve" my husband, and sometimes he "serves" me. We've fallen into our own rituals over the years. And yet, when I do fix Phil's plate or pour his coffee, I experience the truth Mama preached years ago. It truly is better to give than to receive.

The Crime of False Advertising

On the other hand, one of Mama's marriage pointers I've done my dead level best to adhere to is her admonition to keep yourself looking nice for your man. Mama hated to see a pretty young girl marry and then "let herself go." Letting oneself go because you have a ring on your finger is a felony in Mama's book. "Why," she'd say, "it just isn't right."

My Southern Mama told me I should always put my makeup on before I went to bed so that my husband always saw me at my best. As a matter of fact, most of her advice was about keeping your man. I should tell you that my mother is divorced and I never wear makeup to bed.

Deborah Zizzi
West Monroe, Louisiana

The way Mama saw it, neglecting one's appearance didn't fall under the "for better or worse clause." It was simply false advertising. She felt strongly that if a girl was going to dress up, fix her hair, and do her makeup to catch a man, she shouldn't turn into someone else once she gets her hooks in him. (It'd be unfair of me not to mention here that Mama has lived by this same standard. The lady is now in her sixties and there are plenty women half her age who would love to have her complexion, her figure, or both!)

Not all of Mama's messages were taught so clearly. We picked up some by osmosis. For instance, I wasn't very old before I realized that Mama and her girlfriends were good at getting their husbands to do what they wanted, all the while letting the men think it was their own idea. Some people would call this manipulation. Southern women call it charm.

My mama always says, "When you're dealing with a man, you have to make him think it's his idea."

Carey Eubanks Tomlinson
Lake Providence, Louisiana

My parents have been married for more than forty years now. Mama is still teaching us by example and she is still tending to her man, maybe more now than ever. Sometimes Papa ribs her gently about her "tending" getting out of hand but he doesn't fool anyone, not for a second. It's too easy to see the well-worn patterns of a game they've been playing since their courting days. After all these years, they're just two big flirts.

At my grandparents' fiftieth wedding anniversary my grandmother was asked, "How did you do it? Fifty years!" My little grandmother (4'9") looked up and said, "Honey it took a lot of love and a lot of understanding . . . and a whole lot of lettin' it go in one ear and out the other."

Kim Hudson
Gadsden, Alabama

Not long ago my oldest sister was home visiting our parents and checking on Papa, who was recovering from minor surgery. Cyndie said the first morning she was home she found the two of them drinking coffee in the living room. She wished 'em both a good morning and asked Papa how he was feeling. The way Cyndie told it, Papa looked toward Mama and grinned in the way that means the rest of us can enjoy the joke but it's really just between the two of them. "I don't know," he said. "She ain't told me yet."

My New Role

I'm hoping to emulate that kind of loving relationship for my own young married children. My son and my daughter tied the knot with their sweethearts last summer. I remember feeling very philosophical as they headed to the altar. My sense of obligation to assume the right Southern Mama role led me to compose the following suggestions to help 'em get off on the right foot:

> My mama told me that if things got bad in my marriage, I could come home at any time but: "Don't keep the backdoor swingin'!"
>
> Anonymous
> Tennessee

Dear Son: Your wife does not (nor will she ever) look fat. Much can be solved and or avoided by sticking to this proven theme. When y'all decide to have me some grandchildren—and heaven help you if you don't—she might spend much of her pregnancy at the table, where she might take up a good bit of room, but she won't look fat. She'll glow. (You might wanna write that word down.)

Also, you might think your wife cries for no reason. Wrong, there is always one reason at the very least. Sometimes she needs you to ask about it seven hundred times before she is convinced you want to know. Do not grow weary. Yesterday your father and I were leaving your new home for the first time when my eyes filled with tears. Our son, a married man; it was a nostalgic moment that went right over your dad's head. I must say, though, he recovered nicely as soon as he recognized the signs of an approaching meltdown. "You don't look fat," he said firmly.

To my daughter: While it's true your man would rather die than ask directions, this is only true outside the home. Your dear husband will need you to locate common household items and he'll be very willing to ask for your help. He might even stand in the kitchen and ask you if there is any milk. It won't help to roll your eyes and point toward the refrigerator. He wants to hear it from your sweet lips.

Oh, and when y'all decide to have me some grandchildren—and heaven help you if you don't—your husband will be no help getting the wee ones to sleep. This is because he will already be asleep. You'll have a happier marriage if you resist the urge to send him into a deeper one. Call me instead; I'm just a rocker away.

When I was having trouble leaving my babies behind to go on a trip with my husband, my mama said, "Marriage is like silver, you have to take it out and polish it sometimes."

Donna Nix
Shreveport, Louisiana

Weddings with a Regional Flair

Thanks to the grace of God and Tylenol PM, I made it through both of those back-to-back weddings. And for the record, and at the risk of trampling yet another Southern stereotype, there wasn't a shotgun used in either ceremony. Matter of fact, my daughter, Jessica, and her Patrick were so serious about getting things tied up tight they didn't settle for one preacher, they used three!

Some might think the traditional wedding service is pretty

I always heard this one from my mom and grandmother: "When you say your vows, be careful because you can tie a knot in your tongue you can't untie with your teeth." I wish I had listened because boy do I have a big knot in my tongue now.

Patricia Cantrell
West Liberty, Kentucky

much the same everywhere, but I noticed a definite regional flair that summer. For instance, my husband and I went to a wedding in between our son's wedding and our daughter's wedding. (Not so much because we couldn't bring ourselves to skip a week; we were just fond of the young couple getting married.)

Sarah Beth's preacher was my kind of guy, a real country fella. I can say that because I'm a real country girl. You know that line in every wedding where the preacher says, "You may now kiss your bride"? Well, Sarah Beth's preacher handled that with a lot more regional flair.

"Cullen," he said to the groom right after the vows, in the presence of several hundred witnesses. "You know what I'd do if I were you?"

I couldn't see Cullen's face but I think he said, "Sir?"

"If I were you," the preacher said, "I'd haul off and kiss her right in the mouth."

My mama told me to always examine my marriage through the wrong end of a spyglass. That way everything looks small and you can see the big picture without focusing on the tiny details.

Phyllis Frey
Livingston, Texas

I'd never heard the phrase *haul off* during a wedding ceremony, but it wasn't the only original line of the summer. The first came during my son's wedding. Carey's grandfather performed their vows. "Phillip," he said, after pronouncing them husband and wife, "You may salute your bride." Salute?! Did the preacher say "salute"? I wondered if I'd heard him right, but the phrase slipped my mind during the reception.

The next morning I got an e-mail from an old friend. "Shellie," Andy said, "the wedding was beautiful and I enjoyed cutting up on the dance floor like old times. But tell me, did the preacher really tell your son he could salute the bride, and if he did—don't you think he was getting ahead of himself?"

Casseroles to Hold It All Together...

A Southern Mama's marital advice is heavy on learning to give and take, and it's similar to the expertise that goes into the casseroles they teach us how to cook. If necessity is the mother of invention, you can bet your bottom dollar that Southern Mamas hold the majority of the cooking patents. Many a good casserole has been born out of an ability to substitute rather than running to the store when you're short of an ingredient. Here are just a few of our favorites.

~ Mama's Cornbread Dressing ~

SERVES 15–20

The inner workings of a man's mind might remain a mystery despite a Southern Mama's best efforts, but a good dressing doesn't have to be. I've taken Mama's Cornbread Dressing recipe and broken it down to a few very manageable steps.

Cornbread
2 cups self-rising cornmeal
⅓ cup self-rising flour
3 tablespoons bacon grease or shortening
2 eggs
1–2 tablespoons sugar to taste
1¾ cups of milk

Dressing
1 good sized hen
1 pan of cornbread
1 sleeve saltine crackers
4 stalks celery, chopped
1 white onion
5 eggs
salt and pepper to taste
3–4 cups chicken broth

We'll start with the bird. Place hen in a big boiler and cover it completely with water. Bring to a boil over moderately high heat, then turn it down and let it cook on low until the meat is ready to fall off the bones. Take the hen out and let it cool before deboning it, but make sure you save the broth. It's priceless and we'll use it in just a bit.

Now for the cornbread: Sift together the cornmeal and

self-rising flour. Cut in shortening (bacon grease is better if you have it). Add eggs, sugar, and milk. Stir well, pour in cast-iron skillet, and bake in a 350 degree oven for 30 minutes, or until your cornbread is nice and brown.

Now, for the dressing: Crumble cornbread in a large bowl along with the saltine crackers. Add celery and onion, eggs, and salt and pepper to taste.

We're ready to spoon all this into a large buttered casserole dish. (It's important not to work your dressing too much. You'll make it dry.) Last step: gradually add your broth until everything is soft and mushy. This isn't an exact measurement, but you'll use about three to four cups of broth. Cook it about an hour at 350 or until the dressing begins to firm up and the edges get a nice crust, stirring maybe once. That's it! Thanksgiving dressing... Southern style!

~ Hamburger Stroganoff ~

SERVES 8–10

This tried-and-true favorite is hearty enough to satisfy the healthiest male appetite and it's easy to stir up when time is short. Don't be afraid to substitute if you don't have the cream of chicken soup. Cream of mushroom, cream of celery, they'll both do the job.

½ cup minced onion
1 clove garlic, minced
¼ cup butter
1 pound ground beef
2 tablespoons flour
2 teaspoons salt
¼ teaspoon pepper
1 pound fresh mushrooms (or 1 eight-ounce can)
1 can cream of chicken soup
1 cup sour cream

Take a small sauce pan and sauté onion and garlic in butter over medium heat. Brown ground beef in a larger skillet. Once the pink is gone from the meat, drain the grease and return it to the skillet adding the cooked garlic and onion mixture. Add flour, salt, pepper, and mushrooms. Cook another 5 minutes before adding cream of chicken soup. Simmer uncovered for about 10 minutes and stir in sour cream. That's it! Heat thoroughly and serve over rice or your favorite noodles. Ring the porch bell if you want company.

~ Sausage and Cornbread Pie ~

SERVES 8–10

Sausage and cornbread meet each other halfway to create the perfect marriage of flavors. We're talking about soul-satisfying comfort food. The warm feelings will start in the kitchen but they'll permeate the whole house.

1 pound pork sausage
1 cup chopped onion
1 28-ounce can tomatoes, undrained
1 4-ounce can chopped green chiles, undrained
1 cup frozen whole kernel corn
1 teaspoon garlic powder
1 teaspoon chili powder
1 cup yellow cornmeal
⅔ cup self-rising flour
½ teaspoon salt
2 teaspoons sugar
1 egg, beaten
⅔ cup milk
¼ cup vegetable oil

Preheat oven to 375.

Brown sausage and onions together and drain. Add tomatoes, green chiles, corn, garlic powder, and chili powder. Spoon this into a lightly greased baking dish and set aside.

Now to create the perfect cornbread topping: Stir together your cornmeal, flour, salt, and sugar. In a separate bowl combine your egg, milk, and oil. Add to the dry ingredients. Pour this cornbread mixture over the sausage mixture and bake for 40 minutes. Hide and watch—this one is sure to become a family favorite!

~ Easy Cheesy Enchiladas ~

SERVES 10–20

I do hope y'all will appreciate the sacrifice I'm about to make. I'm gonna share my Easy Cheesy Enchiladas with y'all—and in turn risk my husband finding out that I don't actually stand on my feet all afternoon preparing his special dish. You can thank me later.

1 medium onion, diced
1 medium green pepper, diced
1 tablespoon butter
2 pounds ground beef, cooked and drained
6 10-ounce cans enchilada sauce
dash of Panola Hot Sauce
1 teaspoon cajun seasoning
20–24 flour tortillas
1 small can chopped black olives
12 ounces cheddar cheese, grated

Preheat oven to 350 degrees.

Saute the onions and peppers in butter. Combine onions, peppers, and meat in a large pot over medium heat and add the enchilada sauce. Stir in hot sauce and seasoning and simmer. Prepare a large casserole dish with nonstick cooking spray. Build the enchiladas by filling tortillas with meat and cheese, rolling and placing them side by side in your dish. Top with leftover sauce, chopped black olives, and sprinkle with cheese. Bake until the cheese melts and the enchiladas are thoroughly heated. Serve with a nice salad and watch your man hurt himself!

~ Simple Shrimp Creole ~

SERVES 8–10

Diamonds might be a girl's best friend, but Southern Mamas are quick to remind their daughters that a good Crock-Pot will never let you down. If you've got more to do than you can shake a stick at, pull yours out and try this one. I'll walk you through it . . .

½ cup chopped onion
½ cup chopped green bell pepper
½ cup chopped celery
2 tablespoons butter
2 tablespoons Bisquick (biscuit mix)
1½ cups water
1 6-ounce can tomato paste
1 bay leaf
dash of sugar
Salt and pepper to taste
2 pounds frozen shrimp, thawed, shelled, and cleaned
fluffy rice, to serve

Sauté the trinity (onion, pepper, and celery) in the butter. When they're tender and the onions are translucent, make an easy roux by adding the Bisquick and stirring well.

Meanwhile, take your Crock-Pot and combine the water and the tomato paste. Stir in your roux fixings and season with a bay leaf, a little sugar, and some salt and pepper. Set it on low and let it cook for most of six to eight hours. About an hour before you're ready to eat, turn it up on high and add the shrimp. It's that easy. . . . When you're ready to eat, remove the bay leaf and serve over hot fluffy rice.

4

Buns in the Oven

What Southern Mamas Tell Their Daughters About Having and Raising Children (with Bread Recipes for All Your Little Honeybuns)

I'll be the first to admit it: Mama learned a lot while I was off on my honeymoon. Upon my return, I was relieved to discover she was a lot easier to talk to and much more interesting. Over the next weeks and months, as I went about setting up house and learning how to be the lady of it, Mama impressed me with her slow but steady improvement. Her progress was incredible. Less than two short years later I announced my first pregnancy to a transformed woman. My Southern Mama was a wealth of information and the answers were as near as the phone.

> I remember asking Mama when we were growing up how old she was when I was born and she'd always answer, "I don't know, Jan, you've been here all my life." I never thought you could take that two ways until I became a parent myself. It seems like a great part of your life doesn't even start until you become a parent. Mama's a lot smarter to me now than she was when I was younger.
>
> Jan Horne
> Bossier City, Louisiana

From the first day the rabbit died I was cognizant of two schools of thinking: the learned opinions of the medical field concerning pregnancy, childbirth, and parenting—and the Southern Mama's Gynecology and Pediatric Fields of Knowledge. When the two collided, and they collided on a regular basis, Mama was always right.

I quickly discovered there were pregnant women and there were "Stone" pregnant women. Stone is my mother's maiden name. Nothing about my pregnancy was so unusual, so unique, that it couldn't be explained by the females in my family tree. It's been widely noted that Southerners have an unusual fascination with their ancestors. My people are certainly no exception.

> If a girl got married and a baby came less than nine months later, Mama would say, "I think she lost her notching stick!"
>
> Marcia Young-Whitacre
> Sylvester, Georgia

We're all about genes, and I don't mean denim, but DNA: Duly Noted Abnormalities. My family can tie every habit, tendency, or twitch to a predisposed and unavoidable trait handed down from an older relative. The women, in particular, have shown a serious preoccupation with the bloodline. My mama appears to function as head scientist, but her sisters have been knowledgeable and willing assistants. These women bravely identify and document genetic markers the rest of the scientific community chooses to ignore.

For instance, they've traced my sister Cyndie's ability to use her toes like extra fingers back three generations (the girl can practically pick a lock with those nail-polished feet), and they theorize my middle sister, Rhonda, is hot-natured because Grandmaw Stone was. This particular marker has been found in a number of Grandmaw's descendants, and no, according to the family geneticists, it has nothing to do with our famous Delta humidity. My siblings and I, along with our cousins, have tried to convince our elders it's highly improbable anyone could "pass on" the sort of idiosyncrasies they like to trace through the branches of the family tree. Our experts dismiss us with an airy wave.

One of their theories is that the Stones, as a family, have an unusual weakness for tobacco products. Once, when we were teenagers, Cyndie, Rhonda, and I tried to use their solid body of research to our advantage, claiming entrapment by those Virginia Slims Menthol Lights. Unfortunately, Papa was a big believer in rehab.

As amusing as our parents' far-reaching genetic markers are to my generation, we acknowledge that there are worse fates, like the distant cousin whose doings are dismissed with the most damning of Southern pronouncements: "For the life of me, I can not imagine where he got that from!" Such a sad commentary on his lineage is told and retold in hushed tones, like a ghost story or an urban legend. And so it is that we laugh, even though we understand that deep down we too cherish these family connections for they are the ties that bind.

Show and Tell

Showing is a term for that special time when your pregnancy becomes physically obvious. Where I come from, if you're married and you're showing, it's all good. If you've got so much as a bump on the belly without a ring on your finger, it's not so good. Seeing as how I was dutifully observing the accepted order of progression, the Southern belle in me was ready and eager to show. Showing equals attention, Sugar.

My mom's advice on raising children: "If it washes off or grows out, it doesn't hurt anyone. Don't worry about it!"

Peggy Savage
Marion, Arkansas

I suppose women the world over like attention but belles are raised to expect it, enjoy it, perhaps even demand it, without appearing to notice, of course.

Unfortunately for me, I was almost five months pregnant before I began to show. Wait. That's not entirely true. There was one part of my body that appeared to be expecting children. That would be the upper half, and the plural version is accurate. We're talking at least twins, possibly quadruplets. My stomach, however, merely looked swollen. This was not at all what I had envisioned. And if I may digress a moment, indeed my stomach was swollen.

My bowels hadn't "acted" (Mama's polite term) a dozen times in the last couple of months. If you find this an uncomfortable topic of conversation you're probably not a Southern Mama, nor were you birthed by one. Around here, the subject is discussed delicately but often. Medical doctors have yet to fully comprehend the dangers of irregularity, but our mamas have long taught that "a good movement" is critical to one's overall health. Why, even one's skin and hair is at risk. Mama's suggestions had much to do with consistency of time and place, but seeing as the theory resurfaced later when I was toilet-training my own offspring, we'll table it for now.

> My mother always said to wear a maternity outfit with a bow at the neck, "To draw the eye from the stomach to the face." Imagine what she has to say about those T-shirts that have an arrow announcing "baby" or "nothing says lovin' like something in the oven!"
>
> Fran Walton
> Winnfield, Louisiana

We were talking about showing—or not showing, as was my case. After five long months, I wasn't at all pleased with my chest growing three times faster than my belly, but I told myself I probably wasn't showing because of my height (I'm fairly tall). My doctor concurred with this assumption. Not so fast. My Southern Mama corrected us both with one gleeful announcement: *Stone women do not show early.* Mama seemed quite proud of this trait, as if showing early was just a mite too pretentious, even for a belle. I found the news depressing. And yet, as disappointing as Mama's revelation was, it didn't compare to the bad news that lay right around the corner.

A short time later, just when I had begun to wonder if I would ever show, my dear, sweet mama backed me up to the hall mirror. The time had come to end the mystery. Call it the day of discovery. I was about to see where Stone women carry their babies once they do show. Without further ado Mama instructed me to look over my right shoulder. Good Lord in heaven; have mercy on my soul! So, this is how it was gonna be? There would be no cute little pregnant body like I'd seen in all of my mommy magazines, no round little stomach protruding from an otherwise normal figure? My child, my first-born, my long-awaited bundle of joy was right there, on my back—my fat back to be accurate.

My mama told me to never raise my arms above my head while I was pregnant because it can make the cord wrap around the baby's neck.

Patricia Brooks
Daughter of Judith Herron
Edgefield, South Carolina

Looking back on it now I can see that Fat Back Day was only the first in a series of reality checks. With no morning sickness to speak of, I had made it through more than half of my pregnancy with little to complain of other than a case of irregularity. I suppose I could be forgiven for thinking I was coasting through the whole pregnancy thing. But times, they were a-changing.

I spent the next few months trying in vain to keep tabs on my emerging fat-back but every ounce that showed up in front seemed to provide cover for a couple more to slip in the back. I was pregnant coming and going, especially going. Thank goodness I had people to share the blame.

Mama had warned me that Stone women craved fried food when they were pregnant. That was the good news. I found out they also retain water and suffer from hemorrhoids. My doctor said those issues were common with all expectant mothers, but what did he know? This is the same man that said the sex of my child couldn't be determined by whether I was carrying the baby high or low. How silly is that?

Yes, the second half of my pregnancy was all guts and no glory. That is, up until the last moment, and I do mean *the very last moment* when they put that precious bundle in my arms, not the ninety-two hours of painful labor that preceded it.

By all accounts, I should've been prepared to give birth. For some morbid reason known only to our gender, every childbearing female in my dear Southern family had felt compelled to give me a detailed account of her birth experience from the first day the rabbit died. Aunt Marleta might have been the clearest. Her description involved a watermelon and left me sleepless for weeks.

Aunt Marleta is my mother's sister and our family's official eccentric. Most Southern families have at least one eccentric they can count on. Mama's side has always had Aunt Marleta. Now, before you conjure up a stereotype, let me introduce y'all.

An eccentric is merely a fancy name for a larger-than-life individual who isn't afraid to be different, which is why I can call Aunt Marleta eccentric and live to tell about it. While eccentricity isn't confined to the elderly, it usually takes years to perfect the craft. Not my aunt Marleta—she's neither old nor gray. Okay, maybe gray without Miss Clairol, but that's beside the point.

Aunt Marleta mesmerized me when I was a little girl. She was a flamboyant and flashy beautician with rings on every finger. She talked like the rest of us, only more so. On her tongue, Mama's name wasn't Charlotte; it was "Sha-Lut." After thirty years battling cancer, and some nineteen surgeries, Aunt Marleta's valuables now include canes. She doesn't like using a walking stick at sixty-three, but true to form she collects 'em like hats—fancy, jeweled hats.

Aunt Marleta is happily married to Uncle Stan, and they live peacefully in Mississippi. The peace was hard-won. Their early years were right out of the movies, if not the police blotter. During one of their legendary feuds, Aunt Marleta met Uncle Stan on the road in the family car and forced him and his motorcycle into the ditch. Another time she backed over him in the driveway. The story goes that her passenger and their son Little Stan, hollered, "Mama, you ran over Daddy!"

"Is he okay?" Aunt Marleta asked.

"Yes'm," Little Stan answered.

Never one to give in, Aunt Marleta put the car in drive and ran back over him. I should say here that Aunt Marleta has always claimed she tried to put the car in park and it slipped back into gear. Right. In her defense, Aunt Marleta did take her injured husband to the hospital.

Uncle Stan lived to fight another day and over the years it became a story my whole family could laugh at. I realize some people will be mortified by this tale but I doubt they'd be from around here because this is one more of those things that set us apart. We don't merely accept the characters in our families; we adore 'em! Besides, all you have to do is watch the news to see that we Southerners don't own crazy. By way of illustration, I offer the following commentary in light of our birthing-babies discussion. (And you thought I'd lost my train of thought.)

My birthing experience was a noisy affair. It's not my intention to make light of anyone's religious beliefs, but the truth is, there are people among us today, highly intelligent people with no prior signs of mental illness, who believe in something called "silent births." They contend children should be brought into the world silently with no expressions of pain from the mother. They believe it's frightening for Baby to hear Mama cry during birth and it could scar him for life.

I'll tell you someone who needs to be scarred for life—the fellow who came up with this theory. That's right. I looked it up. This whole give-birth-quietly idea came from the founder of Scientology, a Mr. Hubbard. No word on Mrs. Hubbard's reaction. I say, show me a woman who gives birth quietly and I'll show you a woman on drugs. Oh, wait, these people don't believe in drugs during childbirth either. Are you listening, ladies? Your mission, should you choose to accept it, is to stretch your bottom lip over your head and smile.

Mama always warned me not to "eat for two" because "it was a lot easier to put it on than take it off." She was right, again.

Cyndie Rushing York
Hattieville, Arkansas

I'm reminded of a day several years after the birth of my first child. I was exhausted from running after said offspring, who was now a rambunctious toddler, while great with my second child. I was also ranting about all things pregnant with my good friend when I said, "And I'm tired of people grinning at me. Every woman I see smiles when she sees me coming!"

"You know why?" Rhonda asked.

"Yes," I said with a bad attitude, "because my big old belly is so sweet!"

"Wrong!" Rhonda said bluntly. "It's because you're fatter than they are."

Ladies, the truth hurts, just like childbirth. But it's worth noting that with enough time you can usually laugh at both of 'em.

The Science of Bowel Movements

In a perfect world, children would come with an owner's manual full of detailed instructions. Southern girls are blessed with the next best thing: our mamas. My sisters and I relied heavily on our Southern Mama's advice when our children were small. Mama taught us things you don't pick up from the parenting books. For instance, one of her controversial areas of study resurfaced: the science of bowel movements.

After being married for several years, I received a package in the mail containing a bright yellow and black bikini with this note attatched, "I want grandchildren. Maybe this will help! Love, Mom." Now she has five between me and my sister. We got the hint.

Lucy Sanguinetti
Hattiesburg, Mississippi

Mama could read our kids' movements like some people read tea leaves. Let the pediatricians claim teething babies don't have diarrhea. Mama scoffed at their innocence because, "anyone with half a lick of sense can see the poor thing's stools are loose!" Mama's entire body of work in this area was built on color and consistency. She knew which foods to add or subtract in their diets to adjust these characteristics to her high standards. My sisters and I followed her suggestions to the letter, especially during the toilet training years.

Southern Mamas have yet to fall for the idea of letting the child tell you when he or she is ready to begin toilet training. They go by a totally different but highly reliable yardstick.

Belles are reminded that infants are born without shame or modesty, perfectly willing to screw up their little faces and do the do in front of God and everybody. Mama taught us that as soon as the little ones begin "hiding out" to do their business in their diapers, they were signaling us that they were ready to learn to potty. Our toddlers tried their best to blow holes in Mama's toilet training instructions, but we girls stood firm (no pun intended).

Bare Heads and Death Colds

Gone were the days BC (Before Children) when my sisters and I questioned Mama's theories. When it came to raising kids, the woman was simply too good. Was that starve a cold and feed a fever, or feed a cold and starve a fever? 911 Mama. Neither, of course. Southern Mamas don't believe in starving anything! What to do with an earache, a toothache? Call Mama. She knew things—a lot of things. Many of her theories have since withstood the test of time to come out on top.

My Southern Mama is feeling quite pleased with herself these days. New scientific reports are coming out all the time confirming more and more of her theories. If I didn't know better, I'd think she slipped somebody some money under the table. First there was the big chicken soup vindication.

Mama was smug when researches confirmed that chicken soup has a mild anti-inflammatory action, similar to today's cold medicines. And yet, she wasn't completely satisfied because her "death cold" theory was still being discredited. You know—"bundle up or you'll catch your death" cold. That always sounded a bit gruesome.

As teenagers, my sisters and I were happy when we got old enough to report what we were hearing at school: There was

> Upon popping my mouth if I sassed her, my mama would always say, "If it's your mouth that gets you in trouble, it's your mouth that's gonna get it."
>
> April Swaynigm
> Mars Hill, North Carolina

no such thing as a death cold. It was merely an old wives' tale. "Scientists say you can't get sick from not wearing a coat," we said, albeit very carefully, lest we get our jaws popped. But, wait—can you, really?

New evidence suggests some people carry dormant cold viruses. When they get chilled, their blood vessels constrict, which weakens infection-fighting white blood cells and produces—ta da!—a cold. They didn't say death cold specifically, but they didn't have to. Mama was more than happy to connect the dots. It sort of makes a person wonder what else Mama was right about. Maybe swallowing gum *will* make your insides stick together. Maybe you *can* go blind by sitting too close to the TV. Maybe, just maybe, if you cross your eyes your face *will* freeze that way, which reminds me of a good joke: You know the redneck's worst pickup line, don't you? "Sugar, I wish I was cross-eyed just so I could see you twice."

Rules, Routines, and Why a Good Nap Could Promote World Peace

My sisters and I provided my mama with unlimited opportunities to weigh in with her parenting expertise. Among the three of us, we had six children in four years. Do the math. That's a baby for every hip. We were always together too, so the hips and the babies were mostly interchangeable.

My Southern Mama made it a point to help us girls bring each of our newborns home from the hospital on their respective big days and she always arrived for this mission bearing special gifts. Yes, that was sweet, but don't think for a minute she didn't have an ulterior motive. The gifts were lessons in their own right.

For Mama, the opportunity for education here was irresistible. The Hospital Homecoming is a big event in the South. When it was my turn, she brought Jessica Ann, my infant daughter, the ultimate pink traveling outfit: a Feltman Brothers ensemble to be sure—the only name in classy baby clothes. It was complete with a matching smocked bonnet, a coordinating receiving blanket, and personalized bloomers. Lesson given and received: Proper Southern Mamas spit-shine their babies to a fare-thee-well before taking them out in public. FYI: Receiving blankets are critical, regardless of the weather. One can find receiving blankets of varying weights for this reason. Sure, they're meant to ward off the little one's chills, but they also double as a sign of affection. To see a newborn not wrapped in a receiving blanket is to witness a sad state of neglect that almost warrants a 911 call to the proper authorities.

They say the type of car you drive says a lot about what type of person you are. I can't say if that's entirely true or not, but I'll remain forever sold on Mama's Clothes Theory: Your child is a

---

My wonderful grandmother (Emma Young) lived to be 102. She had a funny way of telling things. If we said somebody had an ugly baby, she'd say, "You better not say that about that baby. You know, every ole crow thinks hers is the blackest."

JoAnne Luke
Brandon, Mississippi

My mama used to say, "A person might not be able to help being poor but there is no excuse for being dirty. You can always bathe in a ditch if you can't afford soap and water!"

Nora Hawk
Newellton, Louisiana

---

walking billboard and it's your name in lights. People draw assumptions about you by the way you dress your kids. Oh, not the quality of the clothes. Heavens, no! I was raised to understand that money and class aren't synonymous. The key words in kiddie fashion, according to my Southern Mama, are *cleanliness* and *age-appropriateness.* Blue jeans can wait. Babies should not wear stiff and scratchy miniature-adult clothes. They should be dressed in sweet little garments as soft as their newborn bottoms.

Not dressing your baby in age-appropriate clothes can be overlooked and marked up to differences in opinions, but a dirty baby is without excuse; ditto for dirty clothes, diapers, or bibs. Yes, it means toting extras of everything in your diaper bag but if you don't, eyebrows will be raised. Southern women might say it this way: "Show me a baby with a dirty face and I'll show you a mama with a filthy house." It's just the way things are. If you plan to raise your children down here, you might want to keep this in mind.

Mama taught us to get our babies on a routine as soon as possible. Routines are everything. They not only make for happy babies, but as previously noted, they will keep their little bowels regular. Say no more. I was sold.

For several years there, regardless of where the kids and I had to go and what we had to do, my mission in life was to be back at our house in time for their naps. This was easier said than done but I persevered and my efforts were well rewarded. Mama was right. If I was diligent to see to it that my little ones napped, I could enjoy a few moments of peace while they were down. And here's a big bonus: They were much cuter when they woke up and we could all last 'til bedtime without killing one another. Actually, this worked so well for me I would like to propose it as a plan for world peace. Show me a terrorist and I'll show you someone who could benefit from a regular nap time.

Sweet Cheeks and Happy Meals

My sisters and I loved our babies and we were good little mamas if I must say so myself. They loved us too, but they were no dummies, our offspring. By the time they were old enough to talk they had identified the brains of the operation. When they got sick, we were instructed to "call Nanee."

Nanee was the name our children gave our mother. It was not the name we had chosen. Grandmother christening was not taken lightly in my Southern family. When my older sister Cyndie announced she was carrying the first grandchild, my Southern Mama, along with my two sisters and I, carefully weighed all appropriate grandmother names before unanimously deciding the kids would call Mama "Gan-Gan." We thought that was so cute. We monogrammed it on T-shirts, cross-stitched it on pillows, and religiously referred to Mama as "Gan-Gan" while we toted her grandchildren in our wombs.

As soon as they were old enough to talk, the oldest two thumbed their little noses at us

> Mama always said, "Little pitchers have big ears."
>
> Judy Thomas McDonald
> Daughter of Laura Robbins Thomas
> Jackson, Mississippi

> Here is a quote our mom used so often we still hear her say it twelve years after her death. Mama's advice was, "Love them babies while you can. They'll be grown and gone before you know it."
>
> Leona Cagle
> Keithville, Louisiana

and christened her "Nanee." They called my sister Cyndie, "Nennie," and my sister Rhonda, "Nana." That would be Nanee, Nennie, and Nana. We had birthed comedians.

Nanee could do no wrong in my children's eyes, and vice versa. She excused their every childhood discretion with the Sleep Theory. "Poor thing, Nanee's baby won't eat her vegetables because she needs a nap," or "Bless his heart; Nanee's baby is just cranky because he's sleepy." If that didn't work, Mama stood ready with a second excuse for the perennially sleepy criminals. They were hungry. It should be noted that this was a self-serving observation.

There are few things Southern women like more than feeding their hungry families. As soon as my babies graduated to solid foods, Mama was there with a bowl full of all-purpose grits. Mama believed in feeding grits to hungry kids: grits in the morning, grits in the evening, and grits at suppertime if they were feeling finicky. Nanee's grits were all-purpose comfort food. They still are.

Mama taught me that grits would succeed where all else failed. As our little ones matured, grits even became healing agents. Skinned knees needed mercurochrome for the actual injury and grits for the hurt feelings. I do not know if my children came into this world with a taste for grits or if their little taste buds developed a fondness for ground corn. Nor do I care. They're grown and married now with homes of their own, but as long as we can help it, Mama and I will keep grits in the pantry. One day I'll fix their little ones a bowl. And the rest, as they say, will be history.

If I did not eat everything on my plate, Mama would shake her head and say, "There are starving children in China."

Ginger Bower
Oak Grove, Louisiana

Actually, it wouldn't be a bad idea for the great scientific minds of our day to take another look at the nutritional value of a good bowl of grits. And it'd make a lot more sense than some of the lame-brain ideas one reads in the news. A while back I read where some scientists had come up with a grand new idea to combat childhood obesity, and it has nothing to do with separating Sweet Cheeks and her Happy Meals. Their answer is heavier toys. I didn't stutter. If your toddler is tipping the scales, some experts are suggesting that putting some lead in his teddy bear will keep it out of his pull-ups. I believe I speak for the majority of my gender when I say, "Do what?"

I bring up gender only because this couldn't be more obvious. Such an idea had to have come from a male brain, those among us who prepare for all family outings by dressing themselves and giving periodic time checks. Meanwhile, those of you who will henceforth and forevermore walk with your hips permanently thrust out to one side—you know who you are—pack everything but the kitchen sink, sling it on your backs, and limp to the car. If this catches on, you might as well toss in the fridge, sugar, 'cause we all know who's gonna be toting these trendy toys. Of course, some side effects will be gender neutral. When Little Man has a tantrum and throws a weighted teddy bear from his car seat he has a fifty-fifty chance of opening up either of your noggins. Can you say, "Multicar pileup?"

Far be it from me, though, not to look for a silver lining here. I am Southern and "tomorrow is another day" and all that. Besides, there's a good chance I'll have some grandchildren in the

My Southern Mama told me to teach my children to always say "yes, ma'am" and "no, ma'am," to never go to anyone's house and say they were hungry, sit on their made beds, peek inside their dresser drawers, or run inside the house in case they broke something.

Delilah Waldroup
Commerce, Georgia

next five years and I'd like my suggestions on record. If y'all are determined to go down this road, put that extra weight where we could all enjoy it. Like Barbie's thighs, for starters. After all, the girl is in her forties. It wouldn't hurt if she had a little back fat and upper-arm jiggle. Toss in a big old gut for Ken and we might all sign on. I realize this might give our french-fry eating, weight-training yard young'uns a mixed message. Hey, I didn't start this line of reasoning; I'm just trying to improve on it.

Tan Their Little Hides

Poor babies, it must have come as quite a shock when their dear Nanee went from doling out excuses to encouraging us to get a switch and "tan their little hides." My sisters and I knew it was bound to happen. Our Southern Mama was a firm believer in (shall I say it?) spankings.

> Mama said, "Children should be seen and not heard, and if I hear you, your rear end is going to see me when we get home."
>
> Sally Farr
> Monroe, Louisiana

I'm fully aware that spankings are frowned on in some circles, but that wouldn't be our Southern spheres. We still give spankings, although sometimes we call 'em "whuppings" or "whippings." I've had both. Allow me to clarify for you. A whupping is a personal sort of whipping that promises to hurt your feelings as much as it does your backside. It's very similar to being promised a "real spanking" as opposed to just a spanking. In my experience both a real spanking and a whupping come with a lecture and have repercussions beyond the actual event. And now, to head off the non-spanking committee, let me hasten to add that while my parents straightened us up by bending us over, I will always contend that it didn't affect, didn't affect, didn't affect me.

There are a variety of discretions that warrant tanning a child's bottom. "Talking back to your mama" quite possibly heads the list, but not saying "ma'am" or "sir" ranks right up there. Mama assured us girls that a well-placed switch on the seat of a child's learning would be a more effective reminder than any amount of ranting and raving and time-out chairs combined. Our prior experiences with Mama led us to agree.

My sisters and I weren't bad kids; we were just curious and we lived way out in the country where we had to make our own fun. This was often a recipe for trouble. Sometimes when my papa was harvesting, he'd scare up baby animals in the field. My sisters and I loved it when he brought these guys home for pets. We raised, or tried to raise, several families of rabbits, but field rabbits don't thrive very well in captivity—especially if their captors are three little tomboys. On the other hand, Cyndie, Rhonda, and I found out that baby rats are perfectly well suited to just those conditions. We found the tiny rats in Papa's shed one day and quickly decided the little innocents had been abandoned by their natural mother and needed our help.

I can't pretend we weren't fully aware that Mama wouldn't be as compassionate toward our poor orphans. Why else would we have hid them in a coffee can in the bottom of

I can still hear my mother telling me "Southern ladies speak softly" whenever I'd get rowdy. That was her way of telling me I was being overly loud. I find myself telling our granddaughters the same thing, and it still works just as it did all those years ago. Amazing how I now get that look, a grin, and a quiet, "Yes, ma'am."

Mona Leggett
Denham Springs, Louisiana

Cyndie's closet? Some moments live in infamy. I remember exactly where I was when Mama went to Cyndie's room to hang up some freshly cleaned clothes and accidentally tripped over our wildlife refuge, releasing our rat family all over her feet.

That evening at supper, we noticed Papa's eyes crinkling as Mama recounted how she had tanned our hides and bemoaned our tomboy ways, but even Papa knew this one wouldn't be funny for a long time. I know they say good judgment comes from experience, but a lot of times experience comes from bad judgment.

Mama seemed to take a strange delight in reminding us of those long-ago indiscretions whenever our little kids pushed the envelope. "They're just going through a phase," she'd say with a strange glint in her eye. "You ain't seen nothing yet." Mama had always been a stickler for good grammar. Looking back on it now, we should have realized that double negative was a bad sign.

The Southern Hex

Sure enough, it wasn't long before our children stepped up to the threshold of that special phase of their lives that put my sisters and me smack in the crosshairs of the Southern Hex. Spoken by generations of Southern Mamas, the Southern Hex is a weird sort of cross between a wish, a prayer, and a curse. It has a few variations, but the theme is amazingly consistent. The common theme is "I hope you grow

> My mama said, "I hope I live long enough to see your kids do the same things to you that you do to me."
>
> Terri Hall
> Marshall, Virginia

up and have kids just like you." Sometimes Southern Mamas will attempt to be noble by saying something like, "I hope and pray your children don't cause you the grief you're causing me." It sounds good but no one believes them.

So, what phase was this? Was it the Twilight Zone? Had we traveled into the Bermuda Triangle? No, ma'am. This was far more serious. We were entering the teenage years. Mama had been as guilty as legions of Southern Mamas before her in speaking the Southern Hex on us girls, but as the time of our testing neared, she developed a conscience. We might be grown, married women with teenagers of our own, but we were still her babies. I suppose she had a certain obligation to get in the trenches with us. Mama's actions are all the more commendable when one considers the grief we put her through during our teenage years.

Mama gave us one very important piece of advice: We shouldn't fall into the trap of trying to be our teenagers' friends. They would have plenty of friends. For the next few years they would need us to be their parents more than ever before. Mama said they didn't have to like us—and she said this like it was a news flash. We tried to respond appropriately, but we were way ahead of her on this one. None of us had forgotten the not-so-distant days when our parents were a lot less popular. There were plenty of reasons, but I'll just pick one.

We were raised in a strict Southern Baptist home where dancing was a huge no-no. "Dancing feet don't belong on praying knees." For whatever reason, call it Divine Humor, my sisters and I had a beat in our feet that just couldn't or wouldn't say die. One weekend there was a big dance at the Moose Lodge. I wasn't supposed to go, but once I got uptown with my friends I kinda fell into temptation. And then we got there and found out they were having a dance contest. My ears shot straight up. I was headed the wrong way and shifting gears.

Back then I was dating a good old boy who didn't like to dance but I had a couple reliable dance partners I could count on—John and Jamie. That night, Jamie Wallis and I cut up like a new pair of scissors. The judges kept narrowing the couples down, and the Isley Brothers kept singing until eventually we were crowned the winners. The crowd cheered, a flashbulb popped, and reality hit me. I spent the rest of the night begging my friends to keep my secret.

One week later, I was eating breakfast with my whole family, my indiscretion only a faint memory. Papa was reading our town paper, the *Delta News*.

"Papa," I said, without a care in the world, "pass me the biscuits." Papa lowered the paper slowly. And then, just as I saw the photo of my and Jamie's big win, I heard my papa say, "Sure, Disco Queen." I didn't enter many dance contests after that—at least none close by.

Double-Dog Dares

In our defense, much of the trouble my sisters and I got into could be traced to the double-dog dare. As a young mother, I did everything I could to inoculate my children against this inherent Southern threat. I was no more successful than my parents and their parents before them.

Someone once wrote in to my radio show and double-dog dared me to address a certain issue on the porch. Their suggestion isn't important to our discussion, but their complete mishandling of the double-dog dare is very alarming. People, we need to talk; maybe have one of those national dialogues everyone's always talking about! I'm afraid we're at risk of losing the childhood art of the dare. There is a correct and an incorrect way to ascend the level of dares necessary to prompt someone to act in a way he or she would never otherwise consider. Let us review.

First, of course, there must be a dare. The dare comes after someone's honor has been questioned, as in, "You're a chicken if you don't swim the lake." At that point the challenged might say, "No, I'm not," and the accuser may respond, "Yes, you are." This can go on for an indefinite period until, without warning, the darer fires the inevitable shot. "Prove it," he says. "I dare you."

Only when the daree is seriously considering the dare, can the darer up the ante with, "I double-dog dare you." A double-dog dare that has not been properly reached is like a yard dog with no teeth.

By way of illustration, I once skipped school with my sister Rhonda and a couple of high-school friends in the dead of winter to attempt to swim the width of Lake Providence. I never would've considered such a fool thing had the level of dares not been properly layered. As it was, we had no recourse.

We were three-fourths of the way across the lake when our extremities became so numb we could only float on our backs and kick our feet the rest of the way. Sure I was scared, but we survived. And that, my friends, is the power of the correctly administered double-dog dare.

Mother of the Year

I'm happy to report that I made it through my kids' teenage years without an excessive amount of drama or trauma. They weren't near the handful I had been, which should breathe hope into the hearts of Southern girls everywhere: The Southern Hex can be broken. My two are now terribly neat young married people. And they love their mama, faults and all.

My mom taught me that sometimes a parent needs to do without so that their kids won't have to. When she was the only parent, she stayed up many nights sewing and doing things to make sure our family was taken care of. Even though she remarried a wonderful man, she still works to help make sure the family has nice things.

Karen McKay
Greenwood, Mississippi

I've always aspired to being Mother of the Year, but I knew my chances weren't good from the day I forgot to lock the handle of Jessica's infant carrier and watched my firstborn slip out and onto her head. And I felt sure the committee was watching a few years later when toddler Jessica interrupted my inspection of the fruits and veggies at our local grocery. "Where's Sillup?" she asked, using her pet name for her brother, Phillip. Sillup! I had forgotten my second offspring. Jessica and I found Sillup fast asleep in his car seat and none the worse for wear. Sorry, Sup.

I'm sure I'm shooting myself in the foot for next year's nomination, but it feels good to get these things off my chest. So, let me be honest. Ever since my son, the baby of the family, left for college, I've been having trouble adopting the right attitude with well-meaning people who look at me with a pitying stare and ask, "So, how are you and Phil coping with the empty-nest thing?"

The questions have gotten even more comical since I made it through the Wedding Summer when my little darlings decided to get married a few weeks apart. I try to give these inquisitors a woe is me smile and I never giggle, but I always think they see through me. The truth is, my biggest problem with the Empty Nest Syndrome is the guilt I feel for not having it.

When my grown kids call home, they expect nothing less than my complete attention. I've long suspected that the question "What're you doing, Mama?" is a mere formality, that they aren't really listening, so I tested Jessica Ann recently. "Trying to meet a deadline," I said, in response to her robotical question, "but it's hard with this man standing here with a knife to my neck—"

Jessica Ann interrupted me in midbreath. "That's nice, Mama, but could you e-mail me your Crawfish Etouffee recipe?" thus proving that I will never have a life that cannot be interrupted by theirs. I guess that's how it should be. Right, Mama?

Bread Recipes for All Your Little Honeybuns

Whether giving advice on knowing when to scold a child and when to hold him close, or teaching us how to tell when a child's fever was too high to ignore, Mama taught us girls the key ingredient was learning to trust our instincts. Similarly, trusting one's instincts is also integral to successful baking. Oven temperatures vary too. Always remember the toothpick test: If you can stick it in the middle of the bread and it comes out clean, it's done. Here are a few treasured bread recipes from my home to yours.

~ Hot Water Cornbread ~

SERVES 4–6

It's hard to beat hot water cornbread. It's a perfect complement for most any meal. Your smallest honeybuns will love this Southern favorite as much as your big ones. If you're not careful, they'll run through the kitchen and pilfer 'em behind your back. With just a couple simple ingredients, they could be the original fast food.

2 cups cornmeal
½ teaspoon salt
vegetable oil
2 cups boiling water

Stir together the cornmeal and salt while heating about half an inch of oil in a skillet (the black, cast-iron, been-around-for-ages kind works best). Heat the water to boiling and pour over the salted meal, stirring well. Drop spoonfuls of meal into hot oil and fry to a golden brown. Drain and blot with paper towels before lightly sprinkling with salt. Perfect! (Special thanks to Lillie Hampton for all the cornbread she cooked for the Tomlinson family over the years and for teaching me her secrets.)

~ Pull Apart Bread ~

SERVES 10–15

This is one of my sister Rhonda's recipes; some folks call it Monkey Bread, perhaps because the little monkeys love the bite-size pieces. By any name, we grown-ups love it served with hot coffee. It's so easy and delicious you'll want to keep canned biscuits on hand! (If the idea of canned biscuits scandalizes you and your mama, hide 'em in the vegetable crisper.)

1 tablespoon cinnamon
1 cup sugar
3 cans refrigerator biscuits (10 to a can)
1 stick of butter, melted

Mix cinnamon and sugar in large freezer bag. Cut biscuits into fourths with kitchen scissors, drop in bag, and shake until they're evenly coated. It works best if you shake a few at a time.

Drop coated pieces in a Bundt cake pan. Do not grease pan first. Pour leftover seasoning mix over biscuit pieces and drizzle with the melted butter. Bake at 350 degrees for 30 minutes. Let cool and turn over onto cake plate. Enjoy! (Rhonda would say the calories don't count because everything is broken up.)

~ Hoppin' Jalapeño Hush Puppies ~

SERVES 4–6

Legend has it that hush puppies began as deep-fried treats thrown to the dogs to quiet their barking around the campfire as in, "hush puppy!" If it's not true, it should be. It sure makes a great story. This recipe uses a packaged cornbread mix. You can spend the extra time you save with the kids. And speaking of the yard young'uns, kids of all ages like hush puppies, but you might want to reserve these for the bigger ones. The jalapeños really heat things up!

1 6-ounce package Mexican cornbread
1 egg
1 10-ounce can cream-style corn
4 jalapeño peppers, seeded and chopped
¼ bell pepper, chopped
1 bunch green onions, chopped
½ cup or less of buttermilk (enough to make a consistent batter)
Oil for frying

In a small bowl, combine cornbread mix and egg. Add corn, peppers, and onions. Be careful with this next step. Stir in just enough buttermilk to make your batter stiff enough to push off the spoon. (We're talking a half cup of buttermilk or less.) Once your oil is good and hot, push a teaspoon of batter at a time into the hot oil. When your puppies float to the top, turn 'em over and let 'em brown well on the other side. You've done it! Drain on paper towels and enjoy. HUSH PUPPY!

~ Cheddar Muffins ~

MAKES A DOZEN MUFFINS

We Southerners are trying to watch our carbs like the rest of the country but it's hard. We flat-out love our bread—cornbread, tea cakes, biscuits, hoecakes. These flavor-packed muffins are a great complement to any meal and the leftovers warm up well. I like to serve 'em the next morning with coffee. Think of it this way: carbs are the body's main energy food and who needs energy more than someone chasing kids all day? If you don't have kids, you can still make this excuse work by chasing your spouse around the kitchen. Your marriage will benefit along with your waistline.

3½ cups all-purpose flour
3 tablespoons sugar
2 tablespoons baking powder
2 teaspoons dill weed
1 teaspoon salt
1 cup shredded cheddar cheese
1¾ cups milk
2 eggs, slightly beaten
¼ cup butter, melted

In a large bowl, combine flour, sugar, baking powder, and dill weed. Add salt and cheese. In a separate bowl combine milk, eggs, and butter. Stir this milk mixture into the dry ingredients just until moistened. Be careful not to overwork the dough. (A little hard work never hurt anyone, but it will make your dough hard as a rock.) Fill your greased muffin cups (it'll make a good dozen), and bake 'em at 400 degrees for 20 to 25 minutes or until a toothpick inserted in the center comes out clean.

~ Banana Nana Nut Bread ~

SERVES 8

Mama can't see a spotted banana in my kitchen without trying to save it. She needn't worry. She sold me on saving overripe bananas years ago. Fresh bananas won't make tasty bread. However, the sugar in the older ones will take it over the top. Your kids might turn their noses up at the mushy bananas, but they'll join in with everyone else to devour hot Banana Nana Nut Bread.

½ cup oleo
1 cup sugar
2 eggs
1 cup mashed bananas
1 teaspoon vanilla
2 cups self-rising flour
½ cup nuts

Cream together oleo and sugar. Add eggs; mix well, then add bananas and vanilla. Stir well and add self-rising flour and nuts. Mix only enough to moisten dry flour; overmixing will dry your bread out. Pour into a loaf pan. (You can also use a muffin tin, if you'd like.) Bake slowly in a 350 degree oven for 1 hour. Slice a couple pieces and share 'em with a friend over a good, hot pot of coffee.

~ Aunt Carmen's Party Bread ~

SERVES 8–10

Aunt Carmen's Party Bread is the hit of any gathering and it's hearty enough to satisfy the hungriest appetites. You can divide this bread into po-boys or, if you need it to go further, you can slice 'em into thin party appetizers. Just give it a try. Breaking bread with your loved ones will keep their bodies and their spirits strong.

1 pound hot sausage
½ pound ground chuck
1 onion, chopped
1 green bell pepper, chopped
1 teaspoon oregano
salt and pepper to taste
2 loaves French bread
8 ounces Velveeta cheese

Brown sausage and ground chuck just until the pink is gone. Drain and add onion and bell pepper. Season with oregano, salt, and pepper, and let it continue to cook on low.

Meanwhile, slice French bread lengthwise and scoop out the center of all four sides. Add these removed bread pieces to the meat along with Velveeta cheese. Stuff the meat mixture into one side of both loaves and fold the tops over to make two long sandwiches. Spread butter lightly on top of both loaves, wrap 'em in tinfoil, and bake at 350 degrees for 15 minutes. That's good eating... Southern style!

5

A Wasteful Will Is A Woeful Want

What Southern Mamas Tell Their Daughters About Cooking and Stretching the Budget (with Salad Recipes to Do It Right from Start to Finish)

Few aspects of Southern culture have been as scrutinized and criticized as our food. While we Southerners do walk in lockstep on some things, like the divine flavor of sweet tea, we've grown somewhat weary of the oversimplified descriptions and widely held misconceptions about our cuisine. For instance, much ado is made about us eating pigs' feet and yet no one in my immediate circle of friends and family has ever eaten a single swine toe. And, for the record, this dyed-in-the-wool-homegrown Southerner is perfectly willing to make the following confession: I hate buttermilk.

> My mother would say, "Sweep around your own doorstep before you sweep around others'."
>
> Marsha Adams
> Choudrant, Louisiana

My papa invented a game that amused him when I was a little girl. Milk was a very important staple at our house, both sweet and buttermilk. (Back then, 2 percent and low-fat were unheard of.) Papa was the only one that drank buttermilk. Sometimes, while we were saying the blessing at evening meals, he'd swap his glass of milk-gone-bad for the glass of one of his three easy marks, Cyndie, Rhonda, or Shellie. The moment he loved came when his victim reached for a refreshing sip of ice-cold milk and got a big swig of buttermilk instead. Gag! Have you ever noticed that even good stuff doesn't taste right when you're expecting something else? Mama always scolded Papa about his little game, but she could never break him of the habit.

As forthcoming as I am about the differences in my eating habits as compared to those of my fellow Southerners, I'd never dream of allowing our fine food to be attacked without launching a defense. Toward that end, I once took to the airwaves to address a letter from one of my radio listeners who wrote in asking if it was true that we Southerners eat flitters. The poor thing wasn't from around here, so granted, there's a chance she was legitimately confused, but the tone of her letter didn't set well with me. I took the time to explain to her that no, we didn't eat flitters, more commonly known as cow patties, but that we do eat fritters: fried bites of corn (or anything else we choose to batter). I also made it perfectly clear that we didn't appreciate people suggesting we eat flitters. I didn't say it in so many words, but the Southerners in my audience could read between the lines. They understood what I was really saying: "Girl, you ain't right."

> Here's some good advice passed down for generations in our family: "Whatever cooking mistakes you make can be covered by either gravy or frosting."
>
> Jackie Zink
> Fritch, Texas

"You ain't right" is one of our most Southern expressions.

But, seeing as it is also very complex, perhaps it'd be beneficial if I took a moment to clarify its varied interpretations. "You ain't right" can have different meanings, friends. It's all in the inflection. At the core, it applies to someone who isn't the sharpest knife in the drawer, as in "That Smith boy ain't right." It can also be an insult. When my friends and I heard Madonna, "The Material Girl," explaining to the rest of us Americans that our values are wrong, we rolled our eyes and said, "She ain't right." And anybody can see Michael "I can't find my nose" Jackson and know "that boy ain't right!" And yet, the phrase can also be a form of endearment. When my big sis got mad at her ex-husband and asked me how to attach him to an e-mail and forward him, I said, "Girl, you ain't right." Simply put, if and when someone says, "You ain't right"—one should always take a moment to pay attention to the inflection before insulting their mama. They could be paying you a compliment.

The flitter/fritter discussion didn't heal the nation, but it made me feel better about the critical reviews our cooking methods have endured. I realize we have what other people might consider oddities in our diet, but what region doesn't? I remember the first time I ate fried rattlesnake. Someone told me to "try it, you'll like it—it doesn't taste like rattlesnake! It tastes more like chicken. " Have you ever noticed that regardless of what type of strange new meat people are trying to feed you, their next line is always "It tastes just like chicken!"? For the life of me, I don't know why these people don't serve chicken and be done with it.

The poor fruitcake gets a similar sort of treatment. Most every Southern family has at least one well-meaning aunt who spends the entire holiday hawking fruitcake with a line like this: "I've got a new fruitcake recipe for you. You'll love it. Scout's honor, it doesn't taste anything like fruitcake." Face the music, Aunt Ethel! That dog won't hunt. When was the last time you heard someone say, "You really should try this banana puddin'! It doesn't take anything like banana puddin!" I rest my case.

My sister Cyndie was the first one to use that line on me, way back there on Bull Run Road. I remember the time she found some mussels in the ditch in our front yard, fried 'em up and convinced Rhonda and me that they'd taste just like oysters. You really can trust me on this one; mussels taste like mussels.

Speaking of strange food, I'm a little bit embarrassed by this, but since it's just us, I'm gonna tell y'all what my daughter's new favorite food is. Are you ready? It's sushi, that's right—raw fish. I liked it better when she ate crayons and dirt. Kids, you teach 'em everything you know, and they leave home and eat fish bait. What can ya do? When I called her on it, she was quick to tell me, "Mom, sushi is a delicacy, just like frog legs—and besides, it doesn't taste a thing like chicken..."

Time-Out for Turkeys

Not surprisingly, when it came time for me to run a kitchen of my own, I turned to Mama, not Cyndie. (If you've had one fried mussel, you've had plenty.) Mama didn't give us girls a lot of detailed cooking lessons when we were at home but the woman was a walking cooking school. Her basic philosophy came through loud and clear: Home-cooked food says you care. Mama said she cared twenty-four seven, to

> Mama taught me to never return a dish to a friend empty. Always return it with something you've cooked.
>
> Mary Margaret Minsky
> Lake Providence, Louisiana

friends and family alike. She spoke in casseroles, fresh veggies, cakes, and cobblers. I watched her and understood I was expected to follow suit.

Back then, when my sisters and I were younger, our kitchen time was mostly about prep work. We sliced and diced for Mama and we always handled cleanup, but it was forced labor. None of our hearts were in it at the time. The three of us were grown and married before we became interested in mining the treasure trove that was Mama's knowledge of good down-home cooking.

Mama always has time for these "how-to" kitchen lessons. She enjoyed cooking for her family when we were all at home and she has done her dead-level best to pass that experience down to her daughters. My Southern Mama believes cooking shouldn't be a chore, but a pleasure—and a privilege. We've all seen the commercials where the flustered young bride cooks her first big meal for the extended family. That's a myth—at least it is here in the South. Around here, newlyweds don't host important meals like Thanksgiving. For the first couple decades you're at his mama's or your mama's. And then one year the powers that be decide it's your turn and just like that, you're supposed to be Martha Stewart (without the indictment, of course).

When it came to buying groceries and stretching the budget, Mama taught me to always have some money on hand that you don't have to account for.

Robbin Miles
Hot Springs, Arkansas

I recently discovered how many people missed getting this "cooking should be a pleasure" memo. My education began with some research I was doing for a Thanksgiving column. Hosting *All Things Southern* is not just fun and games, people. I take my hostess responsibilities here very seriously. I was trying to compose a helpful article to make the holidays and all of its shopping, decorating, and cooking chores less stressful for my readers when I ran across a company that seemed to think they had the answer.

This company was releasing several new sodas onto the market. Just in time for the holidays they were offering Turkey and Gravy soda, Green Bean Casserole Soda, Fruitcake Soda, Cranberry Soda, and Mashed Potatoes and Butter Soda. Their ad campaign bragged that their sodas had no carbs, no calories, and zero caffeine. Cuss fire and save the matches! We're as busy down here in the Deep South as the next person, but trust me on this; we make time to cook the turkey. And we might be a little heavy 'round the middle but we take time to eat it too—with a fork, mind you (not a straw) and maybe even our fingers.

See, we Southerners don't look at eating as another item to check off in our organizers. We love food. It's one of our favorite activities. We like cookin' it, eatin' it, and talkin' about it. Heck, while we're filling up on banana puddin', we're usually discussing the culinary delights of our mamas' fried chicken.

I suggested to my fellow Southerners that there was no time for apathy and reminded them that in the not-so-distant past a group of people (most likely all Yankees), had taken Martha Stewart—that one poor woman who was willing to hand-feed the turkey, kill the turkey, pluck, stuff, and cook the turkey—and threw her in the slammer! Could it really be a coincidence that someone is trying to sell Southerners on the benefits of drinking fruitcake? This must be what they mean by culture war.

I've never been one to advocate unnecessary violence but I posted a friendly reminder on my website for any foreigners who might come by. It was polite, but I thought it staked out our position in very clear terms. It read simply: We own more handguns and we'd like for y'all to leave our turkeys alone.

I figured that little skirmish was over, but I was mistaken. Would you believe those folks at Jones Soda got wind of it and got off a shot of their own? The very next year they retaliated by sending me a *large box* of their sodas along with a tube of turkey and gravy lip balm!

As horrible as that sounds, folks, I'm having a difficult time staying upset with the poor things. I feel sorry for 'em. Mama said she's afraid I encouraged 'em! They've even added to their line: Corn on the Cob Soda, Broccoli Casserole Soda, and—dare I say it; my grandmothers are both turning over in their graves—Pecan Pie Soda! I have myself a real communication problem here. I don't know where to begin with these people.

The problem is now that we've written back and forth a couple times, well, they kind of feel like friends. And having their sodas at my house for Thanksgiving two years in a row almost feels like a tradition. Being a true Southern girl, I can usually make a tradition out of most anything but this here was a challenge. It wasn't easy, but I managed to hammer out a compromise. I dropped 'em a short note.

Dear Jones Soda, it read. *We're still not gonna drink this stuff, we tried that last year just for laughs. It wasn't funny. And we're not putting it in our traditional after-Thanksgiving turkey gumbo. That'd just be wrong. However, if y'all agree to get some counseling, I promise to set it out on the sideboard along with our real food and Cyndie and Rhonda have promised to use the lip balm, once. In closing, I think our relationship can set a fine example for the rest of the country. Oh, but there is one more thing—that slogan of yours: "Just like Mom used to make"—Mama says you're gonna have to lose that or the deal is off.*

Can It, Fry It, or Stick It in a Casserole

Surprisingly enough, even though I didn't enjoy kitchen duty when I was growing up, I actually knew a lot more about cooking when I got married than I thought I did. I suppose I got it by osmosis.

Mama always told me that when I got married, I should can what I could and what I couldn't I should fry in a pan. She said this would keep your man happy.

Marleta Crawford
Natchez, Mississippi

Mama's kitchen repertoire was typically Southern and there wasn't anything secretive about her methods: can it, fry it, or stick in a casserole. What Mama didn't do, under any circumstances, was waste it. Wasteful was right next door to sinful. As little kids we were taught to clean our plates because there were other children going hungry. I could never follow that line of reasoning. I may not have been the smartest kid on the turn road, but it seemed to me that shipping my hateful carrots to the unfortunate would be better for all involved.

Anytime someone within earshot complained about having an old "clunker" my grandmother Essie Owen Dunaway would say, "A po' ride is better than a proud walk." Another of her sayings that haunts me is, "A lazy woman can throw more out the back door than a good man can bring in the front door."

Pam Dunaway Bonner
Tyrone, Georgia

And yet, I soon learned that as bad as it was to hide your carrots under your cornbread, there remained a worse crime. When I crossed this line, Mama would scold me because "my eyes were bigger than my stomach." This announcement worried me to no end. My eyes were deformed! How had this happened and how could I fix it? Was it obvious? Was Mama the only one that could see it, or were other people laughing at me behind my back?

Years later, I would hear Mama's words again when my kids balked at their veggies or took too much of their favorite food onto their plates. Only now, the voice was coming out of me. It was one of my first recorded experiences of channeling my mother and I was powerless to stop. (I couldn't help but notice Mama's mealtime tactics had mellowed somewhat when it came to feeding her sweet grandbabies. Unfortunately, "Watch out! Papa's gonna eat your peas" wasn't any more successful at creating vigilant vegetarians than her threats from yesteryear. Papa was welcome to their peas as long as he kept his big paws off their Tator Tots.)

Thanks to Mama, my brother and I became involuntary members of the clean plate club. At almost every meal, she pressed us with, "Children, eat your colors." To this day, I can't look at a plate of broccoli or a bowl of carrots without hearing those words in my head.

Trisha McNeill
Fuquay Varina, North Carolina

By this time, my husband and I were trying to balance our own food budget. The logic behind taking small helpings on the first trip and going back for more if you were still hungry finally came home. Once food goes onto the individual plates, it can't be saved for leftovers. And when it comes to reinventing leftovers, Sugar, I learned from the experts. To be sure, Mama's rules about throwing away perfectly good food is so firmly ingrained in my DNA that one of the hardest things about the whole Jones Soda episode was throwing away all those soft drinks. I kept those fool bottles in the door of my refrigerator for months like I half expected someone to walk in and say, "I'd give my last dollar for a swig of Green Bean Casserole Soda!"

The Unique Magic of Mushroom Soup

Blame it on my heritage. The Southern women in my family have made an art out of stretching groceries. Far be it for me to be sacrilegious, but watching them gives one an inkling of the astonishment the disciples must have felt when they saw the Good Lord feed five thousand people with a couple fish fillets and a few pones of cornbread. These women practiced their magic on their individual families and displayed their skills when unexpected company showed up, which was often.

Mama would start stretching the food as soon as she saw 'em coming. If soup was on, it got diluted with water, broth, or both. Veggies appeared from the freezer like rabbits out of a hat, and canned foods turned into casseroles as fast as Mama could holler "Quick, girls! Hand me some cheese, and a can of cream of mushroom soup."

My mother taught me "to always have something special frozen in the freezer so you can have a good supper ready at the last minute for unexpected company."

Joyce Forssee
West Monroe, Louisiana

These unexpected visits always contained what I fondly call the Southern Good-bye Ritual. Once everyone was sufficiently full and just as convinced they had caught up on the goings on in each other's lives, the company would start leaving a long time before they actually left.

The first obstacle was rounding up the kids. If the head count came close, everyone started for the car. Of course, if the trip home meant the company had to leave the county, much less the state, it was customary for everyone to hold hands and ask the Lord for traveling grace. Something about the requisite group "amen" always seemed to remind the hostess that she wanted to send some homemade jelly, leftover pound cake or banana puddin' with her guests. After eliciting a promise "Don't y'all leave before I get back," she would scurry back to the kitchen.

During her absence, the children would be instructed to go tend to their private business, whether they had any or not. This was usually an empty gesture as that sort of business always resurfaced a mile or two down the road. By the time the hostess returned and the kids were corralled again, the driver would have the motor idling, ready to make a run for it. Except for the waving, huggin', cryin', and promises to come back soon, that pretty much sums it up.

Those unexpected visits are one of the things that I've seen change the most about my beloved South just in my lifetime. There are fewer unplanned gatherings, whether between family, or friends and neighbors. Everyone has his or her own theories to explain this development. Some say it's because everyone is so much busier making a living, that it takes both parents working longer hours to provide the same standard of living, and leaves less time for impromptu visits. Others say it's because people live farther distances from their immediate families. Most of the old-timers, like Papaw Stone, God rest his soul, would blame it on the television. (Papaw called it the one-eyed monster.)

> Mama always told us at breakfast time not to "gouge the jelly!" She would never let us dip jelly with a knife. I guess it stuck. I hear those words in my head every day of my life—as I'm gouging the jelly!
>
> Diane Collins
> Tallulah, Louisiana

I suppose they all have a piece of the truth, but here's my

two cents on the subject: A person could dwell on the past and rue the changes of our busy world—or they can set out to cherish their immediate circle of family and friends and put more effort into planning and attending the larger holiday parties and reunion gatherings. I don't think the sky is falling on family get-togethers. Nor do I believe we've thrown the baby out with the bath water. I say this because for every letter I get bemoaning the loss of the South as a distinctive region, I get five more proving her people haven't really changed. Witness the typical family reunion and notice the similarities to years gone by.

The smaller kids will still play as hard as they can until they get cranky from fatigue and an indulgent parent hooks up *Shrek* on a DVD in someone's vehicle, treating all the young mothers to a few moments of respite. The teenagers will still group together, even if they are checking out the tunes on one another's iPods. The women will still be talking about kids and cooking, even if the conversation is more about how to tend to the family's needs while balancing that demanding job outside the home. Meanwhile the men will still be discussing ball games and farming—along with which network gives 'em the best access to the latest

My mama has a college degree but she still subscribes to Southern superstitions. If you spill salt, you're to throw a pinch of it over your shoulder. And you never give knives as a gift because anything with a blade will sever the relationship between you and the receiver. If you must give an object with a blade, always ask for a token payment in return, such as a dime. This way you're not giving the blade but selling it. Unfortunately, she explained this to me after I was well into my thirties. I guess I've blissfully severed a lot of friendships.

Lisa Elaine Simpson
Seymour, Texas

commodity prices when they're using their new laptop computers on the back forty. Technology hasn't changed the family gathering, just altered it a tad.

While we're on the subject of changes, here's another one with an illustration, just for fun. I've had a lot of older people tell me that many years ago when a big family meal was served, the grown-ups ate first. The kids waited their turn and hoped for leftovers. This was before my time, but I have a good friend who told me a story that hawks back to those days. This one's been handed down in Sam's family for years. One Sunday after church, when Sam's grandfather was a young boy, his mother invited the pastor and his family over for Sunday dinner.

When it came time to eat, Sam's granddaddy and his younger brother were sent away to play with the preacher's kids while the grown-ups sat down to a big country meal of fried chicken, mashed potatoes and gravy, and all the fixings. The boys were impatient and hungry. After a while they grew worried that there wasn't going to be anything left. They slid up to the wall dividing the rooms and the oldest boy put his eye up to a knothole just big enough for him to peek through and see what was going on at the dining room table. The younger boy stood close by and pestered his older brother for regular updates. The meal progressed and the grownups continued to enjoy the visiting and the fine food. And then, just when the boys were convinced that the meal was wrapping up and it was almost their turn, they heard their mother invite the preacher to have another piece of fried chicken!

"Why, thank you," the preacher said. "I believe I will have another small portion."

The younger boy pulled on his brother's pants leg. "A portion?" he whispered. "What part of the chicken is a portion?"

The older boy looked through the knothole and back at his brother, "All of it," he said sadly. "All of it."

Save the Bathwater

Mama stretched more than our food budget. The Southern generation below me has probably never been reminded to "save the bathwater!" Let's just say change isn't always a bad thing, Sweet Cheeks. This is easier understood when you're the youngest in the family and the last child to bathe. It also helps to explain the phrase "Don't throw the baby out with the bathwater." I suppose I shouldn't complain. I did get to bathe with the lights on.

I confess. As the lady of my own house, I enjoy leaving a lamp on to set the mood in a room. This doesn't seem criminal at nighttime, but unless it's pitch dark outside I almost expect to answer the phone and hear Mama say, "Turn off that floodlight, Shellie Charlene. You might as well be burning money." Don't ask me how she'd know. She just does. She always has. When we were younger she got inside information on me and my sisters from a "bird in the neighborhood." My Southern Mama: a cross between Snow White and Al Gore. Scary, isn't it?

Mama was doing conservation years before Big Al got involved. She was just more worried about the bills than saving the planet. (Please save the global warming letters. I know trees are important, y'all, but Mama's always stressed that money doesn't grow on 'em.) Consider her hand-me-down system: Mama would lower the hem on my oldest sister's dresses as Cyndie grew taller until there was no more room to let it out. Then she'd

> My mother always said about people who were living beyond their means: "They have, champagne taste and a beer bottle pocketbook."
>
> Marie Dobrosky
> Jacksonville, Florida

put the hem all the way back up, move it to my middle sister, Rhonda's, wardrobe, and start the process over. By the time these outfits found their way to my back they'd been altered more often than a Hollywood actress.

> Mama taught me that I shouldn't "borrow from Peter to pay Paul."
>
> Pam Geiger
> Donalsonville, Georgia

I was almost a teenager when my parents moved us out of their tiny starter home on Bull Run Road into a medium-size wood frame home a mite closer to the highway. But even as the budget became more flexible, Mama kept a hawk eye on the bottom line. She may have put the sewing machine away and bought our clothes off the rack—but it was always the sales rack.

The Art of Substitution

As a newlywed, Mama's make-do motto resurfaced in many areas of my home, but it was most obvious in the kitchen. My early training came back without any conscious effort on my part. Back when I was under Mama's roof, the nearest town was only twenty miles up the road, but it may as well have been two hundred. Running to the store for this and that wasted both time and money. Such a practice was simply unthinkable. Mama stocked up about twice a month. The rest of the time she cooked from the pantry. Watching her taught us the Art of Substitution. I know people who follow recipes to the letter and wouldn't dream of deviating, but Mama taught us ingredients were nothing more than suggestions.

These survival skills have served me well over the years. And while my family will admit I've created some really good dishes with this method, my husband and kids have long teased me because my recipes morph according to what I have on hand. "This is very good" they might say, before adding with a grin, "What was it supposed to be?" Ah, but sweet satisfaction: Now that my daughter has a husband and a home of her own, and my son has taken a wife, I'm witnessing the art's survival. This next generation is already sharing recipes with me that included instructions like "It called for two cans of Rotel tomatoes, but I used a half jar of salsa and a can of tomato paste and it worked just as well." You don't say?

If the ingredient in question couldn't be substituted—say, flour for instance, Mama borrowed from our neighbors without hesitation, and they in turn borrowed from us. I thought this was the most normal thing in the world. I'll never forget how surprised I was to discover a mini-cultural divide within the Southern region itself. For a while it may have been normal for country folks to borrow, once I married and moved to town (largely differentiated from our rural community by its possession of two red lights compared to our sole caution light), I soon found it wasn't the custom for town people. The first neighbor I borrowed from as a newlywed offered me the commodity readily, but I couldn't help noticing my sweet friend looked totally surprised by my request. If the grocery store was right up the road, why was I borrowing flour? Did we have money problems? Once I realized my neighbors weren't "borrowing back" as we called it, I learned to go to the store.

On the subject of borrowing things, my mom, Margaret Mobley, would say, "If you have to borrow something, be sure to return it in better condition than when you borrowed it."

Sandy Costello
Kilbourne, Louisiana

Our Regional Obsession

It is routinely noted that Southerners are fanatical about extolling the superiority of our food and that we're bound and determined to serve it in large quantities. Some have suggested this fascination can be attributed to the fact that our people remember going hungry during The War, which at least to me, makes about as much sense as Rosie O'Donnell. (That was it. I'm through with that sentence.) We don't remember being hungry during The War, Honey. News flash: We weren't here, and neither were our parents or grandparents.

My mother told me to learn to cook well, because "your looks will fade, but his appetite for food won't."

Susan Rozelle Bezemer
Ontario, Canada

There is a much simpler explanation. If we appear to be bragging about the superiority of our food, it is because our food is superior. If that was too deep, you can reread it. I'll wait. The South is surrounded by some of the best sustenance the planet has to offer. Our rivers and streams offer up bream and catfish while our freshwater bodies produce a variety of seafood. Our weather, as unbearably hot and sticky as it may be during the growing season, consistently redeems itself by supplying our tables with big healthy fruits and vegetables. (Think Georgia peaches and Vidalia onions.)

My mother always said eating meals together as a family would keep your family strong.

Emily Beasley Blais
South Daytona, Florida

We serve this bounty in large quantities for much the same reason: It's good. And besides, it seems stingy and downright sinful to offer someone a plate with nothing but a mouthful of meat and a few carefully chosen green beans stacked up and tied off with a piece of seaweed—not when there's a whole garden where that came from. Southern women take great pride in telling their guests there's "more where that came from." Mama taught us girls that any cook worth her salt would be mortified if someone left her table hungry. Instead, she will repeatedly ask, "if you found enough to eat." The cook is fully aware no one has to labor to find their food; she has spread it out before them in plain sight. She's simply confirming that her guests found it to their liking.

There are a few notable exceptions to the no labor rule as it applies to our cuisine. Heading the list would be that tasty crustacean, that marvelous mudbug, the Louisiana crawfish. Special literary note: Please do not come down here and order crayfish. It might be the same animal in the science books but we won't recognize it, on purpose.

Southerners boil crawfish up by the bucket loads and offer them to guests on nice-sized individual serving trays rather than plates. History tells us that many years ago some creative soul christened these events where we boil crawfish—watch this now—crawfish boils. The name stuck. It has never been confirmed as to whether or not the creative person who came up with that name had consumed a large share of the fermented drink often served at such gatherings, but I for one wouldn't bet against it.

True, it takes a fair amount of time and effort to get full at a crawfish boil. One must completely peel the tail of the tasty crustacean to get at a single mouthful of the delicious meat, but we Southerners feel complaining is counterproductive unless you want the rest of the partygoers to beat you back for seconds. (Besides, we throw whole new potatoes and corn on the cob in the boiling pots along with all those crawfish. They're not only slap-ya-mama-good cooked in all that spicy seasoning, but they help break the monotony and keep your strength up during the long feast.) It should also be noted that the squeamish soul might not enjoy peeling and eating our little mudbugs, or watching people suck the heads to get the remaining flavor. I can't help you there. Southern eating is similar to the Southerner's method of procuring our food: It's rarely for the faint of heart.

Two of our biggest loves are hunting and fishing. They bring food to our table and sport to our lives, and yet we know there are outsiders who see our much loved sports as dangerous and/or barbaric. I'm not gonna sit here and say there isn't a little risk involved here and there, but I will contend that it's worth it.

Consider the lengths we've often undertaken to pull in the legendary catfish. When my sisters and I were little girls we loved to help a family friend named Tez check his catfish lines on Lake Saint John. We'd stick our arms up to our armpits into these big black pipes sunk below the murky water. Tez paid us a quarter for every catfish we came up with. You don't have enough money to get me to do that today! And yet, many of my fellow countrymen do that and more, just for kicks. I'm speaking here of the popular sport known as catfish grabbling, or "noodling" for monster catfish.

Noodlers don't actually eat these huge fish. Instead they break one of their mama's hard and fast rules: They play with their food. In years gone by catfish grabblers have been somewhat of a secretive group as this type of hand fishing continues to be controversial and in some places illegal. But recently the brave folks of Noodlers Anonymous in Missouri have "come out" to lobby their state legislature. Missourians can now jump into lakes or rivers, stick their hands into cold, dark places and hope monster-size catfish will swallow their arms so they can wrestle the cats to the surface. And they can do it all without fear of prosecution. Which is interesting—the fear of prosecution... If I were to take up noodling, I'm not sure prosecution would register on my fear list.

They don't teach catfish grabbing in magazines or on those fishing shows. It's a way of life passed from father to son (and mothers to daughters)! Those opposed to noodling are afraid legalizing it will encourage more people to try the sport. Ummm... probably not, but I digress.

I'm not interested in noodling myself. It sounds like a bad game of Hokey Pokey: "Put your right hand in, pull your right nub out, count your missing fingers and shake it all about..." However, I am very interested in protecting the rights of my fellow Americans. I say: If someone wants to hold their breath underwater while attempting to pull a big Catdaddy from a hollow log, fully aware he could come up with an irritated water moccasin or snapping turtle instead, well, they should be able to. This is still the land of the free! I just have one suggestion. Noodling sounds like a bunch of pasta fans. This is an extreme sport; I think it needs an extreme name. Fearless Fishing, now, that's catchy....

The Great Debate

As a young married woman I had more than enough help in turning nature's blessings into traditional Southern meals for my family. In addition to the wealth of information available to me through my Southern Mama, I had our church's cookbook. Pity the novice that must begin the journey without either.

There's a certain Southern psychology behind our cookbooks. I

> My mama told me, "When cooking cabbage, cook it just long enough to get the squeak out."
>
> Sue Hudgins
> Danville, Virginia

once got a letter from a nice Yankee who said, "Dear Shellie, I don't mean to sound offensive but as an avid traveler and regional cookbook collector, I no longer buy your Southern cookbooks. Many have several versions of the same recipe with only slight variations. Why is this?" I explained to Emily in Ohio that our community cookbooks are usually produced as fund-raisers for church projects or local civic organizations like the Junior Auxiliary and they're as much about the community as they are the cooking. For heaven's sakes, the selection committee can no more choose Mrs. Sally's chicken salad over Mrs. Jane's chicken salad than we could pick one of our children over the other. In the South we find it hard to separate food and family.

My mama said the best gravy or roux was made when the oil and flour mixture was slowly cooked and stirred 'til it was somewhere between "darker than peanut butter and next door to burnt."

Ann Kendrick
Lumberton, Texas

Not only will you find similar recipes in the same cookbook, but you will find recipes similar to many of the other cookbooks from your region. It is the variations to these favorite dishes that we find interesting. We're not looking for the secret to tofu, but that twist on pantry cooking that hasn't occurred to us. We know the variation is the result of a moment of true genius in the Art of Substitution. "Horseradish! Mary Nell uses horseradish in her deviled eggs. I thought they had a kick!"

I left y'all a minute to go to the kitchen and check out my cookbook collection. After a fair amount of research (I scanned a couple dozen cookbooks), I have verified what I'm about to tell you. The recipes in our Southern cookbooks, as a whole, refrain from even touching upon the Great Debate. Perhaps we feel it's too close to proselytizing. By definition, the term *proselytizing* means attempting to convert another person to your faith. Southerners don't believe this to be the same as sharing one's faith, which is not only acceptable but biblical. Around here, proselytizing would be members of the First Baptist Church trying to steal the good long-standing members of the First Methodist Church. Such a practice, with its potential for emotional stress and serious community discord is avoided at all costs, similar to the Great Debate purposely sidestepped in our cookbooks.

From the beginning of time there have been those topics that have aroused such strong feelings, such passionate loyalty, that they've been called the Great Debate. Was the world round or flat? Are we alone in the universe or are there aliens among us? Is that a cowlick or does Donald Trump do his hair like that on purpose? Many of these debates have been settled. Others will live on, destined to be forever fueled by the passion of their advocates. Such is the nature of Miracle Whip vs. Mayonnaise.

It's not pretty. Miracle Whip people—and you know who you are—have been known to ridicule and ostracize mayonnaise people who have done nothing more than marry into their poor deceived families. And I suppose, to be fair, mayonnaise

Mama taught me to always take a dish to a bereaved family and attend the services. You should put identification on the bottom of the dish and understand that this is one occasion when you shouldn't expect it to be returned with something in it, other than, perhaps, a note of thanks. Your note or letter of condolence should always follow.

Ann Love
Maggie Valley, North Carolina

Mama always taught us to be careful about eating other people's chicken salad because it might not be cooked completely, but my sisters and I think she was more worried that they might use Miracle Whip!

Ellen Beth Marks
Dallas, Texas

people have not been completely innocent. The stress has caused these God-fearing right-thinking Americans to go so far as to suggest that Miracle Whip is of the devil.

While researching this important subject I discovered that my video producer and good friend Bubba managed to make it to adulthood without even knowing there was a difference between Miracle Whip and mayonnaise. (Obviously, he hadn't spent time in the kitchen other than sitting at a plate.) However, the first time his bride sent him to the store and he came back with Miracle Whip, he was brought up to speed—quickly. Bubba says it's been years now and he still gets nervous in the condiment aisle when he's sent after mayonnaise. No impulse buys from Bubba; once burnt, twice shy.

In the tradition of my peers, and the interest of civility, I will include at least one recipe in this collection that allows the use of Miracle Whip. The remaining dishes will simply call for mayonnaise. If someone wants to ruin their chicken salad with Miracle Whip in the privacy of his or her own kitchen, it is their God-given right. I am nothing if not open-minded.

I suppose I should admit here that I've never witnessed a Miracle Whip/Mayonnaise debate in my Southern Mama's kitchen, so this is merely a hypothesis, but if such discord were to break out on Mama's territory, I know without a doubt exactly what action she'd take to quell the strife. Mama would serve grits. She'd serve them with lots of butter and a little salt and pepper, and she'd serve them quickly. If mayonnaise is the battle cry, grits is the truce. Southerners may have issues with our mayonnaise, and our opinions on who makes the best barbecue may fluctuate so violently that I'm afraid to even touch the subject, but grits—grits glue us together.

Funeral Foods and Organizational Skills

Our Southern Mamas believe there is never a more appropriate time for the belle to use her extensive training in serving up large quantities of comfort food lightning-fast than when someone she knows and loves goes to meet their maker. Actually, she doesn't really even have to know the deceased soul personally, although the closer the tie the more obligated she may feel about feeding the bereaved.

If the deceased is the daughter of her friend's cousin who used to be married to her ex-brother-in-law's nephew, she can get away with some nice paper goods and a couple liters of Cokes from the grocery store. But if the connection is any closer at all we're taught to materialize at the family home as soon as possible with food prepared by our own two hands. This is no time to be stingy, Sugar. If one dish is good, two is better.

Upon her arrival she will find something to do without waiting to be asked. If the belle happens to be in the first wave of mourners, she'll quickly find an empty notepad and begin documenting the following guests and their accompanying provisions. The next belle will man the phone. The next belle will answer the door, and so on. They'll tend the kids and wash the clothes, tidying, tossing, and cleaning as they go. It's a phenomenon akin to the medical triage one might witness in a state-of-the-art emergency room after a national catastrophe, only more organized. These well-trained women can take an unfortunate sister's house from total disarray to white-glove ready in less time than it'd take that Pennington fellow to scream "Extreme Makeover" in his bullhorn. And when it's all said and done, they'll offer a funeral feast fit for king and loyal subject alike. Not long ago one of my readers wrote in with a beloved family story about just such a spread.

It happened many years ago when the reader's uncle David was in the service. He and his good friend Larry had scored a leave and were hitchhiking home to Middlesboro, Kentucky, from Fort Benning, Georgia. It was cold and snowing most of the way. They'd trudged along for more than sixteen hours without anything to eat when they made it to Pikeville, Kentucky. Walking through the small town, the two weary soldiers noticed funeral cones outside a home. They stopped and watched as a growing crowd filtered through the front door. Their eyes lit up as inspiration hit them both simultaneously. Southern born and bred, the boys were well aware that folks in the South send their dearly departed out in style. David and Larry made their way into the house and headed straight to the buffet. Nodding only if acknowledged and speaking to no one, the boys filled their plates, found a corner, and satisfied their hunger.

Much later, when they were ready to brave the cold for the remaining thirty miles home, they tucked their hats underneath their arms in official army order and filed by the coffin, pausing for good measure. Then, turning to the mourning widow, David gently smiled and said with utmost respect, "Ma'am, he looks the best I've ever seen him!" It may not have been the whole truth, but it was an accurate observation.

I'll wager that, given a reasonable amount of time, even the bereaved family would've pardoned their gate-crashing, for our Southern Mamas truly believe no one should have to mourn on an empty stomach, nor celebrate, shop, travel, or otherwise exert himself without appropriate sustenance, and plenty of it.

Salad Recipes to Do It Right from Start to Finish

Mama taught us girls to serve our meals in full, living color. Every plate should have some green on it. Bonus points for squeezing in a little red and orange. (Sorry, deer meat and mac and cheese don't count here.) Mama's fondness for the color wheel, together with her need to stretch a dollar could go a long way toward explaining why she served green salads and fruit salads in so many varieties. Especially fruit salad—it does come in a kaleidoscope of colors. So she dunked those colors in a little mayonnaise here and a little cream cheese there. I'm not complaining and trust me, if you were able to slide your feet under her table, you wouldn't either.

~ Plantation Dressing ~

SERVES 12–15

Mama says a green salad was only as good as the dressing. Here's a recipe that could've been served in the formal dining room of Tara, before all the unpleasantness, of course. It's called Plantation Dressing and it is guaranteed to make your salad sing.

1 cup mayonnaise
1 cup buttermilk
1 garlic clove, minced or pressed
½ cup sliced green onions
1 tablespoon parsley flakes
1 teaspoon tarragon
salt and pepper to taste

Blend mayonnaise and buttermilk well. Place into your food processor along with garlic and green onions. Season with parsley, tarragon, salt, and pepper. Stir and refrigerate overnight before using.

LA, LA, LA, LA, LA, LA, LA! (You guessed it! That was my salad singin'!)

~ Sensation Salad ~

SERVES 4–6

I have one word of warning about this salad. Be sure to kiss your sweetie before you partake! The garlic cloves and Romano cheese join hands to ramp up the flavor, but they also tend to stick with you like white on rice. Oh, well, as Scarlett would say, "Tomorrow is another day..."

1 large head iceberg lettuce
6 cloves garlic, mashed
1 teaspoon salt
½ cup Wesson oil
juice of one lemon
1 cup Romano cheese, divided

Soak lettuce in cold water before tearing into bite-size pieces. Drain and set aside. Mix garlic with salt. Add oil and mix well. Toss lettuce with oil mixture, lemon juice, and half of the Romano cheese. Top with the remaining cheese right before serving.

~ Hot Chicken Salad ~

SERVES 6–8

If you're the least bit Southern, you've had your share of chicken salad but did ya mama teach you how to serve it as a main dish? If not, here's a delicious twist on an old favorite.

6 chicken breasts
4 tablespoons butter, melted
¼ teaspoon Tony Chachere's Original Creole Seasoning or other season-all
2 cups mayonnaise
4 teaspoons lemon juice
4 teaspoons chopped onion
4 cups chopped celery
1 cup slivered almonds
1 cup grated cheddar cheese
2 cups plain potato chips

Begin by baking chicken in the oven with a small amount of water, melted butter, and a good season-all like Tony Chachere's. That's an important step. Baking the chicken rather than boiling it delivers a much better flavor. Now, chop up your cooked chicken into bite-size pieces and mix with mayonnaise, lemon juice, onion, celery, and almonds in a large mixing bowl. Spoon into a greased casserole dish and top with grated cheddar cheese and crushed potato chips. Bake at 375 degrees for 30 minutes.

~ Bestest Broccoli Salad ~

SERVES 6–8

My Bestest Broccoli Salad is simply delicious and it's a perfect side dish to round off a light supper (say some grilled seafood and a loaf of French bread). Now, on the outside chance that you're siding with the forty-first president of these United States, George Herbert Walker Bush here and you're anti-broccoli, I'm going to have to ask you to try it, please. I just know you'll like it!

2 cups fresh broccoli, cut into bite-size pieces
6 slices bacon, fried, drained, and crumbled
1 cup golden raisins
1 cup chopped green onions

Dressing
1 cup mayonnaise
¼ cup sugar
2 tablespoons lemon juice

Combine the broccoli, bacon, raisins, and green onions. I like to make the dressing and keep it separate so I can mix up the salad right before we sit down. The dressing is simple. Combine the mayonnaise with the sugar and lemon juice. That's it! Good eating doesn't have to be complicated. Put the salad and the dressing in the fridge and stir it up while you slice the French bread and grill the seafood.

~ Frozen Fruit Salad ~

SERVES 6–8

Can you really go wrong when you start with Cool Whip and cream cheese? This chilly dish serves up in pretty little helpings just perfect for that special luncheon. Break out your grandmother's china and do it up right, girl!

½ cup lemon juice

1 6.5-ounce cream cheese, softened

1 10-ounce package frozen sliced strawberries, thawed

3 bananas, sliced

1 21-ounce can unsweetened crushed pineapple, drained well

1 cup pecans

1 8-ounce carton Cool Whip, softened

Add lemon juice to cream cheese and blend until smooth. Add strawberries, bananas, and pineapple. Add a cup of nature's sweet meat (that would be pecans) to lend a crunchy texture. Stir in Cool Whip and pour into a 9 × 12-inch glass dish. Freeze until firm.

~ Summer's Best Seafood Salad ~

SERVES 6–8

You can substitute your favorite noodles in this recipe if you like. I prefer corkscrew pasta. By way of confession I'll admit that I actually use Miracle Whip in this salad instead of mayonnaise. It's one of the few times, and I do mean few times, that I use the sweet imposter, but it combines with the other ingredients to supply just the right flavor. (I try to slide the MW to the back of the fridge to protect my reputation.)

½ cup salad dressing (Miracle Whip)
¼ cup Italian dressing
3 tablespoons Parmesan cheese
1 12-ounce bag corkscrew noodles, cooked and drained
1 cup chopped fresh broccoli florets
½ cup diced green onions
¼ cup finely diced celery
2 cups imitation or fresh crabmeat, chopped

Dressing: In a small bowl combine your salad dressing, Italian dressing, and Parmesan cheese. Mix well and set it aside.

Pasta: In a larger salad bowl, combine noodles, broccoli, green onions, and celery. Stir in your imitation crabmeat along with the mixed dressing, toss well, and chill! That's Summer's Best Seafood Salad, and it's some mighty fine eating! By the way, you do know why you have to be careful around seafood, don't you? Cause you might pull a muscle. (Get it, mussel?)

~ Mrs. Billie's Crunchy Sweet Coleslaw ~

SERVES 4–6

The first time I had this slaw it was served at a Garden Club luncheon. I cleaned my plate in record time, but seeing as I was the guest speaker I decided not to ask for more. I did, however, get the recipe. I promptly dropped by the grocery store for the ingredients and made it for supper. It's that good! Oh, and in the Southern tradition, I name it here after the lady who first served it to me.

Crunchies

1 package Ramen noodles (Oriental flavor), crushed/crumbled
½ cup sliced almonds
3 tablespoons sesame seeds (or sunflower)
4 tablespoons butter

Dressing

4 tablespoons sugar (or 6 packets Equal)
6 tablespoons rice or tarragon vinegar
1 tablespoon soy sauce
½ cup canola oil
1 tablespoon pepper

Slaw Base

1 package old-fashioned slaw with carrots
1 bunch green onions, chopped

Combine the Ramen noodles (and the seasoning pack) with almonds and sesame seeds. Brown this crunchy mixture in butter; let it cool and store it in the fridge in a plastic bag.

For the dressing combine sugar with vinegar, soy sauce, and oil. Season this dressing really well with black pepper and chill.

When you're ready to serve, add crunchies and your dressing to coleslaw and green onions. Have mercy, that's good eating!

6

Baseboards on Display

What Southern Mamas Tell Their Daughters About Cleaning and Keeping House (with Soul-Satisfying Soup Recipes to Help Make Your House a Home)

My dear Southern Mama supplied my sisters and me with an unparalleled education on how to keep house. The lessons she began to preach when we were still under her roof continue to echo throughout our homes today (due at least in part to the fact that she keeps repeating them).

> Mama's rule about housekeeping in general and being prepared for company in particular was a twist on a familiar phrase: "Never put off 'til tomorrow what you can tend to today."
>
> Elaine Boyette
> Natchez, Mississippi

We know that if we "pick up, it won't pile up," and we live under the threat of the irreparable damage our dusting skills, or lack thereof, could have on our reputations because "you can tell a lot about a person from the way she keeps house." There is recent evidence that Mama's lectures—I mean gentle teachings—have finally taken. I know this because I've begun to concern myself with some of her legendary apprehensions.

Lately, it's become important to me to have my personal

items organized so that if—Heaven forbid—I'm in an accident in my clean undergarments, a friend or relative can come into my home and get additional undergarments without bringing shame on the entire family. Mama raised us to understand that leaving the house with so much as a dish in the sink was to invite a potential embarrassment we'd never live down.

Mama said, "Always wear clean underwear in case you're in an accident."

Bettye Kelley
Auburn, Alabama

There was a time when my sisters and I laughed this off; noting we'd never once heard anyone who, while discussing an accident in our close-knit community, let it slip that they had found the victim's home in disarray. To which Mama would insist that people around here are just too polite to discuss things like that. I don't mean any disrespect toward Mama, but I've heard polite people around here discuss a whole lot worse, out of concern of course, and to add the poor things to the Wednesday night prayer list.

"Whistling girls and crowing hens never come to a very good end."

Kitty McGuire
Sylvania, Georgia

I remember once when Rhonda and I were teenagers and our friends were all going out on the lake. We had permission to join them, after we completed our Saturday chores. Papa and Mama left on a short day trip to the next town, warning us not to leave the house until the clothes were done. In our defense, even former president William Jefferson "Bubba" Clinton would say, "There are different interpretations of the word *done.*"

Our version meant sending all the clothes through the washer on the shortest possible cycle and then draping and

> My mom, Judy, always told me before I got married, "No one can make you do what you don't know how to do." That's why I never learned to iron.
>
> Marion Brown
> Lake Providence, Louisiana

hanging them all over the house to dry. After all, a clothes dryer does take time and there was only so much daylight and our friends were waiting. Unfortunately for us, Mama and Papa came home much earlier than anticipated. We paid dearly for that one. And to this day, Mama is likely to take a sick headache just thinking about the indignity the family could've suffered had there been an emergency while she was gone.

The Serious Risk of Greasy Buildup

Mama raised us girls during the height of the feminist movement, but it's safe to say she wasn't greatly influenced by their passion. She had her own priorities. It was fine with Mama that we learn how to bring home the bacon and fry it up in the pan, but it was vital to her that we understood how to avoid the greasy buildup once we were done. She taught us girls that the only way to keep house is to stay on top of it, that it was much easier to keep it clean than it was to face it after the dirt built.

> Mama said, "Don't build more house than you want to clean."
>
> Joyce Dixon
> Claxton, Georgia

Contrary to popular belief, the old saying "cleanliness is next to godliness" cannot be found in the Bible. Many theories abound as to its origin, but since none of them are proven, I'd like to submit one of my own. I wouldn't be surprised if the saying was coined by a Southern Mama trying to coerce her daughter into keeping her baseboards clean. Southern Mamas have baseboard issues. I wish I had a dime for every time I've heard a Southern lady sigh heavily and bemoan the condition of her baseboards. A belle's house might be clean, but if her baseboards are dusty she may as well be living in a pigsty. Heads-up, newcomers: These same women will contend they're only concerned about their own dirty woodwork and feign indifference to yours. Don't be deceived. They may go so far as to say they'd never even consider checking out another woman's baseboards. They're lying like a three-dollar rug. They'll judge you by the dust that is or is not collected there. It may not be fair, but it's fact.

Mama has passed on a ton of housekeeping hints but one in particular was so rigid, so unwavering that it shall henceforth and forever be known as the Cardinal Rule of Housecleaning: One should never, ever leave dirty dishes on the kitchen counters or in the sink. This rule is about much more than appearances. To quote Mama, "Dirty dishes and exposed food will invite roaches and you will never get rid of 'em."

> Mama said, "Always wipe your feet before you enter someone's house."
>
> Evelyn Smilow Hopkins
> Daughter of Ruth Leach Smilow
> Lake Providence, Louisiana

My apologies to the exterminators who might be reading this; I'm sure you know your business, but Mama said you will never, ever get rid of 'em and I have no reason to question her at this time. Besides, I do not want to take any chances. The Southern roach can compete in size with the small dogs you see peeking out of celebrities' purses, without the rhinestone collars of course.

These Southern roaches are big and they are bold. They're loud, in-your-face bugs. We may share the same region, but we do not live in harmony. Often these overgrown insects will not even run when the lights come on. They would much prefer to dance in your face while holding the last cookie in the house. And—because God has a sense of humor—they can also fly. I have been known to hurt myself and other unfortunate souls in my vicinity simply trying to avoid contact with one of these ugly creatures. And I have never identified more closely with a TV sitcom character than I did when the astute Ms. Suzanne Sugarbaker of *Designing Women* fame staked out her position on the issue during a serious feminist discussion with the rest of the cast. "I still say," my heroine stated passionately, "that the male should have to kill the bugs." Well said, Suzanne. Well said.

As hard as it is for me to say this, when I talk about the blessing I would receive from the demise of all cockroaches, I am not speaking for everyone. Oftentimes my work leads me to opine on stupid people. I try to limit this style of commentary, but frankly, it's hard. And I'd rather discuss the stupidity of people who aren't from around here, but alas, stupid grows everywhere. Sometimes it seems to be coming at me from all sides.

Take the Roach-Gate controversy of fall '07. It was hard to take sides on that one. On one hand, you had the brilliant minds at that Six Flags amusement park who were hosting special nights where anyone who ate a three-inch Madagascar hissing cockroach was allowed to jump to the front of the line. Why? Don't ask me, Sweet Cheeks. I can only suppose there was a shortage of people "calling Ralph" on the roller coasters. Perhaps drastic measures had to be taken, you know?

I actually read that "certain health officials" were worried, saying that eating cockroaches increases a person's risk of having stomach problems. Aw, ya think? So does eating mystery foods at church fellowships, friends, but at least it's done for the love of faith, family, and friends. Now, there's an act of courage that should rewarded.

I was terribly upset with Six Flags for encouraging such reprehensible behavior, and yet, it was also hard for me to side with the people on the other side of the Roach-Gate controversy. That would be the PETA people. I haven't done any research on this, but I think PETA stands for People against Eating Trees and Animals. The PETA folks were determined to stand up for the roaches of the world. Roaches, or so they said, were gentle creatures that have been given a bad rap. I tried to get a good quote on that from my Terminix man but he could not be reached for comment, as in he literally could not be reached. The poor fella was rolling around on the floor laughing.

PETA also said cockroaches were complex, intelligent life forms—which doesn't come close to explaining why the ugly geniuses run at you when you flip the kitchen light on instead of darting for cover, unless someone told 'em they were smarter than the other bugs. I reckon that could explain their arrogance.

Being wise in the ways of the world, I was quick to smell a publicity ploy by the Six Flags people, and it succeeded, but here at *All Things Southern* I like to delve deeper into these things. Do you suppose, that with the high gas prices, revenues were down at these parks and they couldn't afford their exterminators? It would give them the opportunity to adopt a new corporate motto: "If you can't beat 'em, get the folks to eat 'em." I have a great idea. This summer

My mom always said, "The outside of your house and your yard are as important as the inside. When people pass by, they judge what type of people live there by their yards."

Mildred Chapman
West Monroe, Louisiana

I'm hosting the first annual Tourist Mosquito Eating Contest, right here in beautiful Lake Providence, Louisiana. Y'all come!

The Roach Reality

If you share my aversion to roaches, Honey, follow the advice of my dear Southern Mama. Keep your kitchen as clean as is humanly possible. Take the trash out regularly and keep everything in sealed containers. If, however, you are fond of the nasty bugs, you might have a future in reality TV.

I'd like to think by the time you read these words reality TV will be a thing of the past. Please, a girl can hope. Even *The Brady Bunch* ran its course. Reality shows weary me half of the time and nauseate me the other half. Granted, the concept isn't all bad. I even liked a few of the earliest offerings, but they lost me when they started eating roaches. Reality TV has been going downhill ever since. Even the name is a misnomer. Here's my idea of reality: If I come face-to-face with a spitting cockroach, I'm hollering at my sweet husband to come squash it. It doesn't cross my mind to close my eyes and eat it!

We have an expression round here about folks "having the good sense to be embarrassed." There's a vanishing character trait if ever I saw one. It's a pity too; some of these reality contestants should be shamed to their knees. Take *Fear Factor* for instance. (I know what you're thinking. In my defense, I barely paused while flipping channels. It's like passing a car wreck. You feel bad for looking but you can't help yourself.)

Can you picture one of those young girls being introduced to her new sweetheart's family? It might go something like this. "Oh, I recognize you," the mother-in-law would say with that decidedly sweet but deadly potent mixture of sugar and acid known so well to our tongue. "You're the girl who carried the most dead rats between your teeth on television! How nice for you..." It might sound like a compliment at face value but if this was to happen in my family, my folks would recognize it for what it really was and everyone in the room would be making those eyes that say, "Take her out with the trash."

There have been a few, a very few, exceptions to the reality TV ban at our house. One season Phil and I got hooked on watching that *Do You Want to Be a Lead Singer for a Rock Band We Never Heard Of* show. In our defense, that first night we thought we were watching a new comedy—and a good one. We laughed 'til our sides hurt.

My Southern Mama taught us to never leave a table after a meal and expect someone to clean up after us. If my sisters and I ate a meal at another house, say at a boyfriend's, we knew the first thing out of our mother's mouth when we returned would be "Did you help clean up?" Once a boyfriend's mother insisted I leave the dishes and I said, "If I don't clean your kitchen, I can't come back."

Edna Durden
Perry, Florida

Then we found out it was real but we kept watching because those people were fascinating (in an E.T. phone home sort of way). We'd stare blankly at the screen while some poor soul twisted and hollered and slid across the stage. And when he would quit, or die (sometimes you couldn't tell because they all fall out on the floor), one of us would mutter, "He's horrible" just as the camera would cut to the male judge wrapped in a white feather boa in time for him to gush, "Genius, sheer genius!" Music critics we are not.

Before we leave this particular thread of conversation—and I'm trying—I'd like to point out that it appears to me my beloved Animal Planet channel is even trying to up the gross factor. I recently watched a story from India, where a man had found two giant cobras under his hut. Doo Doo the village priest (I'm sorry, that was his name) said the snakes were mating. He instructed the villagers to dig up the ground under the hut. Sure enough, they found 150 baby cobras. Doo Doo held them in his hands and showed them to the camera, one big wiggly mass of snakes.

And then the commentator asked, "But what are you going to do with 150 cobras when the neighbors don't want 'em and the zoo won't take 'em?" Before I could even consider such a dilemma he answered his own question. "There's nothing left for Doo Doo to do, but eat them." And that's what happened. Doo Doo commenced to chewing on that wiggly mass even as one of them latched down on his left nostril, its tail disappearing into his mouth. The commentator explained to us viewers that Doo Doo ate them to prove his supremacy over serpents, but I don't know—I blame all of this on *Fear Factor*! Special note to homeowners: Mama said if they would have kept their huts picked up that pileup never would've happened.

The Great Unseen Hand

Mama passed down simple housecleaning decrees: If you dirtied it, you cleaned it. If you pulled it out, you put it back. There was a time when Mama wearied me with her fastidiousness. Then I became head housekeeper of my own little domain. Suddenly I found great value in Mama's anticlutter theory. Persuading my family to honor the concept, however, left me understanding why Mama used to call me back to the living room to

Mama taught me to have a place for everything and everything in its place.

Nell Collins
Longview, Texas

ask, "So, did you think those socks would walk to the laundry room by themselves?" Puleease. We both knew she'd be going that way long before I would.

Though I didn't particularly enjoy Mama's attempt at humor, it didn't prevent me from trying out my own routine years later with my offspring. I developed my own comic bit called the Unseen Hand.

"Excuse me," I would say to halt an exiting child in his or her tracks. "Are you leaving that empty ice cream bowl there? And just who do you think is gonna pick it up? The Great Unseen Hand? Do you really think a Great Unseen Hand swoops through this place picking up after everyone?" I'd close with my best attempt at Mother Guilt: "Well, mystery solved, Honey. The Great Unseen Hand belongs to me. I'm the one who picks it up." For the most part, neither my son nor my daughter seemed moved by these monologues, except for that brief period when Jessica Ann became... a stuffer.

It began, that tragic season, when Jessica was a preteen. It lasted for less than a year, but there were a few times there when I thought I was going to have to send her to reform school, aka Mama's house.

Tired of the Great Unseen Hand routine, but not yet willing to pick up after herself, Jessica Ann fell prey to a tendency she seemed almost powerless to control. Upon first inspection, the living room would look clean but first impressions can be deceiving. I would find candy wrappers stuck in the houseplants and dirty socks stuffed between the sofa cushions. I would scold gently (rant and rave 'til my eyes bulged). Jessica would come clean, repent, and promise to reform—only to repeat the offense at the first opportunity. It got so bad that the child would spend twice the energy and time finding new places to stuff than it would have taken to pick up.

I was afraid I wasn't getting to her at all. I began to worry about her future. I could see my poor Southern child risking everything to stuff. I had nightmares of her standing before a group of strangers and confessing, "My name is Jessica and I stuff. It all started when I was a little girl and I was afraid of my overbearing Southern Mama and her pick-up rule. One day I stuffed and it felt good. That's the truth. I was sorry when Mama caught me, but only because I had been caught. I knew it was wrong, but I liked stuffing. I tried to quit. But it grew on me. Sometimes I can go for days without stuffing and then—just like that, I stuff one little peppermint wrapper and I'm hooked again."

Mama said, "Beaus won't go where cobwebs grow."

Rena Dillman
Louisburg, North Carolina

Jessica finally quit stuffing but only after I resorted to the last line of reasoning I had learned from my own dear mama. In short, I threatened to "beat her within an inch of her life." Today Jessica Ann is one of the most fastidious housekeepers on the planet. Oh, the power of a well-turned phrase.

Clutter Alert

If one aspires to be a good housekeeper, one must be constantly aware of the many forces at work trying to bring clutter into your home. Can you say junk mail? How about magazine subscription cards? Exactly! We're going there in just a minute. But first, speaking of magazines, I must tell y'all about the most amazing headline I read while picking up my *Southern Living* at the checkout stand. Someone had taken the first ever pictures from H, E, Double L and sold them to one of those tabloids! It must be true. It said it right there on the front of the paper! Yes, I know—I have my tongue in my cheek, Sugar. And that begs my next question, who's buying those magazines?

Who sees a headline screaming, EIGHTY-YEAR-OLD GRANDMOTHER GIVES BIRTH TO FULL-GROWN ELVIS IMPERSONATOR WHILE SINGING "I DID IT MY WAY"—PHOTOS INSIDE, and thinks "I've just got to read that article!"

Fess up, y'all. Somebody's buying that stuff or they wouldn't keep selling it. I'm just curious. Your choice of reading material isn't bothering me. However, there's a second group of folks I'd love to identify who *are* bothering me, and the rest of your friends and neighbors. It goes back to the subject at hand here (which was clutter in case you've forgotten), and frankly, y'all need a whooping. I'm talking to whoever is mailing in those annoying renew-your-subscription cards that fall out of the magazines. Someone's using 'em for something other than coasters or they'd disappear as many times as the rest of us have cursed their existence. This is clutter in one of its most unredeeming forms. It is also one of my biggest pet peeves.

I don't know what your personal gripes are, but I do have some fascinating news on the subject from the Internet. I have discovered a company out there hoping to capitalize on whatever issues you find annoying. You can now "rent a mob" to put on your own customized protest. Are you mad as a hornet but crazy busy? Too tired to whine? No problem, Sugar. Tell them what's bugging you and a good-size mob of protesters will show up to do all the sign waving and name-calling for you; for a price, of course. The company says business is good and I'm not surprised. We are a consumer-driven society. Hire a mob if you must. I'm just saying, the day this Southern girl can't work up a good hissy fit of her own will be the day she purchases a tabloid magazine full of magazine subscription cards and featuring the first-ever photos of H, E, double L.

Mama the Houseguest

In addition to monitoring clutter, my Southern Mama stressed the importance of having a place for everything and having everything in its place. I've always tried to do right by my raising but last year I had a little extra incentive to get my household in order. Scratch that. I had *a lot* of extra incentive. I was scheduled to have surgery and Mama was coming to stay with me when I got out of the hospital. Have you ever known someone to clean up before the maid comes? That's the idea here.

Mama always said, "Never sweep the porch in your company's face," meaning if you saw someone walking up to the house, it was rude to grab a broom and start sweeping.

Boo Robinson
Bastrop, Louisiana

I wasn't looking forward to surgery, but as far as having some of your insides removed goes, I guess things went according to the medical community's twisted little plan, beginning with check-in, when a sweet little lady led me to a nice private room where I put on one very public gown.

Surgery went okay too, or at least my worst fears weren't realized. I had read where some hospitals right here in the good old US of A were using harp players to calm patients and reduce their pain. The harp's vibrations were supposed to calm the nervous system, lower the heart rate, and in some cases lessen the need for anesthesia before surgery. Well, I was hoping my doctor wasn't on that bandwagon, so to speak. I'm old-school on this one: If you're gonna be cutting anywhere in or on my body, I don't care to be serenaded, thank you very much. I want drugs, a heavy dose of legal drugs, before, during, and after. Besides, I figured if I woke up to the sound of a harp, I might be thinking I'd had a slight change of address, if you know what I mean.

Come to find out, I didn't have a thing to worry about. My house and I both received excellent care. While I recuperated Mama, aka Marshal Dillon, waged war on my dust bunnies and made sure I didn't lift anything heavier than the telephone. I was waited on hand and foot and I didn't cook a meal for weeks. I'm not proud of this, but I ended up playing the game for all it was worth. Oh, don't be like that. You would have too. I mean, for heaven's sakes, the Good Marshal cleaned the tracks on my sliding patio door, sanitized my refrigerator, and waxed the leaves on my houseplants—the leaves on my houseplants! I tried to bribe my doctor into not releasing me before Mama got to my closets, but he got all professional on me. Whatever.

> Mama gave us girls a great housekeeping tip I've since passed on to my daughter. She told us, "Clean your toilet bowl with Lysol and people will think your whole house is clean!"
>
> Judy Patrick
> Vicksburg, Mississippi

Germs and Bumping Elbows

Perhaps you noticed something a little unusual when I mentioned Mama cleaning the tracks on my sliding patio door and waxing the leaves on my houseplants. Yes, Mama can be a bit of a neatnik. I'm not joking, Sugar. I am purposefully limiting this chapter on her housekeeping hints to a few handy overall rules. If I were to be true to my raising, it'd be a three-volume work, all its own.

Included in such a collection would be Mama's detailed

instructions on how to care for those special household items, like the valuable cast-iron skillet. Never, ever desecrate this symbol of our heritage by placing your skillet in a sink full of hot, sudsy water. Any Southern girl worth her raising knows that soap and man-made scrubbers will both remove the precious seasoning of a perfectly good skillet. So, how do you clean stubborn messes in your skillet? It's called salt, Sweet Cheeks. God had two good reasons for making salt. It's a fine seasoning when used in moderation (yes, we've heard some of you put sugar on your grits, but the subject is too distasteful to address), and it will help scrub stubborn food from your cast-iron skillet. Shake a little salt in your skillet and get a little aggressive with a wet rag. Simply put, anything that won't come out doesn't need to be removed.

My Southern Mama schooled us girls on when to clean, what to clean, and how to clean: all the time, everything, and thoroughly. If pressed, Mama will admit that sometimes it can be necessary to give your house "a lick and a promise," meaning a quick cleaning with a promise to be more meticulous next time but this type of cleaning should be the exception. "Top to bottom" is the rule, and it covers everything from the crown molding to the aforementioned baseboards.

Mama said, "Always light a fire in the fireplace. It doesn't cost much and it warms things up, calms people down, and brings the family together."

Becky Melton
Cincinnati, Ohio

Let's look at kitchen work, for instance. There is the general breakdown behind the rule known as "clean as you go," and then there are Mama's more thorough customs. I would tell you to return seasonings to their rightful place, wash empty pots and pans, and throw away trash as it accumulates. My Southern Mama wouldn't stop there. She'd suggest wiping down the seasoning jars, tidying up the pots and pans cabinet, and disinfecting the trash can while waiting for the cornbread to brown. Good housekeeping is about germs, people, and germs don't stand a chance against Mama.

As a matter of fact, I believe the Good Marshal could be of great use to humanity in the right position, say as CEO of the World Health Organization. I'd put her ideas on how to slow the spread of infectious diseases up against theirs any day of the week. Mama and I are still snickering over one of their latest suggestions. The serious folks at the World Health Organization have gotten so worried about the spread of bird flu they'd like people to stop shaking hands and switch to "bumping elbows."

We Southerners are as interested in preventing disease as any other region, but I don't know if this'll catch on down here. We don't just shake on things in the South, this is hugging country. We hug hello and good-bye and nice to meet you. Heck, we're even willing to risk the occasional misfired hug when our necks aren't coordinated and we end up smooching strangers. We're affectionate like that.

> You don't invite folks to your house and then berate them.
>
> Anna Marie Bess-Bleich
> California, Missouri

Anyway, I'm a little bit afraid of what might happen if Bubba goes to shake your hand and you throw an elbow at him. He's liable to throw one right back atcha. See, we judge folks by their handshakes. If you give us a tentative elbow, we'll think you're weak. Bump us too hard, and well, there you go, again. FYI, Bubba says he's cool with the hip bump, but that's Bubba. He loved the seventies!

Still, I wouldn't want it said that I'm unwilling to help the cause. Let it be a matter of record that should there arise a truly drastic worldwide epidemic, here at *All Things Southern* I will do my part to protect the public's welfare by supporting the use of face masks (Mardi Gras style) and gloves (pretty white ones).

In the first place, I'm patriotic, and hence, quite willing to sacrifice for my country. And in the second place, we Southern women do love to accessorize. True, gloves might be uncomfortable if our old pal Al is right about the planet warming up, but our great-greats wore 'em and by golly we can too. Besides, if someone gives me an aggressive elbow bump, Bubba says I can pull my glove off, slap 'em in the face, and challenge 'em to a duel. Our great-greats did that too. Isn't tradition beautiful?

Cleaning Feat or Dancing Feet?

I grew up hearing some of the women in my family discuss the difficult days, those trying times, BE, Before Electrolux. Not that there weren't vacuum cleaners out there, but they were once—get this, Sweet Cheeks—luxuries. I don't recall my late paternal grandmother having much to say on the subject, but then, she'd also be the one who as a newlywed set up house in a tent with dirt floors. Grandma swept those floors every day until they were packed as hard as a brickbat. Had Grandma owned a good vacuum cleaner, I dare say the woman would've sucked the dirt smack out of China.

My own mama purchased her first Electrolux in the sixties, when my sisters and I were three little stair-step tomboys. We grew up listening to its whirl, but we were preteens before she anointed us to run this hallowed appliance. (The picture is not unlike that of the Queen Mum knighting an officer.) I must say, though, once Mama finally gave us the reins, she seemed quite pleased with her decision. One of us girls was always being instructed to either put the vacuum cleaner up or take it out. I believe she would've left the blame thing in the middle of the floor had it not been such a valuable possession.

"Be careful with that," Mama would scold, if we accidentally bumped its precious gray case. "I didn't always have an Electrolux, you know." Yes, we knew. Mama taught us to vacuum very slowly so we could listen as the machine picked up debris. If you couldn't hear this process, Mama thought you were going too fast. We felt it much more likely that there was simply no more dirt to be found. Hello?

Mama's preoccupation with vacuuming reached epic proportions in the seventies when she had that fashionable shag carpet installed. Suddenly cleaning the carpet wasn't enough; we girls had to rake it. That's right. I said rake it. Mama's new shag carpet came with a carpet rake, designed to make the nap stand up. Mama liked it standing up in one direction, at all times. She would have done well in the armed forces, my mama. Go ahead. It's easy enough for you to laugh, but the whole experience left me with a lifelong distaste for vacuuming. Unlike Mama, I consider it more of a chore than a hobby.

Mama always told me to keep house as if the preacher and his wife were coming to visit.

Mary Alice Goss
Pennsylvania

Imagine my delight then, when I first heard that Electrolux, the reputable company of my childhood, was coming out with a brand-new development to help us with our household chores. "Whatever could it be?" I wondered aloud. "And will the Yankees steal it?" Okay, that's not exactly what went through my mind. It's just fun playing Scarlett now and then. But enough, I won't keep you waiting any further. Drum roll, please...

Electrolux has created shoes that will vacuum the floor as we walk. Um, if we could briefly postpone the wild celebration, Sugar, I have some concerns. First, does this mean multitasking is in again? I remember when it was all the rage. Then they decided the practice led to stupidity—and I'm quoting *Time* magazine here—"because doing too many things at once prevents you from concentrating on the task at hand." Which proves my point: I need to clean out the refrigerator.

I remember the first time I heard the buzzword of the millennium. Big deal, I thought, I've been doing that all my life. Technically, multitasking is the ability to execute more than one task at the same time. In my world it's known as brushing your teeth with one hand, putting on mascara with the other, while cleaning the bathroom floor with your big white athletic socks soaked in Scrubbing Bubbles.

This Southern Mama was simultaneously engaging in different activities a long time before they glamorized it with a name. I'm overqualified to share what the organizational experts don't always tell you: multitasking has a dark side.

I once read about Diane Sawyer making good use of her desk time by sitting on an exercise ball. She said it engaged her abs. Well now, I was spending countless hours at my desk, and I was all for engaging my abs. It sounded like a multitasking miracle!

I swapped my padded desk chair that lets me slump comfortably toward the screen for a big gray exercise ball. I balanced myself on top of it, booted up my computer, and engaged my abs. We had a short, yet very painful relationship.

I'd forget about our commitment and slump, causing me to fall off the ball and bond my chin with my desk instead.

I was more than willing to give up multitasking when they finally decided that it led to short-term memory loss and lapses in concentration. It made sense to me. In computer terms, I had too many programs open with too few resources available to run 'em.

Evidently we've gone full circle because the evil geniuses at Electrolux are now giving us the aforementioned footwear that will, and here's another precious quote: "Help us combine cleaning and exercising as we suck up the dirt while walking, running, and dancing through our homes." The people at Electrolux have either been drinking or they've managed to miss the memos about all of us being overweight and out of shape, otherwise they'd know scant little running and dancing is being done in the homes of overworked Americans.

Of course, these multitasking shoes do have rechargeable batteries, which I suppose could recharge one's personal battery if one stepped in the right household mess, but that's another subject and a possible lawsuit.

I like new shoes as well as the next woman, but I'm not grasping the advantage here, even if I get a pair for me and the hubby. The way I see it, this should allow Phil to vacuum a path from the fireplace to his recliner, back to his office, through the kitchen, and toward the door, which would leave me to personally lay my size eights on every other inch of the house. I can't be the only one seeing a serious design flaw here.

Supposedly, these shoes were invented after designers asked consumers what they wanted. All I can say to that is, I bet that hyper little Richard Simmons voted twice.

Soul-Satisfying Soup Recipes to Help Make Your House a Home

Anyone can set up a house but it takes a lot of love and attention to make it a home. One tried-and-true way to make the most of your time is to set a big pot of soup cooking on the stove top. While you tend to the laundry or any of the other myriad chores that keeps your house running smooth, that pleasing aroma will waft through your home and create just the right atmosphere. Here are a few of our family favorites. Try 'em and see if they don't say "I love you" to your bunch too.

~ Crawfish Étouffée for Cheaters ~

SERVES 4–6

Short on time and long on cravings? Coming pretty close to the old-fashioned start-from-scratch version, this one's a winner for that harried soul who has a to-do list a mile long. Take a few simple ingredients and a little bit of time and you can check supper off before you know it. And here's the bonus: you'll soon be enjoying some fine dining, Southern style.

1 white onion, chopped
1 green bell pepper, chopped
1 stick butter
2 pounds crawfish tail meat, washed and drained
3 cans cream of celery soup
1 can Rotel tomatoes
salt and pepper to taste
Tony Chachere's Seafood Seasoning or other season-all

In a small saucepan sauté onion and bell pepper in butter. Add veggies and crawfish to a large stockpot. Combine with soup and tomatoes and season well with salt, pepper, and season-all. Cook over medium heat for 45 minutes and serve over hot fluffy rice.

~ Cheesy Vegetable Soup ~

SERVES 6–8

My family raved the first time I bumped plain old vegetable soup up a notch. Yours will too. Feel free to experiment a little with the amount of cheese if your group isn't as crazy about the commodity as mine. Just do me a favor and refrain from telling anyone how simple this recipe is; I'm resting on my laurels here.

6 medium potatoes, diced
3 to 4 onions, diced
5 cups water
1 16-ounce package frozen mixed vegetables
1 can cream of celery soup
1 can cream of mushroom soup
1 pound of Velveeta cheese, cut into cubes
salt and pepper to taste

Place potatoes and onions in about five cups of boiling water. As soon as they're fork tender add frozen mixed vegetables and stir until the heat comes back up.

Stir in both soups and Velveeta cheese. Season with salt and pepper and let it cook on low about 30 minutes. All that's left for you to do is ring the dinner bell and say the magic words—soup's on!

~ Four-Bean Soup ~

SERVES 10–15

Want a hearty meal without spending all day in the kitchen? My Four-Bean Soup is just what you're looking for, Sugar. It's delicious and nutritious. (And I'm a poet and don't know it. That's my papa's line. He always followed it with "every verse gets worse.") Throw this one together and let it simmer on the stove while you round up the troops.

1 medium onion, chopped
2 whole bell peppers, chopped
3 tablespoons butter
2 pounds ground beef, browned and drained
1 can kidney beans
1 can pinto beans
1 can navy beans
1 can Great Northern beans
1 can Rotel tomatoes
1 can whole tomatoes
salt and pepper to taste

In a large stockpot sauté onion and peppers in butter. Add ground beef, kidney, pinto, navy, and Great Northern beans along with the canned tomatoes. Oh—and don't even think about draining the juice off those beans. For goodness sakes, that's the good stuff! Mix all this well and cook over a medium-high flame for at least 30 minutes, although it won't hurt to turn the heat down afterward and let it simmer a good while longer. Salt and pepper to taste. Happy eating!

~ Ann's Taco Soup ~

SERVES 6–8

Sometimes you know in advance that the week is going to get rough. Maybe you've got a big report due at work. Maybe every kid in the family has a ball game on opposite ends of town. Regardless, I've got some help for you. This recipe lends itself to making two great meals from one. The first night you serve tacos, taking care to make a double portion of taco meat. You'll be ahead of the game the next day. Just add the following ingredients along with the meat to a big old pot and let it simmer in a Crock-Pot while you're out. Brilliant!

1–2 pounds ground chuck or venison
1 package dry taco seasoning
1 package dry ranch dressing mix
1 cup water
1 can red kidney beans
2 cans pinto beans
1 can whole-kernel corn
1 can diced Rotel tomatoes with peppers
1 can stewed "Mexican recipe" tomatoes

Prepare ground beef according to taco seasoning instructions. Add dry ranch seasoning and a cup of water. Stir in beans, corn, and tomatoes with their juices and bring to a boil. Simmer at least 30 minutes. (I usually rinse out the bean cans and pour this water into the pot too. I get all the goods from the beans and cut down on smelly garbage at the same time.)

Serve with cornbread, crackers, or Fritos chips. Top with grated cheese and enjoy.

~ Here's Looking Atcha Potato Soup ~

SERVES 8–10

How about some trivia? I learned a lot of cooking tricks from my mama, like planning a meal based on whatever ingredients are on hand and according to which ones are about to expire. So, whenever I look into the pantry and notice that the potatoes are looking back at me, it's time for Here's Looking at 'Cha Potato Soup. (The potatoes' eyes, get it?)

Soup

6–8 potatoes (or as many as are looking at you)

2 tablespoons of flour

1 cup milk

1 can cream of mushroom soup (or any other cream soup flavor)

salt and pepper to taste

Topping

ham or bacon

chopped green onions

grated cheese

Peel and chop potatoes into chunks. Cover with water and bring to a rolling boil. Turn the heat down to medium and let the potatoes cook until they're tender.

Meanwhile, put flour in a small bowl and gradually add milk, stirring constantly until it's blended. Add this thickener to the tender potatoes along with soup. (It can be any cream of soup flavor. And if you don't have canned soup, you can leave it out. It'll be okay.)

Add salt and pepper and cook on low until you're ready to eat. 'Course, we like to top it with ham or bacon. Just don't forget the grated cheese and chopped green onions. And remember, waste not, want not, folks.

~ Clean the Pantry Swamp Soup ~

SERVES 6–8

Learn to keep these ingredients on hand and you can do a little magic whenever unexpected company shows up. No one has to know it comes from cans, Houdini Mama, I'm not telling. Just think of it as tricks of the trade.

½ cup chopped onion
½ cup chopped bell pepper
4 tablespoons butter
1 pound of leftover chicken, shrimp, crab, or crawfish
2 cans of evaporated milk
One can each of:
cream of celery soup
cream of broccoli soup
cream of mushroom soup
cream of potato soup
cream of onion soup
cream of chicken soup
3 8-ounce rolls garlic cheese
3 8-ounce rolls jalapeño cheese (I have a hard time finding the jalapeño; sometimes I substitute the Mexican Velveeta cheese instead)
salt and pepper to taste

In a large stockpot sauté onions and bell peppers in butter. When the onions are translucent, add whatever meat you're using (in any amount). Add evaporated milk and the soups. (Side note: try to find the low-sodium variety on those cans since we're using so many. It's better for you.) Cut up garlic cheese and jalapeño cheese. Add cheese to pot and bring the heat up slowly. Add salt and pepper. You're done. Let it simmer on the stove until it's heated through and through—or until the family is banging on the table, whichever comes first. This makes a big old pot! Serve with your favorite hot bread. That's good eating, Southern style . . .

7

Spit-Shined in Public

What Southern Mamas Tell Their Daughters About Beauty and Fashion (with Side Dishes to Complement the Main Course)

My poor mama had her work cut out for her when it came to teaching her daughters about beauty and fashion. Mama, a proper Southern belle if ever there was one, ex–"Miss Forestry Queen of Natchez, Mississippi," herself, gave birth to three little girls whose idea of high fashion was to clamp green lizards on our ears and wear discarded locust shells on our noses. This could not have been easy for someone who wore lipstick to drive her husband's bean truck.

Indeed, there must have been plenty of times when my Southern Mama wondered if she'd ever live to see us girls grow into young ladies, but to her credit, she began beating the belle drum early on and never gave it a rest. Times were hard on Bull Run Road, but Mama has always believed good taste can triumph over a thin pocketbook. She determined early on that her girls would be dressed as well as the next one. To that end, Mama taught herself to sew, producing girly little outfits out of sale fabric, complete with ribbons and lace. The very sight of these costumes drew eye rolls from me and my sisters.

Dress rehearsal was bad, but nothing compared to the main performance. Mama soon doubled our shame by sending us to school in those abominable outfits, even having us sleep in pink sponge rollers every Saturday night to better create a week's worth of ringlets in our crowning glories. Shirley Temple who?

As embarrassing as this girly-girl gear was for me and my sisters, fate wasn't through offering me extra opportunities for personal humiliation. I must've had a bull's-eye painted on my chest at birth.

> Mama always said, "Never let the holes in your socks show."
>
> Joan Bullard
> Lake Providence, Louisiana

Remember me saying I was born with crooked feet? I don't recall the heavy metal braces I had to wear as a baby, but I haven't been able to forget the corrective shoes of my elementary years. Can you say emotional scars?

At the beginning of each school year Mama guaranteed me an embarrassing outing by taking us girls shoe shopping together. My oldest sister, Cyndie, the least fashion conscious among us, went with whatever Mama and the saleslady suggested. Rhonda, the middle child—the one they called "Pretty Woman"—chose more discriminately, having come to the purchasing event with an eye out for the latest fashion. (This is truly off the subject, but the same people that called

> I'll never forget the day in junior high school when my classmates voted me "Cutest Girl." I called Mama to tell her the news, to which she calmly replied, "Well, Honey, just remember that beauty is only skin deep. It's what's on the inside that counts." My bubble was popped, but years later I learned to appreciate it.
>
> Rhonda Rushing Parker
> Dallas, Texas

Rhonda "Pretty Woman" nicknamed me "Coon Dog." I'm just asking, do you think that's fair?) As for me, the unfortunate one forever separated by the shape of her poor arches, I had to do my shoe shopping on a completely different side of the store (cue the horror music), where the corrective shoes lived.

While my sisters and our school friends were purchasing the latest fashions, my feet were being forced into larger versions of those bronzed baby shoes you see on bookshelves. This footwear made a statement, y'all, and it wasn't about fashion. It was more like, "U-G-L-Y, we don't have an alibi. We're ugly, hey, hey, we're ugly." They came with a fortified toe-box and they were indestructible. That's not conjecture on my part—I know that for a fact.

Mama always said I was "hard on my shoes." Bless her heart; she had no way of knowing I was hard on purpose. I did my dead-level best to destroy those clodhoppers! When I was warned not to drag my feet, lest it ruin my new shoes, I dragged those ugly puppies from morning to dark. I sought out mud puddles like a pig in the sunshine. I walked on the insides of my feet to break the arches. Alas, it was all in vain. Seriously, the people whose job it is to design earthquake-proof buildings should consult with whoever is churning out these corrective shoes.

The only thing I ever got for my trouble was a lecture from Mama about some little girl on the other side of the world who would've been proud to have my shoes. While I doubted this, had I been given the chance, I would've gladly struck a deal with my foreign friend. This might be a Mama book, but it was Papa who always said, "The best sermons are lived, not preached."

Suck Your Stomach In and Put Some Color On

As we grew older, we girls outgrew our taste for green lizard jewelry and locust nose rings and Mama retired her sewing machine, but we still had trouble bridging the great fashion divide that separated us.

In her determination to shape us into Southern belles, Mama seized every opportunity to repeat the Southern Mama's Manifesto, that well-known, oft repeated mantra every Southern girl knows by heart: "Suck your stomach in and put some color on." Color is another name for lipstick, and proper Southern ladies develop the lifelong habit of reapplying regularly. Of course, the importance of having color on your lips wasn't taught until later in our teen years, but I literally cannot remember a time when I didn't hear "suck your stomach in."

> When I wanted to pierce my ears, Mom said, "If God had wanted you to have holes in your ears, he would've put them there!"
>
> Teresa Hayes
> Staunton, Virginia

My Southern Mama seemed to think holding in your stomach fixed most anything. If you came home from school upset because someone called you Four-Eyes, Mama told you to hold in your stomach. If you called home to say you made cheerleader, please, girl, of course you needed to hold in your stomach! I think I slept with my stomach pulled in until I was grown and married and nine months pregnant with my first child.

Southern women are fully convinced that we look ten pounds lighter with our stomachs sucked in. Our mamas said so. The challenge is in implementing the practice. I realize the good women in other areas of this fine country suck their stomachs in too, but I will go to my grave contending that it is much harder for us belles. Why? Surely you jest. Sit your skinny bones down to a fine meal of fried chicken, mashed potatoes and gravy, black-eyed peas, homemade biscuits, and peach cobbler and see if you can suck your stomach in. It just has to be easier after a light meal of tofu and alfalfa sprouts. And yet, like other things in life that promise to either kill you or make your stronger, sucking our stomachs in has become a matter of pride for the Southern belle, a symbol of sorts of the will required to forge ahead in the face of adverse conditions. I think it'd make a great T-shirt, "When life throws you a curve, suck in your stomach."

When Mama wasn't stressing the importance of developing strong stomach muscles, she was encoding a variety of other beauty tips into our DNA. Some of these rules were firmer than others. Soaking our elbows in lemon juice to soften the skin was merely encouraged, not necessarily required, and I'm not convinced it was even expected. (I've always suspected Mama used that one to set the bar high from the get-go.) Cracking our knuckles was heavily frowned upon as it would give us big, ugly knuckles and boyish hands. But slouching—slouching was strictly forbidden, in any form. This is back when slouching referred to body posture. Today it describes an interesting fashion style where oversize clothes hang off the body as if the wearer inexplicably lost twenty or thirty pounds between the time he finished dressing and the moment he showed up in public. These incredible shrinking

One of the things my mama used to say that has stuck with me was, "For goodness sakes, girl, sit up straight and put some lipstick on!"

Keena Grissom
Pearl, Mississippi

people are constantly tugging at their poor britches because they can never permanently secure them.

Just for the fun of it, please take a moment to imagine how fond my dear mama is of today's pants-around-the-knees look. Alas, very few people have their pants up around their waists the way Mama and the Good Lord intended. Lord, have mercy. Hand me the smelling salts, Scarlett. It's bad enough to see young girls in those super-low riders revealing way too much in the rear-view department, but I've seen my share of grown women who were old enough to know better showing this "new cleavage." Someone should really tell 'em it hardly looks "new."

When it was time to take a bath, Mama told me to "wash as far as possible and then wash possible."

Muriel Meredith
Lake Providence, Louisiana

In the face of all this skin, I'm happy to report there are still Southern Mamas out there trying to teach their little girls about modesty. Not long ago, I got a letter from a reader named Cynthia Wolfe in Columbus, Georgia. She wrote, "Dear Shellie, I've had a problem with my little girl wanting to wear the hip-hugger jeans and provocative clothing she's exposed to at school. Rachel is only four! I've explained to her that we're supposed to keep parts of our bodies secret for our future husband, and Jesus doesn't like it when we share all our secrets. Well, we were in a restaurant a few weeks back, and two teenage girls were sitting in front of us. They had on the low hip-hugger jeans and their little cheeks

I am the youngest of three girls. Our mother would not let us wear red shoes because "red shoes indicated the wearer was a loose woman."

Marjorie Reyes
Shreveport, Louisiana

were just a shining at everyone. I could see it brewing up in Rachel's little mind, and before I could clap my hand over her mouth, she busted out "Jesus don't like that mama. Those girls are sharing all their secrets!" I'm now working on teaching Rachel restraint and tact, along with the meaning of the word *whisper*.

I told Cynthia that I understood the need for tact, but I was on little Rachel's side. Heaven knows if anything needs to be shared today, it's a lesson on modesty. My Southern Mama pounded that one into our heads from day one. We belles have always been told to leave something to the imagination. This tenet's value becomes even clearer as we age, bringing to mind the Southern Mama's twist on an old saying, "A mature woman's greatest asset is a man's imagination."

"Be Pretty"

Neither our clothes nor our body parts were allowed to slouch in Mama's presence. She schooled us consistently on how to carry ourselves in public. A tight stomach was just the half of it. Everything we had was supposed to be sucked and tucked. If we dared slump, Mama was there to remind us to "sit up pretty."

Being pretty is a multidimensional message Southern belles hear from birth. That, and "Don't be ugly." Neither admonition is all about looks. While we've been trained to do everything we can with the looks the Good Lord gave us, we try not to judge those who are less fortunate in the looks department. As a matter of fact, I believe the subject is serious enough to bring up

> "Pretty is as pretty does." Didn't everyone's mama say that?
>
> Leslie Lee
> St. Joseph, Louisiana

a recent news story that I found very alarming. It concerned the plight of Ugly Sheep everywhere and it's not a frivolous discussion. Australian farmers have been asked to turn in the ugly sheep in their flocks. Scientists want to study them to isolate the ugly gene. The campaign is designed to improve the overall wool quality but, I ask you, is this how we want to repay those poor things who have given us the sweaters off their own backs?

And don't tell me the sheep are too dumb to notice. We Southerners are a mite sensitive about stereotyping. Besides, if all the ugly people around you started disappearing, wouldn't you get just a little curious—if not flat-out nervous? Well, news flash, folks, they always start with the animals. I think you can see where I'm going. Ugly Reports could be headed to your hometown. And what if they attach a finders' fee? We could be on the brink of something that makes the Middle East look like a deacons' meeting. The thing is, ugly won't kill you. That's something you can't say for stupid people. The very same day I read that article I saw a news report about a woman in China who was arrested for letting her dog steer the car while she worked the pedals! Police say he collided almost immediately with another vehicle full of Ugly Sheep on the lam. Okay, the sheep part isn't entirely true. I was just checking to see if you were still with me. All I'm saying is: Turning in ugly people is flat-out wrong. APBs for stupid people—now how's that for an idea whose time has come!

My point, and I'll get back to it, is that here in the South being pretty refers as much to the way one acts or carries herself as it does to her appearance. One should stand up straight, pull her shoulders back, and suck her stomach in. While this procedure does make the, um, "girls" stick out, belles understand it to be a mere bonus, never the goal.

As previously noted, by the time I turned twelve, my

girls had come of age in a big way. They stuck out regardless of whether I slumped or not. The adolescent me found this extremely embarrassing. I tried rounding my shoulders in public to counter this obscene development but Mama was having none of it. She said I should stand up tall and be proud of what the Good Lord gave me. I wanted to, but when the boys gave up talking to my face in order to make better eye contact with other things, my gut feeling was confirmed. Someone up there had been a mite too generous.

Spit-Shined in Public

One of Mama's biggest fashion rules concerned the small window of opportunity in which one can wear white shoes. In recent years, the fashion world has tried to blur the lines on this one, but well-raised Southern girls haven't fallen for it. We'd rather spit on our ancestors' graves than wear white shoes before Easter or after Labor Day.

It's not like we haven't bent a little on other issues. There was a time when we wouldn't have considered leaving the house without a slip, that flimsy little piece of fabric that protected our virtuous reputations. Okay, so we latter-day belles may have been willing, but we sure weren't able; our dear mamas served as constant border guards between us and a world

Mama made sure we were dressed modestly by making us do the "sunlight test" before we went out. We had to stand in front of a sunlit window with our legs spread apart. If you could see through the dress, you had to put on a second slip! This felt good in the winter, but it was a bummer in the hot summertime. It's been a long time since I did the test but I'd love to have my mama test me one more time.

Frances Parker George
Foley, Alabama

of gawkers. "I hope you don't think you're leaving this house without a slip. Why, you may as well be nekkid."

And where we once would have taken two pair of panty hose, cut the bad legs out of each, and combined the remnants to make a single run-free pair, rather than go bare-legged, we're now quite comfortable sans the hose. Which reminds me, this is sort of off subject, but did you know men's panty hose are selling like hotcakes in France? When I first heard about this I was all prepared to give those funny Frenchmen the benefit of the doubt, hoping that maybe men with poor circulation problems were buying 'em, but I ran across an article that confirmed my worst suspicions. Oh, just let me quote Pierre: "We are watching the birth of a hybrid man. He is looking for a more radical affirmation of who he is."

Hmmm... Let's see if I can break that down in terms we can understand. A hybrid male would be a mixed breed—kinda like the mule that's produced when a male donkey mates a female horse, only a lot prissier. Yeah... that's close enough.

I couldn't resist calling my friend Bubba. I called him on his cell phone taking down his deer stand and told him about these panty hose–wearing hybrids, just for fun. Bubba wasn't laughing. 'Course Bubba's always in a bad mood after deer season.

"Don't mess with me, Shellie," Bubba said. "This is another one of your jokes."

I told Bubba I was for real and then I asked him if he'd prefer his panty hose in a thick mannish knit or as sheer tights—they're offered in both.

I can't repeat what Bubba said about that. "Look here," he grumbled. "Every dad gum thing they start over there manages to get here eventually. The last thing I want to see is a panty hose commercial with some hairy-legged man prancing around. It just ain't right."

I reminded Bubba that panty hose–wearing men probably shave their legs too. Bubba just snorted. "Tell you what," he said. "Someone tries to put a pair of panty hose on one of my boys, there's gonna be trouble, big trouble."

"I bet I know what they'd say to that," I said.

"What's that?" Bubba asked.

"I bet they'd say, 'Look here, my good man, you don't frighten us. You put your panty hose on one leg at a time, just like we do.' " All I got for that little funny was a dial tone. Sometimes Bubba doesn't have a sense of humor.

Indeed, we Southern ladies may have relaxed some on the panty hose and slips, people, but that's far enough. The White Rule remains nonnegotiable. Pay attention, wannabe belles. There is absolutely no wiggle room here. Mama used to take my sisters and me shopping for our Easter finery weeks in advance. The whole experience was like purchasing hot property. I can almost imagine Mama in a trench coat, looking both ways before addressing the sales girl. "Keep this on the down low, honey, but we're looking for something in . . . white." Once the deal was done, we had to return home with our white patent-leather shoes and matching white patent-leather purses and stash them out of sight until the big day.

> My mother said, "Don't go barefoot until after Easter!"
>
> Geraldine Tillus
> Calhoun, Louisiana

Like all good Southern Mamas, mine considered Easter a mini–fashion show opportunity. We generally made the two-hour trip home to Mama's folks' house in Natchez, Mississippi, for the holiday. My proud Mama dressed her three little girls in ruffled dresses, with white shoes, bonnets, and gloves and herded us from the parsonage to her father's church next door.

Our similarly dressed cousins would be waiting outside the church house door but all we could do was stare at each other in well-heeled pain. We were whistle clean and expected to remain that way, and this was one time when our mamas had our full cooperation! Their saliva glands were at their most productive on Easter. We kids knew from experience that arriving for last-minute inspection at the church's door with a hair out of place or a smudge on our face meant buying ourselves a dreaded spit shine.

Cyndie claims Mama held on much too long to her Easter traditions. For proof, she offers a picture of herself at thirteen, holding an Easter basket and glowering at the camera. In light of one of my recent experiences with Mama, I would have to say she is still having a bit of trouble letting go.

Mama goes with me to a lot of book signings and speaking engagements. I love Mama traveling with me, really I do—but you have to watch her. She can get caught up in the moment.

The following event occurred at a lady's conference. As I was being introduced, Mama observed that I needed some color on my lips. She motioned to me to reapply. Granted, Mama does this with a very subtle movement, sort of drawing her forefinger across her lips. Nine out of ten people would miss it. Nine out of ten people were not raised by my mama. I smiled at her and touched up my color. This was a mistake on my part for it only encouraged the mother mood. Mama reached over and smoothed my bangs. I grimaced politely, y'all, but when she wet that finger and leaned toward me—no doubt to remove a bit of leftover luncheon—I

> My mother said, "A Southern lady never goes anywhere without lipstick." I blew that one, but Mary Kay would be proud of my mom.
>
> Ginny Marsh
> Tallulah, Louisiana

drew the line. I am too old to be spit-shined in public. Thank the Lord.

Our Crowning Glory

As little girls, we offered Mama scant resistance to the White Rule. Perhaps both sides were subconsciously reserving precious ammunition for the teenage mandates she was about to deliver. Soon there were plenty of skirmishes, but one of the biggest battlegrounds concerned the proper upkeep and style of our hair or, as Southern Mamas say, our "crowning glory."

A lot of belles remember being told to give our shining tresses a hundred strokes per night but, for the most part, that particular mandate came more from our grandmothers. Our mamas didn't harp near as much on the time-consuming practice. They did, however, toe the line on the main point: Protect your crowning glory at all costs.

While we agreed with Mama on the importance of our tresses, we took serious issue with her as to the best fashions for our personal crowns. If Mama liked it out of our face, we liked it in our eyes. At the time, the coolest girls wore their hair straight as a board, parted down the middle, with each side tucked behind an ear. Mama didn't like it so she told us the practice would make our ears stick out like monkeys, permanently. Smart. What Southern belle wants to look like Cheetah? The middle part wasn't the only hairstyle we tried that Mama disliked. I don't remember her caring a lot for The Farrah, either.

> My mama had a law: "The hem of your dress or skirt had to be level."
>
> Evelyn Walker
> Jasper, Texas

It should be noted that Mama was no longer playing fair. Before entering these teenage years, we had known Mama to be straight-up in her dealings with us girls. Her tactics were changing. She had now become subtle—freight-train subtle. My sisters and I could spend hours getting ready and stride boldly toward the door with confidence in our coolness, only to second-guess all our efforts when Mama said, "So, that's how you're gonna wear your hair?" She'd smile and walk off while we looked for a mirror to double-check our crowning glory. It's that natural protective instinct, and it brings us to something I've been needing to get off my chest.

While we Southern girls are growing tired of the jokes about our hair, they're not having the slightest impact on our grooming habits. The truth is, despite prevailing stereotypes, most of us have given up "big hair" but we will defend to the death our sisters' God-given, American-born right to back tease should the urge hit 'em.

On the other hand, as for our infatuation with hair spray, that's no myth. We couldn't care less if we lead the whole world on hair spray consumption. Let the ozone layer fend for itself. We took physics too: Objects in motion stay in motion. We spend a fair amount of time on maintenance each morning—and we like to find our hair right where we left it. While we're on the subject of misplaced hair, perhaps we should revisit the whole Bald Britney season. Remember that one?

As soon as I heard about Ms. Spears's head shave, I could've told you on a stack of Bibles that she didn't get that look back home in Louisiana.

I'm sincerely hoping by the time this book comes off the presses, Britney Spears will have her act together, but I must be honest with y'all, I'm not holding out a great deal of hope. Britney's bald look is just the outward manifestation of a troubled little girl. And, frankly, as lathered up as the media was over her shaved head, they missed the point entirely.

Let me shed some Southern perspective for y'all. The girl didn't just shave her head. She removed her "crowning glory"! This may have been fine for Demi Moore and Sinéad O'Connor, but in the words of a good family friend, here in the South it meant Britney had officially gone straight running crazy. (Straight running crazy is someone who's no longer detouring from more lucid behavior. Think of it as full-steam ahead.) That's why I'm not expecting a full recovery anytime soon. Blood will tell. That little saying simply means that while it is indeed possible for a girl to be born in the South and not become a true Southern belle, (à la Louisiana Britney), it's hard to completely shake your DNA. I'm thinking every cell in her body knew that beauty-shop moment was a bad idea, as evidenced by her first recorded comment when she took in her new look in the mirror, "Sweet Lord, Mama's gonna die!" (I cleaned that up for y'all.)

Speaking of Britney's mama, let's do. Perhaps the woman had been trying to rein the girl in earlier; who's to say? But if, by chance, she wasn't fully convinced her baby's butter was slipping off the biscuit, she got up to speed when Britney went bald.

Color Me Southern

Perhaps this would be a good time to give you a visual of my mama. She's always been tall and slim. My sisters and I like to call her Jackie-O after the late Mrs. Kennedy. Mama's name is Charlotte, but her style is reminiscent of the First Lady's. They were both born with class to spare. Mama's one of those women who can eat whatever she wants when she wants and she still has an hourglass figure. We girls love her anyway. (I've always thought that says a lot for us, don't you?)

Mama's hair used to be jet-black, but over the years the need to color the gray without it looking harsh has moved her toward a lighter brunette. Premature gray runs in our family, but the outside world would never know. (At least they didn't. Sorry, girls.) But, speaking of hair color, let's do.

A while back I heard from a Georgia porcher who had moved up north. She was amazed (okay, she actually said horrified) at the number of women she met there who were willing to go gray gracefully. I've thought about it a lot since then. Maybe it's regional, maybe not, but most of my friends sound like Mr. Charles Heston on this one: They'll have to pry that little hair color box from our cold, dead hands (Miss Clairol—medium natural brown here).

My hairdresser thinks I should issue a disclaimer here. And she's right. For the record, self-coloring can be tricky. I remember once when my friend couldn't find her regular shade of red so she tried another brand and called me in tears. "Oh, my gosh. My hair! It's burgundy!"

I did my dead-level best to console her, thinking surely it was just a deep red, but in the face of her continued theatrics I drove over to her house. It was burgundy all right. Burgundy may be big in the grunge and hard-rock circles but it's not the color of choice among young Southern Mamas.

Later that evening, while my friend was out Wal-Mart hopping for her real color, I left a supportive message on her answering machine. It was sung to the tune of "Delta Dawn" (with my apologies to Tanya Tucker): "Delta Red, what's that color on your head? Could it be a pretty shade of bur-gun-dy?" Yes, we're still friends.

The thought of self-coloring breaks my hairdresser's heart. I really should listen to her. She knows things. Once, she told me that people were getting implants in their gluteus maximus. She said they called it the J-Lo look. I called it "ignorance gone to seed." If you'll forgive a weak pun, I'm always on the tail end of a trend. After years of squats, lunges, and starvation diets to reduce that particular area, I couldn't believe folks were actually PAYING to have it expanded, so I did some research. And of course, I found out buttock surgery was "so over" before I even heard of it. Welcome to my fashion world.

Buttock surgery and whether or not to have it is typical of the discussions a belle can look forward to when visiting her beautician. The small-town Southern beauty shop is the belle's idea of a continuing-education course. Once we get past our teen years, we have standing appointments written in blood, our own. It's never a good idea to stand up your beautician.

In many ways, a belle's hairdresser becomes as important as the man in her life. It's a unique relationship that stands the tests of time, if only because, as one mature belle recently put it, "Sugar, it's easier to divorce your husband than it is to leave your hairdresser." I know a lady who handled this sensitive issue with so much class, that if she were to decide to return to her beautician, my guess is she'd be received with open arms. So, how did she do it? Simmer down, girls. I knew you'd want to know. She sent a small gift with a most sincere note that read in part, "Dear [blank] (insert name of your beautician), I want you to know that I am not in any way upset with you. I appreciate all the time you have invested in my hair. That's why I wanted to be the one to tell you I've decided to let someone else do my hair for a while. It's not that you've done anything wrong. It's

Mama said, "You might as well be out of state as out of style."

Jean Metcalf
Conway, Arkansas

me. I just feel like I need a change. Thank you again. Love, Carla." Yes, I know it sounds a little like a Dear John letter, but that's the sort of relationship a belle has with someone who takes care of her crowning glory.

A belle counts on her hairdresser to be the voice of reason. She's talked many a desperate woman off the ledge who burst into the salon holding a picture torn from the pages of a fashion magazine, featuring a hairstyle suitable only to fifteen-year-old girls and models who weigh between twelve and thirteen pounds. "Put the paper down slowly, Lori Elizabeth, and back away with your hands up where I can see 'em. You know you've got that wedding next month and you know as well as I do that you don't want to look like a French poodle with mange."

I'm one of four daughters and one son. With four daughters, going to the beauty shop was unheard of, except for a haircut. Our permanents were given at home and it was truly a torture test. I can remember my mother telling us girls that you have to suffer to be beautiful.

Bobbie Cox
Tallulah, Louisiana

My Mother's Daughter

They say the apple doesn't fall far from the tree. I suppose they're right. Try as I might, I can't leave the subject of beauty and fashion without adding a few of my own thoughts to Mama's rules. They spring from a certain incident that's fresh in my mind. So, before the next holiday season comes around, I'd like to offer a true story and a few suggestions that could take the mystery out of dressing for various occasions.

This past season I was invited to the KNOE-TV Channel 8

Christmas party. My husband wasn't going to be able to attend so I asked a good friend to accompany me. I also asked the morning show producer for advice on the proper attire. This man (I admit here in black and white this was my first mistake: asking a man) told me the dress code usually ran anywhere from cocktail dress to Daisy Duke. Being true Southern girls with a flair for drama, my friend and I leaned instantly toward cocktail. When we showed up in sequins and sparkles it was immediately apparent that it was a "one bling" night. We felt somewhat conspicuous.

> Mama taught me to buy the most important clothes items in a classical style and do the accessories by trends.
>
> Pamela Smith
> Clarksville, Tennessee

And that brings me to what I'd like to offer as the new and improved and much clearer dress code. The four categories are: two bling, one bling, no bling, and anything.

"Two bling" means sequins and sparkles (shine, sister, shine!).

"One bling" is khakis or slacks and nice jewelry.

"No bling" is clean blue jeans.

And "anything" well, it says just what it means.

It's not easy to start a new cultural awareness program but I think the need is obvious. If you were to get a two-bling invitation next year, you'd know exactly how to dress and you wouldn't feel the need to hide in the car and scope out the other partygoers in the headlights of your vehicle. Not that any one would do that...

> Mama said, "Just because it fits doesn't mean you oughta wear it."
>
> Tracy Nicholson
> Thomasville, North Carolina

Southern Side Dishes to Complement the Main Course

Just like a good pearl necklace properly complements a little black dress, Southern girls know a few carefully chosen sides will accent your main meal. They're also good for stretching your offering out to feed an army. Of course, that's just a phrase. We've been burnt, if you will, by invading armies in the past, so don't be surprised if we check credentials at the door. Here's a sample of my and Mama's side dishes. A few of them are hearty enough for you to serve in lieu of the big course without hearing a single complaint.

~ Cheesy Green Beans ~

SERVES 8–10

While it goes against the traditional method down here, it really is possible to stir up a delicious green bean casserole without a single can of cream of mushroom soup. My version has tons more flavor than the old standard and it pairs nicely with your favorite beef, pork, or chicken recipe.

1 large onion, chopped
1 stick unsalted butter
¼ cup flour
2 teaspoons soy sauce
1½ cups milk
3 cups grated cheddar cheese
dash of hot sauce
3 14.5-ounce cans of green beans, drained
4 ounces canned sliced mushrooms, drained
1 8-ounce can sliced water chestnuts, drained
salt and pepper to taste
½ cup chopped almonds

Sauté onion in butter. Once the onions are translucent, slowly stir in flour, soy sauce, milk, and cheese. Of course, it'll need a kick. A dash of your favorite hot sauce should do it. Blend this mixture well and pour it into a greased baking dish. Fold in green beans, mushrooms, and water chestnuts. Salt and pepper to taste and top with almonds. Bake for 30 minutes in a 350 degree oven and enjoy!

~ Mama's Skillet Potatoes and Onions ~

SERVES 6–8

Some people call these breakfast potatoes. I'm sure they're good anytime, but I remember Mama serving 'em on Sunday evenings after church. If Papa happened to invite a few extra guests, and he usually did, we simply peeled a few extra potatoes and a couple more onions. Regardless of when you serve this dish, it's sure to become a favorite at your house too.

¼ cup butter
4–6 large white potatoes, peeled and diced into quarter-inch cubes
1–2 large onions, peeled and diced into quarter-inch cubes
garlic powder to taste
salt and pepper to taste

Melt butter in a heavy cast-iron skillet. If the skillet's been around for ages, well, that's all the better. Put potatoes and onions in skillet and season with garlic powder, salt, and pepper, and toss 'em to coat. Turn with a spatula every few minutes until they're lightly browned and then cover the skillet and steam 'em for another 10 minutes or so until they're good and tender. Ummm . . . ummm . . . That's soul-satisfying comfort food.

~ Sweet Freedom Fries ~

SERVES 4–6

Because confession is good for the soul, I am ready to come clean with y'all. I'm not a big fan of sweet potato pies, casseroles, or even muffins. I know, I know, but please don't try and pull my Southern credentials, because I'll be the first to gobble up this fried version! If you're not a sweet potato eater, do me a favor and try 'em this way. I have a feeling you'll be a convert too.

4 sweet potatoes
vegetable oil
salt and pepper
pinch of ground cinnamon

Take four cleaned and scrubbed sweet potatoes and slice 'em into lengths about a quarter-inch thick. (I like 'em even thinner, but sweet potatoes are notoriously hard to slice.) Heat vegetable oil and fry the slices in batches until they're nicely brown. Drain well on paper towels and sprinkle with salt, pepper, and a touch of ground cinnamon. Here's a hint—mix that cinnamon with your salt first; it'll sprinkle easier. Have mercy, child! Ring that porch bell and let the good eating begin.

~ Farmer's Omelet ~

SERVES 3–6

There might be six eggs in this omelet, but when my son was at home, the six foot two baby considered it a single serving. If you aren't feeding a bottomless pit at your house, try serving a slice of this hearty omelet with grits and cathead biscuits.

2 tablespoons butter
2 cups finely diced, uncooked potatoes
¼ cup finely chopped onion
1 cup diced ham or bacon
6 eggs
2 tablespoons milk
salt and pepper to taste
½ cup shredded cheddar cheese

Melt butter in a 10-inch nonstick frying pan. Add potatoes and onion, cover and cook over medium heat for 20 minutes, until potatoes are tender and golden brown, stirring now and then to brown evenly. Add ham. Beat eggs, milk, salt, and pepper together in a bowl and pour over the potato mixture. Cover pan and cook 10 minutes or until eggs are almost set. Check frequently, lifting around edges with a spatula and allowing egg mixture to run under omelet during cooking. Sprinkle with cheese. Cover and cook until cheese melts. Fold over once and serve.

~ Southern Beef and Beans for a Crowd ~

SERVES 8–10

I like to serve these beans as a side dish when we're grilling hamburgers. Some people prefer 'em as a dip. All those folks need is a bag of chips and some time. Try them and you'll see your family isn't nearly as interested in how you serve 'em as they are in how often you serve them.

2 pounds of ground beef
1 white onion, chopped
2 30-ounce cans of pork and beans
1 cup sugar
1 cup barbecue sauce
dash Worcestershire sauce
couple shakes Cajun seasoning
6 strips of bacon

Preheat oven to 350 degrees. In a sauté pan, cook beef and onion until meat is browned. Transfer to a large, greased casserole dish. Add pork and beans, sugar, and barbecue sauce. Season with Worcestershire and Cajun seasoning. Mix well. Top with bacon and bake in a 350 degree oven for 45 minutes to an hour, depending on your oven. You want to make sure the bacon's done. That's good eating!

~ Baked Garlic Grits ~

SERVES 4

It goes without saying that we Southerners like grits just about anyway you cook 'em. In this version, a roll of garlic cheese takes 'em right over the top. This versatile dish knows how to play dress-up in an elegant serving dish but it can also kick back and deliver a great breakfast right off the stove top.

1 cup grits (not instant)
1 garlic cheese roll
½ stick butter
1 egg
½ cup milk
dash hot sauce
1 cup grated cheddar cheese

Preheat oven to 350 degrees. Cook grits according to package instructions. While they're still hot, stir in garlic cheese and butter. In a small bowl, whisk together egg and milk. Stir into the grits and add a dash of your favorite hot sauce. Pour into a buttered 8 × 8-inch baking dish and bake at 350 degrees for 45 minutes. Top with cheese and return to oven to brown.

~ Rice Consommé with Mushrooms ~

SERVES 4

Here's my family's absolute favorite way to eat rice (and for a group of rice growers, that's saying a lot). We like it with pork, beef, or chicken but we LOVE it with grilled fish. You can double or triple this side dish as long as you make sure you have one can of consommé for each cup uncooked rice.

1 cup uncooked rice
1 can beef consommé
1 can water
1 stick butter, melted
1 can mushrooms (pieces or whole)
½ teaspoon hot sauce
salt and pepper to taste
2–3 tablespoons of Worcestershire sauce

Preheat oven to 350 degrees. Combine uncooked rice, beef consommé, water, melted butter, and mushrooms in a greased casserole dish. Season to taste with hot sauce, salt, pepper, and Worcestershire sauce. Cover and bake at 350 degrees for 30 to 45 minutes or until rice is fluffy. Enjoy!

~ Down-Home Mac and Cheese ~

SERVES 4–6

Lean in close. I've heard a rumor that some people have never had macaroni and cheese that didn't come from a little box. What a foreign idea! If you're one of those unfortunate souls, don't be embarrassed. I'm here to teach you how to make the real stuff.

1½ cups elbow macaroni
3 tablespoons butter
2 tablespoons all-purpose flour
1 cup light cream
½ cup milk
2½ cups grated sharp cheese, divided
salt and pepper to taste
¼ teaspoon paprika

Preheat oven to 350 degrees. Boil and drain macaroni according to the directions on the package. In a large pot, melt the butter over low heat, gradually stirring in the flour, cream, and milk, in that order. Turn your heat up to medium and continue stirring for about 2 minutes until the mixture boils and thickens. Remove it from the heat and add 2 cups of sharp cheese along with your seasonings. When cheese is completely melted, gently fold in your macaroni until coated. Transfer to a buttered casserole dish and bake at 350 degrees for 25 to 30 minutes. Top with the remainder of the cheese and serve to a happy family. Be forewarned: your group will turn their noses up at the blue box after this, so don't start something you don't mean to continue.

8

Neither Papa Smurf nor Elvira Be

What Southern Mamas Tell Their Daughters About Acceptance, Growing Young, and Watching Ya Figah (with Vegetable Recipes to Balance the Scales)

Now that my sisters and I are all in our forties, my Southern Mama's lessons have changed somewhat, but they keep coming as regular as death and taxes. They're just age appropriate. Mama doesn't spend as much time telling us not to pick at our faces as she did when we were younger. The face-picking rule remains in effect, but she's a lot more concerned about our crow's feet and laugh lines. And speaking of aging, I'd like to go down on record as saying this is wrong on so many levels. I'm referring to this precious time of life where the morning mirror reveals either a new wrinkle or a new zit, or, lucky day, both. Both! Wrinkle cream and zit medicine do not belong in the same medicine chest. (Note to the Creator:

> A pearl of wisdom from my mom: "A lady never reveals her age. A lady who will reveal her age cannot be trusted to keep a secret."
>
> Debra Phillips Vannucci
> Keithville, Louisiana

I've really tried to see the humor here but it comes across as straight injustice.)

These days Mama's beauty tips revolve around the when, why, and where of moisturizing—always, because, and everywhere—with heaviest emphasis on one's face and neck. And she doesn't just tell her daughters. No, ma'am. Mama has been known to preach moisturizer to anyone who'll listen. Not that she'd ask a totally moisture-starved stranger what type of skin care they're using. Please. She'd introduce herself first.

Put Your Face On

My Southern Mama taught me to put my face on first thing in the morning, regardless of whether or not I plan to leave the house. Putting one's face on refers to applying my makeup, or as I like to refer to my current routine, "the extreme makeover." Only in recent years have I begun to see the wisdom behind this first thing in the morning tenet. There comes a time when a belle notices it's taking more and more mirror time to get the same if not substandard results. This is when she learns to appreciate the value in a good head start.

> My mama told me ladies never answered the door barefoot!
>
> Brenda Johnston
> Springfield, Virginia

When this time comes, and it comes for us all, Sweet Cheeks, there are things you should know. If you're not there yet, you will be someday, so grab a highlighter pen and listen up. I'm about to share a very important nugget from my own personal beauty experience file. This one didn't come from Mama. I learned this quite by accident. If you are my age or older, you may have already made this mistake, but if I can

Dear Shellie, You talk a lot about sucking it in. Here's a story for you. Not long after my bladder suspension, I sneezed so hard I was afraid I'd torn something. I mentioned this to my doctor when I went back for my checkup. I told him to look and see how the sides of my stomach were uneven. "The left side sticks out," I said,"even when I'm sucking in." That sweet young doctor said, "Yes, ma'am, I see... Can you suck in for me?" I drew myself up and replied with great dignity, "I am sucking in!"

Fran Walton
Winnfield, Louisiana

save one belle or wannabe-belle from this tragedy, it will be well worth it. Here goes: Never again, for any reason, should you bend over from the waist and look in the mirror at the same time, unless of course you'd like to see your late great-grandmother again—in said mirror.

I have always dried my hair upside down to create fullness. Big hair may come and go, but belles know flat hair is never acceptable. One morning I was drying my hair without too many cares in the world when I turned toward the mirror and saw a very old lady had joined me. Funny thing was, she looked like family.

At times like this, it is important for a belle to remember that old saying "With age comes wisdom." Yes, I've seen age show up all by itself too, but these little sayings can't help us if you won't let 'em. For instance, one of my good friends passed me some sage advice she could never have discovered in those golden days of youth and innocence. It's similar to the "don't look in the mirror upside down" rule. She came to this realization a couple years ago after falling off a horse and breaking her ankle in more places than Joan Rivers has Botox.

My friend Red (yes, she of chapter 7's burgundy hair fame) called me one morning post–ankle surgery and asked,

"Remember when we learned not to look in the mirror upside down?"

"How could I forget?"

"Well, friend, it gets worse. Trust me. If you're ever forced to jump on one foot toward the bathtub without any clothes on—"

"Yes?"

"Cover all mirrors with a sheet first."

"Gotcha," I replied solemnly. " 'Nuff said."

When We Want Plastic Surgery, We'll Ask for It

My Southern Mama has set a fine example for her daughter on how to age gracefully. I'm trying, but belles don't appreciate seeing their bodies succumb to the aging process any more than the next woman. I know I am personally disappointed every morning when I notice that sometime in the middle of the night yet another part of my body has given up the good fight against gravity to party with Smokey the Bear. "Stop, drop, and roll, y'all!"

For the record, my immediate plans to combat this intimate betrayal don't include anything beyond my heretofore inconsistent stabs at proper diet and exercise. I'm not saying I won't ever go under the knife. I'm just saying when and if I should ever choose cosmetic surgery, it will be my own idea. Not long ago I read where plastic

> Mama said, "If you don't buy it, you can't eat it."
>
> Ann Tucker
> Horse Cave, Kentucky

surgeons were reporting a rather interesting trend. It seems in recent years men have been purchasing plastic surgery as holiday surprises for their loved ones. Did you catch that? I said holiday *surprises*, as in "Look, Honey, I saw this face-lift on sale and thought you could use it." Note to men married or dating a belle: If you're considering that move, I'd proceed delicately if I were you. If Penny Sue hasn't asked for cosmetic surgery, gifting her with a nose job will be considerably less popular than household appliances for anniversary presents.

It's not that hard to find the right present for your sweetie, fellows. She begins dropping hints weeks and months before all special occasions. (Yes, that's what all those big red X's were on the appliance ads in the paper.) If at all possible, you should refrain from saying, "I haven't gotten you anything for [*insert occasion of your choice*], so I hope you haven't gotten me anything." This will always be an unpopular announcement on the morning of the big day. Trust me here. So is, "You're not expecting a big deal today, are you?" She's expecting a deal, Romeo, and the bigger the better.

Frankly, I don't understand why men think women are difficult to understand. I can rattle off three quick lines guaranteed to build a bridge across any communication gap. They're mostly interchangeable and extremely effective, especially when used together: "I love you," "I'm sorry," and "Have you lost weight?" Let's say she says, "My bank account is overdrawn. The man could choose, "I'm sorry. Have you lost weight?" and immediately set the stage for a more productive financial discussion.

My grandmother advised me to marry a man my age or a little younger, "because they don't improve with age." I now know what she meant.

Elizabeth Gaines
Monroe, Louisiana

Mama's Tough Love

Where our men fall short in communication, the belle's mother is there to take up the slack. They're usually adept at combining tact and truth, but they can be as blunt as necessary if the situation demands it.

For instance, my Southern Mama encourages us girls to keep ourselves up for our husbands and for our own selves, and she's always sharing advice on the subject, but she has a real tough love attitude about us learning to accept things we can't change. A few years back, I took her bathing suit shopping with me. My mistake.

This was one of those critical times in a woman's life too. I was coming upon my twenty-year high school reunion and, because the organizers were predominately male (pronounced *clueless*), one of the events was to be a pool party. My goal was to find a bathing suit that would make a thick version of Olive Oyl look like Beach Barbie. Let it be noted that I have no waistline, as in zilch, nada, none, never have. It makes no difference if I'm underweight or overweight; I go straight down.

Mama went willingly, but then I hadn't been entirely honest about the day's objective. Somewhere after the nineteenth store and the eighty-second bathing suit, I came out from the dressing room in yet another solid black number with a wrapped bodice and diagonal cinching guaranteed to create the illusion of a waistline. I twisted and preened in the mirror. Then I turned toward Mama. But this time when I dared to ask, "Does this make me look like I curve?" Mama rolled her eyes and told me how the cow eats the cabbage.

"Shellie, honey, that bathing suit can't make you curve because you don't curve. I'm sorry to be the one to break this to you, Sweetie, but you didn't curve when you were eight and you didn't curve when you were eighteen, or twenty-eight, for that matter. And now that you're thirty-eight you're old enough to realize it's just not gonna happen." Now, Mother, tell me how you really feel.

As always, Mama was way ahead of the medical community. I wasn't the least bit surprised to find a new medical study designed to help all of us accept our physical differences by once and for all resolving our bad body images. Hear this: The experts suggest we become pen pals with the attributes we don't like.

Let's say you're unhappy with your nose. You might write, "Dear Nose, you're ugly and you take up too much room on my face!" Once you own your feelings, you're supposed to compose a reply from the body part. You might have your nose say, "I'm sorry you're so disgusted with me, but a lot of famous people have large noses. I mean, if Barbra Streisand can accept her nose, well, it can't be that hard. And don't forget, Michael Jackson's life didn't just fall apart all at once. Things started going badly years ago when he first started messin' with his nose." I hope y'all aren't laughing. We professionals can't help you if you won't listen.

Once, when we didn't have enough pillows to go around for visiting relatives, I was forced to go without. My aunt told me that if I slept without a pillow I would grow up to be beautiful. I never slept on a pillow again until about five years ago when I had a breathing problem. I'm in my late sixties now and that beauty has eluded me completely, but that's okay.

Margaret Jacquelynn Bryan
Westminster, California

Well, friends, I tried it. I took out a pretty sheet of floral stationery and wrote, "Dear waistline, why are you so chunky?

I've done everything possible to trim you up and I want abs—do you hear me?—abs!"

To my surprise, I got a group response! "Dear Shellie," my waistline began. "I've been in contact with some of the other members of our body. With all due respect, the eyes have mentioned seeing a lot of bar-b-cue potato chips and the nose reports smelling more than a couple chocolate caramel lattes. And the mouth—well, the mouth was a wealth of information! In short, we think you should write back when you're ready to take the thighs for a walk."

Well, I never. Can you believe the gall? The article said we should correspond daily until we work things out, but I'm not sure about my new pen pals. What's that old saying? With friends like these, who needs enemies?

The fact is, I've made real progress accepting my body, and yet I realize I still have a way to go. I know this because I grinned all over myself when I heard the fashion world was banning super skinny runway models! (Sweet, huh?) They're staging public weigh-ins, like boxers. If Skinny Minnie doesn't reach the magic number, she's outta there. Their stated goal is commendable—to discourage aspiring models from developing eating disorders. But I can't help wondering if there are sour grapes at the salad bar. Who started this? Would she be female? Is she older than, say sixteen? Please. They don't call that big landing strip a cat walk for nothing.

Don't get me wrong, I'd be heartily endorsing this if I thought it would really combat the eating disorder epidemic in this country, but you can't take these fashion folks seriously. They're not ready to endorse normal people. By the new rules, if you're six foot tall you must weigh at least a hundred pounds soaking wet—or something like that—which means the models can still save plenty of money on X-rays.

Note to fashion authorities: I suggest holding off on the whole "protecting the public" spin. Y'all sound a mite ridiculous. Here in the real world, I believe I speak for my fully grown friends when I say, "We don't need protection from ninety-pound women." We have bigger fish to fry, so to speak. When we see their ribs poking out, we just go back for seconds. No doubt this can be traced to our early raising. "Yes, Mama, I know there are starving people all over the world. Pass the biscuits please."

Besides, I've never liked public weigh-ins. I have a favorite nurse at my ObGyn's. When we pass the scales, she politely asks what I'm weighing these days. I shoot her a reasonably believable number and she records it, no questions asked. It's just a little deal we have.

Now that I've had some time to think about it, I believe the whole skinny model thing could possibly be one big publicity ploy. I bet those designers aren't selling enough of those ridiculous clothes and they think they're gonna pan 'em off on us. Well, we're on to you, folks. Have a Twinkie and try again.

Neither Papa Smurf nor Elvira Be

It'd be easier to accept my body and age gracefully and all that if Father Time would just go a little easier on my crowning glory. The belle's obsession with her tresses doesn't fade with her natural color however. It only intensifies. As long as I can remember, Mama and her cohorts have been setting the stage for this one. Listening to them, it became apparent that there was a time when a lady could no longer wear her hair long or her skirts short. I asked a lot of questions early on but I couldn't get any firm answers on what was too long and when the rule went into effect. It looked to me like the line wasn't very clear, but the women in my world always seemed to know who had crossed it.

When Mother Nature started stripping the pigment from my hair, I bowed to these knowledgeable women and their all-important Color Code: "lighter, never darker." That's the rule, girls, and there are no exceptions. Blondes have it easy; once they finally begin to gray, they can simply frost 'til their dying day. Redheads and brunettes find it a little tougher to hold on to a semblance of their natural-born tresses, but again, lighter shades only, please. Here's a tip. You're aiming for something between Papa Smurf and Elvira.

My grandmother and my mother always told me, "Even an old barn looks better with a little paint on it."

Susan Hovinen
Cambridge, Minnesota

Once the pigment has gone from your hair completely, a mature woman has to face the big decision. Should she or should she not go in for the controversial mystery blue? Some people say mystery blue is a hair rinse some older ladies agree to in order to cut the yellow tone from their tired gray crowns. While this could very well be true, I have my own theory and it's much more fun. Maybe there's a secret society and only blue-haired ladies need apply. Could these mischievous matrons be choosing blue hair as a symbol of sorts? Wait, think about it. I mean, at their age, there's not that much convention left to defy. Perhaps mystery blue is their way of thumbing their

Mama said, "Don't go looking for a fight, but if you're backed in a corner, come out swinging!"

Jody DeLancey
Eden, North Carolina

noses at society for choosing youth over wisdom. While the young things are considering purple hair and dragonfly tattoos, these fed up belles are throwing caution to the wind at their local beauty parlor. "Oh, what the heck, Marcy—color it blue!"

Whatever the case may be, these are definitely thc days when a belle will be rewarded for solidifying her relationship with her loyal beautician. Were she to suddenly earn her Great Reward, she can go to her eternal rest confident that the implicit instructions she has left behind on what to do and not to do to her hair will be carried out to the letter. No self-respecting Southern beautician would allow these last wishes to be violated.

One day, my beautician got an anxious phone call summoning her to the funeral home for what we Southerners like to call the viewing. On the other end of the line was the distressed daughter of one of her former clients. The girl's mama had passed away out of state, where her body had been prepared and returned. Unfortunately, some unknown person had "doodie-rolled" the woman's bangs. I realize that's an impolite term, but you can't beat it for giving the proper visual, now can you? Talk about adding insult to injury, the poor woman was about to go to the great beyond with a perennially bad hair day. Knowing full well that had the deceased only known the indignity she was suffering, she would've reached up and closed the casket herself, Vicki sprang into action.

After gathering the necessary supplies, she made the trip to the funeral home in record time. Once there, she employed the deceased's anxious daughter to guard the door to the small room where her former client rested. Armed with a water bottle, extension cord, blow dryer, and flat iron, and assisted by a handy folding chair, Vicki repaired the damage. Then she and the aforementioned relative opened the door and left the room. To anyone looking on, the sight of the two women holding each other up and dabbing their respective eyes would've been seen as poignant evidence of their private and emotional good-bye. Only the two of them knew they were tears of laughter. At least, it used to be just the two of 'em. I realize that story may sound extreme if you're not from these parts, but we Southerners believe it's never too late to make a last impression.

Seeing Clearly from a Distance

I now know why I couldn't see the invisible line Mama and her sisters saw so clearly, the one that tells a mature belle when she is one sad summer past short shorts and halter tops. The answer is ridiculously simple. I was just too young. At the time, I thought everyone over the age of twenty-five had one foot in the grave.

I now see that the line becomes more pronounced the closer a belle gets to it. And frankly, this is a darn good thing because once you're there you can't see worth a flip. Please notice the wording there. Not a cuss word in the sentence. I realize I'm not very edgy, Honey, and the only envelopes I push on a regular basis are bills and thank-you notes. By the way, I picked up those terms from the entertainment field. They're used to describe people who flaunt

Never curse; there are always other words to get your point across. (For instance: What a rear end of a mule's first cousin he is.) Cursing is for the illiterate and ill-educated.

Madeleine Watt
Highlands, North Carolina

Whenever my mother or grandmother heard someone use a bad word they would say, "You have something in your mouth I wouldn't hold in my hand!"

Nina Dixon
Chrisman, Illinois

convention. My Southern Mama taught me to flaunt a few things, but convention wasn't one of 'em. She felt strongly that coarse language was trashy at any age, but she reserved her strictest objections to women of a Certain Age who talked like sailors. And if I haven't reached the Certain Age, I'm close enough to reach out and touch it.

When I turned forty, a few of my slightly older friends said my eyes would be the first to go. They were plum looking forward to me paying for those jokes I had enjoyed at their expense. (One of them would hold the menu at arm's length and I would crow, "Hey, if you wouldn't hold it so far away you might be able to see it." Okay, you had to be there, but I thought it was funny.) Despite their warnings, I felt sure my eyesight wouldn't go that quickly. I hate it when I'm wrong.

Less than six months later their words came back to haunt me. I was in the shower one morning when I opened a bottle of body wash my then-college-age daughter had left behind on her weekend visit. As I twisted the top off the sweet smelling stuff, dozens of delightful little iridescent bubbles escaped and immediately filled the air around me. I was curious. Was this a special wash designed to pamper a girl with little bubbles each time it's opened, or was it a one-time thing from being closed up or shaken? I turned it over to read the back, but—surprise, I couldn't, read it, not a word. I strained and squinted. Nothing. This couldn't be. I mean I absolutely for the first time in my life could not read a single letter on the bottle, not even at arm's length.

My heart sank! I sure figured it'd be more gradual. Sighing with resignation, I leaned out of the shower and held the bottle up to the light to try yet again. That's when I realized I'd been trying to read French and the only French I know is, "Oui, oui, you can't see!" Jessica Ann and those gosh-darn Frenchmen! If I were a conspiracy theorist, I'd swear they were in on it together.

I was even less amused by my next failing eyesight experience, but then, as I noted in chapter 5, I find nothing funny about roaches. I detest the big brown bugs that love our Southern lakes and cypress trees and—despite our best efforts—our homes. Some folks call 'em waterbugs, but that's spin. Call 'em what they are: demon insects! While I'm stridently opposed to the cockroach's existence, it takes everything in me to squash one. I know I sound like a girly-girl, but look here: I can slap spiders all day and stick a tree frog on my nose. Can I help it if squashing a roach makes my stomach roll?

I first spotted him behind the couch when I went to plug in an extension cord. He was pretty small. That was good because Phil and Phillip weren't home and it was up to me. I couldn't let him (or her) grow up and make babies! I snuck up slowly, clutching a crumpled paper towel. Ignoring my roiling intestines, I swooped bravely in for the kill, ran to the bathroom, and threw the hideous thing into the toilet—where he promptly morphed into an innocent dustbunny. Were there to actually be a moral to this story it'd go something like this. If you've got a roach problem, call Terminix. However, if you're being harassed by a dangerous horde of dustbunnies, I'm your girl.

Here's my last note on the subject of fading eyesight. When I was younger I used to see an older woman with a hair sticking prominently from her chin and I would wonder why on earth she didn't do something about it. News flash, Sweet Cheeks! She can't see it. Cut her some slack, will ya?

Cradle to Grave

A part of me wants to believe that I'm still in the neutral zone on a lot of these age-related fashion and beauty decisions, that I can sort of dance step all over the line without really crossing it. The rest of me knows that, should I err in judgment, my Southern Mama will be right there to point it out. Our mamas' voices go with us from cradle to grave, plus some.

Sometimes I wonder about heeding the backup beauty plan of a woman who once sported the Beehive, but she has seldom steered me wrong. Okay, so there was that red flowing number she talked me into wearing my sophomore year in high school when I was elected to the Homecoming Court, the one she borrowed from my older cousin that made me look like Count Dracula's Date, but I've let that go. Really.

For the most part, I realize that I would have made a lot more fashion mistakes in my lifetime were it not for Mama's influence. I was going to say I'm not much of a trendsetter, but that'd be an understatement along the lines of, "Elvis has a few passionate fans." The truth is, by the time I recognize a trend, you can usually find it on the History Channel.

For instance, I've just recently learned about one of the stranger trends in "body modification." This may be old hat to you, but humor me. Did you know there are people having their tongues slit right down the middle, voluntarily, and letting it heal that way, on purpose? They tell me it's the "reptilian" look and it's not new—they've been doing it for years.

I can't begin to imagine why, but I see some real disadvantages here and at least one big plus.

The disadvantages would be for the forked-tongue people. They'll never be able to say "Peter Piper picked a peck of pickled peppers," they can't whistle "Dixie," and they're gonna have to give up soup. The advantage is for the rest of us. Sometimes you can't identify stupid people right off. So, you mess up and hire 'em or even worse, let 'em date your son or daughter! Now you'll be able to avoid some of that with one simple request, "I'm gonna have to ask you to open your mouth, and stick out your tongue."

Men-Oh-Pause

Because I understand that I suffer from chronic fashion shortcomings, I'm willing to entertain my Southern Mama's age-appropriate rules—within reason. I don't plan to cut my layered and shoulder-length crowning glory off anytime soon. I would like to believe that I have a few sleeveless-shirt years ahead of me. And if I have to have reading glasses, they're gonna be those cute and colorful ones I saw at Wally World. I'm aiming for that balance that says, "I may not be a teenager, but I can still be a hot mama when I want to be."

Then again, these days I'm also a hot mama when I don't want to be. But that brings us to a completely different subject, menopause; or as one female comedian put it "men-oh-pause." Not that she was implying men aggravate our hormone-challenged emotions. She didn't say that outright. I, however, am willing to do just that.

My Southern Mama taught me to love, honor, and respect my husband—and I do, I really do. I've also learned to laugh

My mom always said if a man treated his wife like a Thoroughbred, she wouldn't turn out to be an old nag.

Judy Sorenson
Rockdale, Texas

at him over the years to keep from choking him. Our men do not mean to frustrate us, ladies, no more than we mean to confuse them. It is what it is.

There has been a lot of discussion over the years about the differences between men and women. There was even a book about women being from Venus and men from Mars. Well, being the astute Venusian that I am, I'd like to toss in an observation I haven't found addressed anywhere else.

Men grow uncomfortable ordering at drive-thru windows. I do not say this without documentation. I've done extensive research; all of my girlfriends agree. Our husbands get uneasy ordering from drive-thru windows. Actually, *uneasy* is too mild a description. Many Martians sweat profusely when they have to order for more than one person.

I can trace my experiences with this behavior back to the days when my sisters and I were backseat diners with Papa and Mama. That's when fast-food meals were a big treat. It was also in the "have it your way" day, but we didn't—have it our way, that is. We had it however it was easiest for Papa to order it and took off what we didn't want.

Like all good researchers, I have a few theories to explain this. One, our men can't hear. I have no idea why we can't use the same technology that lets us call Russia on our cell phones and develop a little more clarity on those drive-thru speakers, but my research suggests this is a contributing factor to MSS, Male Speaker Syndrome. Of course, the biggest problem is that ordering at the drive-thru window requires our men to listen to two voices, the one coming from the speaker and the one in the car. That's about one more voice than they can process at a time. We hear the lady saying, "Would you like fries with that?" Our men hear Charlie Brown's teacher, "Wonk, wonk, wonk, wonk, wonk."

When I first discovered this condition I was convinced it was caused by the male's inability to listen to two voices at one time. As evidence mounts, I've become aware that the problem is even bigger. It's not so much that they can't hear, and more like they're just not paying attention.

Exhibit A: I was in a home improvement store recently when I overheard a conversation between two men. One of 'em was supposed to purchase a load of two-inch wood plantation blinds for his wife. I listened as they discovered the store was out of two-inch wood plantation blinds and cringed as they discussed the wisdom of bringing the wife one-inch metal blinds instead. I was trying to stay out of it but in the end one of 'em got cold feet and asked for my opinion. (Ma'am, I don't know who you are, but you owe me.)

The second incident occurred at Wal-Mart over the recent holidays. A man and his little daughter were out on a mission to buy an artificial Christmas tree with tiny white lights. The daddy was leaning toward purchasing a multicolored, fiber-optic, revolving tree. It might sound like it called for an intervention, and it did, but not from me. As I pushed my cart off, I left the dad in the capable young hands of a miniature female who warned in her sweet singsong voice, "Mama's not gonna be happy..."

Gold Slippers and White Perch Jigs

My Southern Mama may have sold me on dressing my age, but there are still some things I hope to put off as long as possible, say, orthopedic shoes. They're too much like the corrective shoes that scarred my childhood. To use a tired old phrase, been there, done that.

I also have a few "never evers" on my list. Topping the list would be dusters, those buttoned-up floral dresses modeled by the women of my childhood, followed closely by gold slippers. My sister and I once watched an older lady take her seat at church wearing a pair of those infamous geriatric slippers. "If I ever get so weak," Rhonda began, "as to put on a pair of those gold slippers, even if we're sharing a room at the old folks home, I hope you'll take 'em off my feet and hit me over the head with 'em." I promised to oblige on the condition that she would do the same for me.

Southern belles know that aging gracefully doesn't mean surrendering your charm. Sparkling is an attitude. If you think you're sparkling, you are. Perhaps this attitude can best be explained with a little story. Once, a reader named NaKole wrote in asking me how she could become a Southern belle. Before I could reply, another lady named Marcy asked if one could be Southern born and not be a Southern belle. I typed, "Yes, Sugar" and referenced poor Britney Spears as Exhibit A (see chapter 7). While the belle can't be defined in one sitting, if you'll allow me, I'd like to offer a few distinguishing belle characteristics and that story I mentioned for illustration.

By definition, the Southern belle is alive and kicking. She might have given up hoop skirts, but she still knows how to leave something to a man's imagination. She loves her God, her family, and her country. She's skilled at putting folks at ease, but it's no act. She's genuinely interested in people. Not that the belle doesn't flirt! Heck, if she's breathing, she'll keep her hook baited.

One summer day my friend John found an old man in our community named James Henry standing near the highway by the lake. The man was leaning against Mama Ruth's car, sweating bullets in his khaki pants and huge white cowboy hat. Now John knew that his grandmother, known to the town as Mama Ruth, and James Henry weren't sweethearts. (The butter had slipped too far off his biscuit for her liking.) But she considered him a good friend and quite handy.

John asked James Henry what he was doing. James Henry said Mama Ruth needed him to count the passing cars while she fished! Appalled, John marched down the bank to confront his grandmother. He found Mama Ruth with a pole in one hand and a Mountain Dew in the other.

She offered a weak explanation, claiming she was afraid the poor man would fall in the water. John observed that she hadn't been too scared to let him bring down the ice chest, minnow bucket, tackle box, and coffee thermos! Busted! Dressed to kill in her Bermuda shorts, sleeveless shirt, and baby blue fishing hat with the white perch jigs, his grandmother came clean, "Honey, supposin' a man wanted to stop and take me for a boat ride? Ya think he'd stop if he saw James Henry?"

It's worth noting: Mama Ruth was seventy-eight at the time, which is one of the most intriguing characteristics of the Southern belle. Even when the world can no longer see her beauty, she's always convinced the charm's still there.

Vegetable Recipes to Balance the Scales

In recent years we Southerners have been accused, tried, and convicted of ruining the nutritional value of vegetables by deep-frying 'em and/or cooking 'em to death over a steady flame. Granted, we've made some concessions since that little witch hunt began, but don't confuse us with true converts. We may fry less and steam more, but our modifications are all about adjusting the time-honored methods of our mamas and grandmamas, not abandoning them. Even as I type, there sits in my refrigerator a pot of snap beans I cooked for the better part of yesterday afternoon, simmering with a few cloves of minced garlic, a diced onion and a big fat hamhock. They'll be even better today than they were last night. What follows are a few tried and true recipes from me and Mama, but be warned, there is some breading involved right at the get-go.

~ Cornbread Fritters ~

SERVE 4

Y'all, I am thrilled to death to have a multicultural group on my cyber porch (allthingssouthern.com), but sometimes it can lead to confusion. I've had a ton of letters about flitters and fritters. It appears a segment of the population has confused those completely inedible and unappealing cow patties called "flitters" with the "fritters" they hear us Southerners talk of eating. I can think of no better reason for including a good cornbread fritter recipe in with the veggie section.

1 cup self-rising cornmeal
½ cup all-purpose flour
1 egg, well beaten
½ cup finely chopped onion
1 14.5-ounce can cream-style corn
2 cups vegetable oil

Mix cornmeal with flour. Add egg, onion, and corn. Drop by spoonfuls into hot oil and fry until golden brown. The oil is hot enough when a fritter floats back to the surface after you drop it in. Remember, that's a fritter you're eating. If you see someone eating a flitter, you're probably watching a reality show.

~ Heavenly Hominy ~

SERVES 4–6

Hominy is misunderstood. There are folks who swear it's the same thing as grits. Bless their hearts; they have a right to be wrong. Hominy is not grits, and vice versa, even though they both start from corn. (Similarly, I'm not Dolly Parton, although we both started as an embryo.) Grits are made from ground corn. Hominy is made from soaking corn in lye until the outer hull of the kernels fall off and the remainder swells ups. Here's a recipe that lets poor old hominy make a name for itself.

¼ cup chopped onion
1 tablespoon butter
2 15.5-ounce cans hominy, drained (white or golden)
2 4-ounce cans diced green chilies
1 cup sour cream
1½ cups shredded Monterey Jack cheese, divided
salt and pepper to taste
1 teaspoon chili powder

Preheat oven to 400 degree. Sauté onion in butter. Meanwhile, grease a casserole dish and pour in hominy and green chilies. Once the onions cook down, stir them into the hominy along with sour cream and half of the Monterey Jack cheese. Season with salt, pepper, and chili powder. Bake in a 400 degree oven for about 20 minutes. Before serving, sprinkle with remaining cheese. Bake another 5 minutes or until the cheese is melted. That's it! (Heavenly Hominy is delicious with a piece of grilled meat and a light salad.)

~ Tasty Tomato Appetizer ~

SERVES 6–8

My grown daughter showed me this tasty and unique tomato dish. I like to substitute it for the salad in my menu. It makes a nice presentation too. If you're expecting company, make a couple and arrange the slices on a pretty serving dish with a little parsley garnish. Perfect!

one frozen pie shell
1 tablespoon olive oil
6 or 7 slices of mozzarella cheese
2 to 3 fresh tomatoes, thinly sliced
1 10-ounce bag fresh spinach, torn into bite-size pieces
salt and pepper to taste
1 teaspoon garlic powder
1 cup Parmesan cheese

Preheat oven to 400 degrees. Take a frozen pie shell, let it thaw slightly, and poke holes in the sides with a fork. Next brush a tablespoon of olive oil in the bottom and around the sides. Evenly layer the mozzarella cheese, then the tomatoes, then the spinach. Sprinkle with salt and pepper, garlic powder, and Parmesan cheese. Cook at 400 degrees for 8 to 10 minutes and serve in pie wedges.

~ Zippity Corn Relish ~

SERVES 4

We Southerners love a good vegetable relish. My Zippity Corn Relish recipe can top veggies and a whole lot more. It complements everything from steak and potatoes to fresh peas. Oh, and you'll also like it over a nice piece of grilled or blackened seafood for those days when you're eating light.

½ cup vinegar
¼ cup sugar
¼ teaspoon hot sauce
½ teaspoon salt
½ teaspoon celery seed
¼ teaspoon mustard seed
2 tablespoons diced green pepper
2 tablespoons chopped Vidalia sweet onion
1 12-ounce can whole-kernel corn
1 2-ounce jar pimientos

Stir together vinegar, sugar, and hot sauce in a small sauce pan. Add salt, celery seed, and mustard seed. Let this come to a boil and continue rolling for a couple minutes.

Place green pepper and onion into a good-size bowl along with the seasoned vinegar and sugar mixture. Add corn and pimientos. Chill in refrigerator until ready to serve.

~ Broccoli and Cauliflower All Dressed Up ~

SERVES 4–6

We're going to add a little cream cheese and a bit of cheddar to our broccoli and cauliflower, but here's something you should know. The healthy veggies totally negate the butter and cheese. It's far too scientific and complicated to explain. You'll have to trust me.

1 head broccoli, broken into florets
1 head cauliflower, broken into florets
2 teaspoons grated onion
4 tablespoons flour
½ cup margarine, melted
2 cups milk
1 8-ounce package cream cheese, cut into cubes
salt and pepper to taste
2 cups grated cheddar cheese

Preheat oven to 450 degrees. Place broccoli, cauliflower, and onion in a large stockpot. Cover with water and boil until veggies are tender. Drain. In a small saucepan gradually stir flour into the melted margarine. Once the flour dissolves, add milk and stir until smooth. Add cream cheese and stir well. Layer broccoli and cauliflower in a greased 9 × 13-inch baking dish and pour cream cheese sauce over the top. Sprinkle with salt and pepper. Top with the cheddar, cover with foil, and bake at 450 degrees for 30 to 35 minutes. You're gonna love my Broccoli and Cauliflower All Dressed Up!

~ Skillet Cabbage ~

SERVES 4–6

This dish is good, stick-to-your-ribs eating. Sure, you can make another ordinary slaw with that head of cabbage, but this is a whole lot heartier. Skillet Cabbage is hard to beat.

6 slices of bacon
1 10-ounce bag of frozen onions, celery, and bell pepper mix
one head of cabbage, shredded
2 tomatoes, chopped
2 teaspoons sugar
1 teaspoon red wine vinegar
salt and pepper to taste

Fry and drain bacon, saving a couple tablespoons of bacon grease in your skillet. Once cool, crumble bacon and set aside. Add mixed vegetables to reserved grease. (You can start with fresh veggies here, but I'm trying to save you some time.) As soon as the onions become translucent, add cabbage to the skillet along with tomatoes and the crumbled bacon. Season this with sugar and vinegar. Salt and pepper to taste and cook over medium heat for 15 minutes. Skillet Cabbage is good eating, Southern style.

9

Bless Their Hearts

What Southern Mamas Tell Their Daughters About Manners and Social Graces (with Dessert Recipes to Sweeten the Deal)

My Southern Mama's lessons on manners and social graces began with the Golden Rule: Do unto others as you would have them do unto you. This precept may have been introduced when we were mere toddlers, unwilling to share our toys, but it would be repeated many times in the coming years. Mama coupled the familiar portion of Holy Scripture with that infamous Southern equivalent "be sweet," an admonition that leaves very little wiggle room no matter how it's interpreted. Taken together, those two tiny commandments could squeeze the joy out of listening or sharing a juicy bit of gossip. After all these years, I still run into people who tempt me to interpret those rules as leniently as possible.

> My mother used to say, "If a dog will carry a bone to your yard, he'll carry it to someone else's yard." It was her way of saying that if someone tells you a tale on someone else, they'll also tell others a tale on you.
>
> Carolyn Moss
> Oak Grove, Louisiana

It is at these moments that I hear Mama's voice saying, "Pass and repass." Sometimes she's even in the room when this happens. From the time we were little girls, Mama has used this line anytime we complained about the way someone was treating us. She would listen and nod but her standard answer was, "You're just gonna have to pass and repass with her." This confused us at first. As none of us Einsteins were old enough to drive at the time, we figured out it couldn't have anything to do with the family car, but what was she saying? Cyndie thought it sounded like a square-dancing call. "Dosey do; promenade your partner, pass and repass." Maybe. Rhonda and I had taken Mrs. Clark's square dancing class, too, but we were skeptical, and rightfully so. It wasn't long before Mama's real message got through: There would always be people you couldn't get along with no matter how hard you tried. With these people we were told to pass and repass. The interpretation, speak and move on when you see 'em but don't look for or expect anything else. (Side note: Spell check said "repass" wasn't a word. However, my extensive professional research, and by that I mean I searched Google for it, revealed pages of references to the phrase in classical literature—so there!)

If I told Mama about someone greeting me in an unfriendly manner, she'd say, "Now, did you check yourself first?" Oh, how I hated that one. What she meant was, had I slighted the person previously without realizing it, or given the person any reason to keep me at a distance? Maybe I had been in too big a hurry to stop and talk before or something similar. It irritated me, but it worked. I think this comes under, "Do unto others as you would have them do unto you."

D. Raven
Columbia, South Carolina

As I was saying before I got all technical, I am often reminded of this phrase when I encounter difficult people. Such was the case of a recent visitor to my cyber porch. Most of the people I hear from are nice, y'all, but occasionally some

My wise Southern mom gave us four girls some great advice when we got ruffled by someone's unkind remark: "Let it roll right off of you, Honey, like water off a duck's back!"

Christina Caruso
Burbank, California

poor thing comes by who has obviously not had any raising. One Saturday morning, while replying to a ton of reader e-mail, I found a note from a testy little surfer who had come upon my website by accident. And he'd obviously been in a foul mood at the time.

Mr. 2bad2b@aol.com wrote in to say we Southerners are trigger-happy rednecks always worrying about someone taking our guns. If you're Southern and that doesn't light your fire, your wood's wet. I'll be honest. Several thoughts came to my mind and none of them could've been filed under "be sweet." It took me several false starts before I was able to compose a polite response. Mama would've been proud.

"We're not worried about someone taking our guns, Mr.2Bad," my note read, "but the people who think they're big enough to take our guns should be, worried that is, for while you're woefully rude and shaming your mama, you're right on one point. Pulling triggers does make us happy.

"Just yesterday," I continued pleasantly, "my friend was having a rotten day. Did she write ugly letters to strangers? Heavens no! She took her shotgun down to the lake bank and blew some water mocs out of the water. Like many of her fellow Southerners, she spells relief, 'BOOM!' And pretty soon, 2Bad, my hometown will host a snake rodeo where contestants will load up to see who can take the most of the slithery reptiles, along with the biggest, and the baddest."

By this time, I had gotten over my fit and was feeling right neighborly, so I even offered Mr. 2Bad the following invitation. "You ought to drive down, 2Bad. We won't have any bronco-busting or bull-riding at this rodeo, but if a snake falls out of the cypress trees into a boat, we might see someone walk on water."

My little visit from Mr. 2Bad brings to mind a good gun story. Several years ago, one of our more mature steel magnolias had a run-in with some fishermen from out of town who tied their boat up to her dock. While allowing folks to fish around your dock is customary in these parts, these particular fellows were cussing and acting a fool, and making Mrs. D. generally uncomfortable. What's more, they were littering the water and Mrs. D.'s lake bank with the remains of their alcoholic beverages!

Mrs. D. stepped off her patio, where she'd been enjoying her afternoon coffee and the weekly edition of the *Banner Democrat*, and politely asked the boys to move on. That should've been enough. It wasn't. Their response went something like this, "It's a free world, Grandma, and our lawyers said we can fish anywhere we want to on this lake." Mrs. D. turned her back and went inside quietly. That wasn't the end, either.

My mother said, "A lady doesn't raise her voice or point her finger."

JoAnn Beavers
West Monroe, Louisiana

Several minutes later she returned with her own announcement. This time she walked right down on the dock, real personal like. "Friends," Mrs. D. said, as she patted a small loaded handgun in her palm. "I consulted my lawyers too. Misters Smith and Wesson here said y'all needed to move along." I reckon that's just the type of story that would cock Mr. 2Bad's pistol—if he was toting.

To Ma'am or Not to Ma'am

Mama built upon the foundational and open-to-interpretation teaching of "be sweet" with more specific social graces. She taught us about proper greetings. "Hay is for horses." We should say "hello" instead, and we were expected to speak to our elders first, as a sign of respect. During these conversations we were to make good eye contact, refrain from mumbling, and stand up straight. Slouching was direct evidence of poor breeding and just slightly less criminal than neglecting the necessary "ma'am" or "sir."

> Mama said, "If you don't remember your manners, everyone else will!"
>
> Lisa Hilbers
> Alba, Texas

Southern children are taught from birth to address their elders with "yes, ma'am" and "no, ma'am," or "yes, sir" and "no, sir." They are not only instructed to use these proper addresses when answering adults but they should also remember to use the proper address when asking their elders a question.

For instance, let's say an adult speaks to a child. Little Johnny doesn't understand so he says, "What?" This is when Little Johnny should begin counting his lucky stars that he's hypothetical, because someone's asking for a hypothetical whuping. (Mama used to say that a lot: Are you asking for a whuping? While the answer does seem obvious, I speak from experience when I say sarcasm would be the wrong choice. This was one of my earliest lessons in rhetorical speaking.) In our example Little Johnny should have said, "Ma'am?"

My mama could get us girls to change a "what?" to a "ma'am?" by slightly arching an eyebrow. I'm all for it too. "Huh" is as offensive to my ears as the sound of a fingernail scraping on a chalkboard. And yet, as supportive as I am of the "ma'am" tenet, I've often wished the same women who taught us to start would teach us when to stop. They kind of hang us out to dry on this one, don't they?

Once Southern Mamas get this response firmly ingrained in your DNA they send you out into the world, where you soon grow up and find yourself in need of some guidelines. Raise your hand if you've ever made the mistake of saying "yes, ma'am" to a lady who doesn't feel like she's your *elder,* (note key word). Uh-huh, no doubt you paid dearly for that infraction. I know I have, many times over. A little clarification, that's all I'm suggesting.

My gramma, Mayebelle Bond, was the typical Southern matriarch and had strict rules regarding "acceptable behavior" for her daughters and granddaughters. Two things that were forbidden were whistling and using toothpicks in public. I can still hear my personal favorite: "You never pick your nose or your teeth in public—nobody wants to see what comes out of either one!"

LaJuana Green
Dothan, Alabama

Along with "ma'am" and "sir," my sisters and I memorized the magic words that grease the wheels of social interaction: "please" and "thank you." Momentarily forgetting these niceties would draw a stern look from Mama. Ignoring them completely could earn you a trip to the back bedroom.

Southern Mamas are diligent about teaching these and other good manners because they know their children will benefit from them many times over, in many varied social opportunities. Rare are the times when good manners can't improve a bad situation, but I suppose there is the isolated incident. My little friend Savannah Grace can attest to that. Savannah is a sweet, if somewhat sassy, little belle who epitomizes the steely charm of the Southern woman. I tell a lot of Savannah Grace stories on my cyber porch. People like her so

Mama always said, "Sit up and be pretty." This was usually at church or at a family event where she had me dressed up and she didn't want me to wrinkle my clothes.

Peggy Chapman Duncan
West Monroe, Louisiana

much I've sort of christened her as our mascot. One day I called her mama to see what Savannah had been up to lately.

"Plenty," Julia said, sounding more exasperated than amused, "but I'll be brief. Last week, Savannah fell on a piece of her dad's farm equipment in the barn and had to have stitches, which led to a tetanus shot at our pediatrician's. Savannah is notorious at the pediatrician's for her aversion to a shot needle. I actually think the nurses draw straws to avoid administering it. That day, as soon as the unlucky winner entered the room with the shot in hand Savannah began kicking and screaming, 'NO! NO! NO!'

"Savannah Grace!" Julia said in her sternest voice. "That's not polite behavior and you know it!"

Savannah paused before continuing, even louder this time, "No, thank you! No, thank you! No, thank you!"

Blessing Hearts and Heavy Legs

While we're discussing manners, I'd like to take the opportunity to correct an errant assumption I've noticed making its way around the World Wide Web. I've read the silly forewords about how Southerners think we can say anything ugly we want to about someone as long as we tag "bless her heart" at the end of it. Well, yes, and no . . . There is a subtlety to "blessing someone's heart." I will now attempt to explain the difference to any wannabe belles out there.

Someone who's not from around here might try to use that

phrase and out herself as a non-Southerner immediately by saying, "I saw Betty Jo's girl at the wedding. She has gotten so heavy—bless her heart." Now, that would be plum rude and such a tagged-on blessing would be useless. It'd be blatantly obvious the commentator was being insensitive to the girl's plight. Watch and learn.

> My granny said, "Never try to be something you're not. Be genuine and be yourself."
>
> Ramona Johnson
> Green Pond, Alabama

A true Southerner would say the same thing this way: "Bless her heart, Betty Jo's little girl inherited those heavy legs from her mama's side." See... you can put it at the front, middle, or close, but this way the speaker is simply commiserating with the genes running in that poor girl's family. (That reminds me. "Poor Thing" needs the same careful handling.)

I understand that people around the world laugh at Americans because we tend to think anyone can speak our language as long as we talk slowly in a LOUD, CLEAR voice. That won't work in the South, either. A person can use our sayings like a tourist with a guide book. They can even drawl if they want to, but they won't be socially acceptable 'til they master the subtleties of the language.

Those Darn Little Ladies

My Southern Mama was determined that we girls become "little ladies." She talked about these mythical females incessantly, never missing an opportunity to extol their social graces. My sisters and I quickly found ourselves growing weary of hearing about the many things these little ladies did and did not do.

Some of Mama's rules on manners were: chew with your mouth closed, don't talk with your mouth full, and don't say "ain't." (Ain't fell in a bucket of paint.) If we didn't hear a question we were supposed to say, "ma'am?" in the form of a question and not "what?" If you said "what?" Mama warned you with "What, what, chicken squat!"

Pam Holliday
Yazoo City, Mississippi

We understood that little ladies kept their elbows off the table, they didn't talk with their mouths full, and they didn't eat so fast that it looked like they were afraid someone was going to snatch their plates away. They spoke when they were spoken to, they crossed their legs at the ankles; they never, but never straddled a chair, and they didn't fidget at the table or anywhere else for that matter.

Yes, I know. My sisters and I found these little ladies a little too good to be true as well. Had we been able to locate 'em, we would've been sorely tempted to ignore Mama's "be sweet" rule and knock the prissy role models off their high and mighty perches. Bear with me as I continue. Little ladies didn't interrupt grown-ups and they didn't go to the bathroom; they excused themselves to *use the restroom.* They didn't balance on the back two legs of their chairs and they didn't sneeze or cough without covering their mouths. And, lest I forget, here's one of the big ones: If at all possible, little ladies broke wind in private, although it was preferable that they not break wind at all.

My mother told me that a real Southern lady knows better than to clean her plate while dining in public.

Ruth Beavers
West Monroe, Louisiana

Mama may have disproved of breaking wind in public, but at least we weren't penalized for the accidental infraction. From what I read in a recent news report, today's children in China aren't so fortunate. I know you're gonna think I'm making this up, but cross-my-heart-hope-to-die-stick-a-needle-in-my-eye the following story is ripped straight from the headlines.

Chinese schools are now *fining* students for breaking wind in class. Can you imagine? I hope this never catches on here in the good old U S of A. As my mama's daughter, I understand wanting to discourage the practice of intentional flatulence, but I've got more questions than answers. As it is, no one but teenage boys like to claim ownership of these less than aromatic public moments. Add a fine and who'll ever 'fess up? And just who determines there's been a violation, and by whom—surely not the poor overworked teacher. If so, is there a smell test involved? Will the falsely accused sue for mental anguish, requiring teachers to carry accidental wind insurance? See what I mean? Mark my words, friends. This is like kicking a cow chip on a hot summer's day. We'd better leave well enough alone.

My aunt Judy had a trick she often resorted to when entertaining guests in her home. She'd kindly excuse herself to the porch to give a generous sample of the leftovers to her beloved cat. On most occasions she'd call its name out loud, come back in murmuring about where he'd gotten off to, and then drop the subject. Funny thing was, I never saw a cat at her house. Years later Aunt Judy explained to me that it was a pefectly acceptable way to break away from your company to break wind. The louder you called for your kitty, well the louder the wind.

Angela Hopper
Monticello, Louisiana

Side note: My paternal grandmother, God rest her soul, never developed the gas problems that often plague mature people. Many times, however, as she walked across the floor or lowered herself into her recliner, one could hear an unexpected but familiar sound. "Oops," Grandmaw Rushing would say with a shy grin, "I must have stepped on a frog," which is ironic really, because lately I've noticed an increasing number of those same amphibians around my house.

To be honest, I have my own reasons for wanting to discourage the type of surveillance the Chinese are engaging in. I had a truly bad experience in the bodily function area recently. Although I had spent a delightful weekend visiting my daughter and her husband, I was leaving her fine city with a complimentary case of food poisoning from a well-known Mexican restaurant and one major goal: preventing my insides from staging their own boycott in Houston Intercontinental Airport.

My Southern Mama taught me that a lady never puts her elbows on the table. To this day, I have a heck of a time not doing it.

Pamela White
Henderson, Tennessee

My queasy intestines and I arrived at the initial security checkpoint where a poker-faced lady discovered my first security violation. My driver's license had expired. Great. I apologized, silly me. Miss Rumsfield Wannabe frowned. Apparently, I was the newest threat to national security. Did I know I was traveling with an expired license? Why had I let it expire? While cramps shot through my shoulder blades, and moisture began beading on my brow, I reminded myself that sarcasm wasn't attractive at any age (thanks Mama). Countless stomach rolls later, Miss Rumsfield's supervisor jotted something on my boarding pass and waved me, his ex-problem, toward the next security checkpoint.

My new friends read the coded note on my pass and seized my luggage from the X-ray machine for in-depth screening. I was passing silently through the metal detector, hallelujah, and smelling the first hint of freedom—or blue cheese enchiladas—when I heard a heart-stopping announcement, "She has a knife!" Who has a knife? I don't have a, wait, yes I do. The good folks in Farmerville, Louisiana, had put one in my gift basket at that last speaking engagement. I, Public Enemy Number One, had inadvertently dropped it in my purse! It had gone undetected when I flew out of my hometown airport, but just like the famous movie line suggested, Houston had a problem.

My best friend's mom always said, "Horses sweat, men perspire, women glow!"

Betty Reid
Petal, Mississippi

A second man spoke directly into the microphone mounted to his shirt collar. "We have a knife," he told someone somewhere. Correction, Crocodile Dundee, you have a utility tool with a corkscrew. (Hush, Shellie.) I didn't want it. I didn't need it. And I desperately needed a restroom. I begged 'em to just throw the blasted thing away, but I quote, "Ma'am, once security has been breached we must follow protocol." Protocol! I haven't seen such blatant suspicion since I was fifteen and told Papa I was carrying those cigarettes in my purse for a friend.

I managed to navigate my own intestinal problem without a fine, and I'm back in my own home bunker now, but I thought you should know how difficult it is for a fortysomething, green around the gills writer from Lake Providence, Louisiana, to threaten the world with concealed fingernail clippers. Rest easy, America.

Scary Female

The whole thing hurt my feelings because I'm really quite harmless. Why, I haven't threatened anyone with bodily harm since...since the days I lived under one roof with my sisters. Cyndie, Rhonda, and I found it much easier to live up to Mama's "be sweet" expectations in our dealings with strangers than we did with one another. We knew where each other's buttons were, how to push 'em, and how long to hold 'em in. Mama, however, meant every rule in the good manners book as a sweeping pronouncement. She made it clear from the get-go that family members were not exempt. A belle's instruction on manners and social graces always includes a teaching on loving and appreciating family members, immediate and extended.

One thing my mother always told my brother, Chris, and me during our sibling arguments was, "If you can't say anything nice, don't say anything at all." That usually stopped the argument in a heartbeat because we sure weren't thinking of anything even remotely nice to say. Another thing she told me about my brother was, "If you just ignore him, he'll go away." I'm not sure if her philosophy is true because I could never seem to ignore him.

Amy Wiggins
Mer Rouge, Louisiana

Mama and her three sisters were very close and she wanted us girls to share the same pleasure. Let's just say the attachment didn't form overnight. We had to fight our share of sister wars first.

We grew up clashing over everything from mud pies to boyfriends, trying desperately to establish boundaries that would help us figure out where one of us ended and the other one started. And then, somehow over time, a shaky peace started forming. I remember the first time I realized Mama's teachings were beginning to take.

My sister Rhonda and I were carefree teenagers, just set free from another long, boring day at high school. She was waiting in the car. I was standing in line at Mrs. Dorothy's Dairy Bar when I heard the most awful commotion. Someone was giving someone the what-for! Looking back around the corner, I was surprised to find a strange girl shouting obscenities at my sister. For her part, Rhonda looked confused—and terrified. My protective instincts took over. "Hey," I yelled, "what's your problem?"

> Mama said, "Simple courtesy and gentleness help to grease the wheels of social interaction."
>
> Betty Martin
> Natchitoches, Louisiana

And that's how I bought myself a confrontation with one scary-looking female who had me by a couple inches and more than a few pounds. Scary Female turned to me and continued the ugly discussion she'd been having with Rhonda. I tried to "be sweet" as Mama would say (although, I thought to myself, Mama might change her tune right about now if she heard the names this girl was calling her!).

Scary Female attacked my looks and my paternity. Then she called me a name I was honor bound to take issue with. (If you must know, it suggested that I was way too free with my favors.) I politely asked her not to call me that again.

"Don't tell me what to do," she said, (her face only an inch from mine). "I'll knock your *#$@^% off." Have mercy, what language! Where I come from, there is talk

> My mama said, "You shouldn't let it be known that you even know a four-letter word, much less use one . . . ever!"
>
> Jo Pate
> Marietta, Georgia

of a moment in everyone's life when they realize they have to put up or shut up. With a sinking feeling, I realized that this was my moment. Meeting her stare, I jutted my chin toward hers.

"Knock it," I said.

Scary Female was only slightly less surprised by this move than I was. While she tried to decide if I was dangerous or bluffing, I went into silent prayer, *"Dear God Almighty, puleease don't let her knock it."*

Several stressful moments later Not So Scary Female abruptly backed down and walked off. It was a miracle! I braced my jellified knees and yelled, "And don't you forget it!" After all these years, I still don't know what she was supposed to remember, but this I do know: Some things are worth fighting for. With Elvis, it was those blue suede shoes; for me, it will always be my sisters.

Deadly Respect and Tombstone Twitch

We didn't share that story with Mama for a number of years, but when it did come out, it was obvious she was proud, even if she couldn't bring herself to admit it because "little ladies don't fight in public." The Southern book of manners and social graces makes exceptions when one's family is accosted. A belle grows up under the constant and remedial teachings about the importance of tending to those in the family tree. Being Southern, this includes everyone, dead or alive.

We don't sit up with the dead any longer, but we still pay our respects regularly. It'd be mighty poor manners to do anything else. I should note here that my Southern Mama has truly practiced what she has spent a lifetime preaching. It's an example she continues to set, even at her own peril.

A couple summers ago my sisters and I got really worried about Mama. We got together and diagnosed her with a bad case of the dreaded Tombstone Twitch. We'd seen it coming for a while, ever since she began locating and documenting the graves of our kinfolks in long-forgotten cemeteries all over the South. Oh, I'm sorry. In case you're not familiar—Tombstone Twitch is a Southern expression for being bitten by the genealogy bug. Happens to a lot of people when they realize they're on the backside of the hill, but I'm convinced it's more rampant in the South.

That fall Mama's twitch prompted her to organize a big Stone family reunion. Now, we've had plenty of reunions. We're Southern, for goodness sakes. But this wasn't just any old reunion. This was the mother of all family reunions.

Mama went on a self-imposed mission, digging up old photos for the welcoming table. She not only tracked down black-and-white pictures of our solemn ancestors but bits and pieces of interesting family artifacts. No one knows where she found it all but her research lab, formerly known as Cyndie's old bedroom, began to look like another of those crime scene investigator shows, *CSI Louisiana*.

Mama expected everyone to be at the reunion, whether they were twitching or not. I'm not implying that she used her famous guilt trips. She just said things like, "One day, when I'm dead and gone, you'll wish you had come, just for me," little things like that.

The other day Mama took me out of our way to see a graveyard that my mama's daddy's grandmother's mama's cousin is buried in—just so I'd know, when I need to. Funny thing is I figure that one day I probably will.

As of this writing, Mama is still alive and well. That's the good news. The bad news is her condition appears to be contagious. Mama and Aunt Patsy, my papa's sister, have spent the last week or so here at our hometown cemetery, staking out their burial plots. As far as I know, neither of them are terminal, at least no more so than the rest of us. I suppose I could go before they do. I, however, am not twitching. They are.

Years ago when my grandfather on Papa's side bought graves for himself and my grandmother, he purchased a number of extras for the family. Other than the present occupants, these remaining graves are unmarked. Mama and Aunt Pat are preparing to seize this opportunity. The two of them are quite a sight stalking around the graveyard in their pedal pushers with their makeup intact and color on their lips. It's their intention, and I'm quoting here, "to make sure they claim the best spots before the rest of the family gets ahead of 'em." Gives a whole new meaning to racing for the finish line, now doesn't it?

I grew up hearing my mother say, "Never leave the house without lipstick." Even in later years when her own mother would forget and try to go to choir practice without it, Mama would say, "Mother, go put on your lipstick. You look like a ghost." My sister and I say we'll put on her tombstone: "She died with her lipstick on."

Jan Forester
Longview, Texas

Unfortunately for the Deadly Duo, they've hit a snag. They can't claim their final resting spots until they find the grave of a baby who, according to family lore, is buried in the family plot without a headstone. Yesterday they were probing the ground for that coffin using a steel rod. Unfortunately, it wasn't long enough. Did you know they used to bury people deeper than they do now? Neither did I; this is the kind of thing one discovers when one's twitching, or knows someone who is. The hunt was called off while they await the delivery of a custom-designed probing stick they've ordered from a local welder. I'm not making that up. When you have a family like mine, you don't have to.

The Deadly Duo's efforts remind me of a family friend. Miss Jane—not her real name—has hit the centennial mark. She's been prepared to go to her eternal reward for some time. She chose her music, colors, and so on a few decades back. However, Miss Jane recently discovered the funeral home of her choice had been remodeled. The news forced her to update her arrangements because, as Miss Jane said, "That new carpet would have completely clashed with the lining of the casket I had chosen." Now, that might not sound like an issue to some people, but to a good Southern woman, it might possibly be a fate worse than death.

Thank-You Notes

I'd be remiss if I discussed manners without mentioning one of the belle's specialties, that all-important thank-you note. Southern girls are known for their notes. This is not by accident. Our mamas expect us to write them, write them well, and in a timely manner. Their reputations are at stake as well as ours.

Southern Mamas swell with pride when an acquaintance says something like, "I got the sweetest thank-you note from Mary Elizabeth." The acquaintance knows this. It's why she mentioned it. This is just one of our little Southern dances.

The same sort of gratification applies to the Southern Mama's daughter-in-law. She takes credit there as well, knowing she will be found innocent or guilty by association. Last summer my daughter and my son got married a few weeks apart. The only thing that possibly made me prouder than

Mom always insisted good Southern ladies write thank-you notes. Whether you've been invited to a meal, a party, to spend the night at someone's home, been given a job reference, received a gift, or any other courtesy, a real Southerner will handwrite a thank-you note. And make sure the recipient gets it in a timely manner. I don't believe the time frame is written in stone (especially in regards to wedding gifts), but for all other occasions Mom said the note should be received within a week of the courtesy given.

Melanie Howle
Idalou, Texas

the "I do" moments was knowing Jessica and Carey both got their thank-you notes out promptly.

On the opposite end of the spectrum lies the dread that strikes a Southern Mama's heart should the acquaintance ask, "Do you know if Mary Elizabeth got that gravy boat I sent?" Now, the acquaintance knows full well what she is doing here as well. And most of the time, she isn't trying to embarrass the lady. She's simply trying to save her from a more widespread catastrophe by letting the Southern Mama know all is not right in the thank-you world. That's why the question is often followed by a gracious disclaimer that allows the poor thing some wiggle room. "Oh, I'm sure she did; it's just that I haven't heard from her. It's probably the post office. They're slow as molasses."

Southern Mamas catch one another's backs on this type of thing. I remember once when my own dear mama came by my house with a thank-you note in her hand and a missionary gleam in her eye, determined to avert such a calamity.

"Read this," she said, thrusting the note toward me. "It's from Sharon's daughter." I scanned the pretty card. It had all the right parts—recognition, appreciation, and affection. And yet, when I looked up, Mama was watching me with raised eyebrows. Obviously I was missing something. I reread the note, more carefully this time. Yep, there it was: a grammatical error. Mama had been reading my face just as close. "Uh-huh, you see it, now, don't you? Bless her heart. And it was such a nice note too. But still, her mother would be horrified."

I agreed, and went to change the subject, but Mama was having none of it. She wanted to know if I thought she should call the woman and tell her, because, and I'm quoting fairly accurately here, "What if she really doesn't know any better, Shellie? For heaven's sakes, what if the poor girl is making that same mistake in hundreds of these notes? If her mother knew I knew and didn't tell her while she could do something about it, why, she may not ever speak to me again."

I had to admit I hadn't considered the widespread catastrophe angle. Mama's been at this longer than I have. Suddenly, I felt guilty for questioning her motives but I still felt compelled to point out the chance that the opposite could apply. The woman could see it as interference and be offended.

"And she'd never speak to me, again," Mama said. "You're right. It's a pickle, isn't it?"

In the end, Mama threw caution to the wind and spilled her guts with as much tact as possible. I'm happy to report that not only was the Southern Mama very appreciative, she was able to intervene and avert further embarrassment, which just proves that sometimes things do work out for the greater good.

Every so often someone comes by my website to ask me if e-mail thank-you notes are appropriate. Let me be clear. An e-mail thank-you card is to a U.S mail thank-you card what paper plates are to fine china: poor imitations. Even when they get the job done (and some of them can flat-out create a mess), they're sorely lacking in presentation. Ditto the new fill-in-the-blank thank-you cards I've been reading about. You heard me. There are companies out there offering cards that allow Little

Suzie to check off this chore in record time. Dear_____, thank you for the_____. Some of these cards must assume Suzie is totally clueless for they give her multiple-choice gifts that allow her to circle one or more. Thank you for the a) jewelry box, b) sweater, c) radio, d) what-cha-ma-call-it.

I've been told these cards are thank-you note training wheels, but I'm not falling for it. Let Suzie draw Great-Grandma a picture if she can't write, and you sign it. But please don't give a Southern Great-Grandma a multiple-choice card. It might just do her in.

I had no idea the situation had gotten so dire. Due to the seriousness of the subject, I've prepared a little rhyming checklist to help wannabe belles remember the ingredients of writing the proper thank-you note. We'll call it: name, exclaim, fame. Name: A successful thank-you note shouldn't give the impression of mass production. The gift giver's name should be used and the gift recognized. "Thank you for the wedding gift" is far too generic. "Dear Aunt Madelyn, Thank you for the tray" is adequate, but barely. "Dear Aunt Madelyn, Thank you for the lovely Arthur Court bread tray with the magnolia handles and vine border" is belle to the bone. When it comes to thank-you notes, it's hard to use too many details, but one should be wary of redundant adjectives. "Thank you for the nice sweater. It should be nice and warm this winter. It was nice of you to think about me" sounds like you run on batteries.

> Mama taught me that upon receiving a gift that I didn't like I was to remember to accept it with the grace it was given in and to never, ever let the giver know I didn't like it.
>
> Dana Sieben
> Oak Forest, Illinois

Exclaim: A belle knows a good thank-you note includes the enthusiastic mention of her future plans for the gift. "I look forward to displaying it on our buffet when we're not using it for parties."

Fame: Fame simply means to show regard for the gift giver's time and affection. "It was so thoughtful of you to remember me at this special time" acknowledges that the gift giver acted out of generosity rather than obligation. It should be followed by "With love" or "With much affection." Belles reserve "Sincerely yours" for more formal occasions.

Finally, there are differences of opinion on the appropriate time frame for getting one's cards out but the last word on the subject is "better late than never." Seriously, if it weren't for the lack of personal detail, a belle would have a stack of thank-you notes prepared to be mailed postmortem. Unfortunately, there's always the chance Mary Alice will bring sweet potato casserole to the bereaved family instead of her customary fruit salad. While this unknown element forces the belle to leave the funeral thank-you notes to her family, I doubt she truly rests in peace until they're in the mail.

The Gracious Hostess

A large part of a belle's education in the social graces is devoted to the art of putting people at ease. Our famed hospitality depends on our ability to make others feel comfortable in our presence. These tried and true methods include looking people in the eye and expressing genuine interest when they're speaking to you. No one likes to feel like they're a bus stop on your way to the more interesting person at the next table.

Our mamas teach us that people like to talk about themselves. Ask questions they can answer easily, perhaps about their work, their families in general, their mamas and children in particular. They can usually speak on these subjects with little effort. As a result, they begin to relax and enjoy themselves. Never do these rules apply more than when the belle is acting as hostess of her own domain. A belle will go to any lengths to make sure no one is uncomfortable in her home.

I'm reminded of a good story that features a couple of interesting belles and their unwavering hospitality. Both friends and relatives around here called 'em Mama Ruth and Aunt Eddie, two roommates that put the *e* in *eccentric.* Even in their late seventies and early eighties Mama Ruth and Aunt Eddie loved nothing more than packing supplies and fish bait in Mama Ruth's old truck and heading for the hunting camp. Alone in the woods, they'd cook, fish, and argue till the cows came home. The two of them thought nothing of picking up a stick and whuping a poor defenseless rattlesnake or cottonmouth simply because it had the nerve to sunbathe in their path.

One unbearably hot Fourth of July, when they'd been gone for days, Mama Ruth's grandson went to check on 'em. He arrived as Aunt Eddie decided to bathe in the old bathtub they used to catch rainwater. John followed Mama Ruth inside to put the evening coffee on.

Barely had the sounds of splashing water and snatches of "Amazing Grace" begun when a truck started bearing down the camp road. Mama Ruth ran to the screen door and hollered at Aunt Eddie, "Get your clothes on, Eddie, someone's coming! Instead, Aunt Eddie panicked and dashed for the door, au natural. Although her towel wasn't big enough to cover any part of her anatomy Aunt Eddie was bent on covering all her parts simultaneously. While she ran, she flapped that rag from top to bottom so fast it looked like she might lift off the ground. Unfortunately, this struck Mama Ruth's funny bone.

Aunt Eddie ran up the steps just as the truck pulled in and reached for the door handle—only to see her loving, laughing, sister lock the latch. Aunt Eddie went from singing "Amazing Grace" to cussin' like a sailor! While a very tickled Mama Ruth sat down to keep from falling down, John jumped to unlock the door. Moments later, Mama Ruth welcomed her unexpected company as if it wasn't the least bit unusual to have an eighty-year-old bare-naked woman leading them in.

"How about some fresh coffee?" Mama Ruth asked sweetly, for neither rain nor shine nor a nekkid relative can make a Southern hostess forget her manners.

Mother said, "The reason some people use so much profanity is that they don't have a very large vocabulary. Enlarge your vocabulary and you won't need to curse." I took her at her word, which isn't to say that my vocabulary doesn't include some pretty good cuss words!

Delese Cannon
Odessa, Texas

Dessert Recipes to Sweeten the Deal

I wouldn't be the least surprised if one day we found out there was a Southern Mama somewhere in Mary Poppins's family tree. Belles know that a little sugar will do a lot more than make the medicine go down. It's why we don't mind the ridicule we take for the "darlings" and "honeys" we're famous for sprinkling in our conversation. We know they soften the hardest hearts and sweeten everyday life. Our dessert tables benefit from the same philosophy. Here are a few dessert recipes guaranteed to enhance the affairs of your heart and home.

~ Phil's Banana Pudding ~

SERVES 10–16

Our mamas taught us that the way to a man's heart is through his stomach. I'd like to add that the road is most likely paved with banana pudding. This is my husband's favorite dessert. It wouldn't be Christmastime at our house without banana pudding in the refrigerator. Try it once and see if it doesn't get your man's attention.

5 cups milk
8 tablespoons flour
2½ cups sugar, plus extra for meringue
4 eggs
1 stick butter
1 teaspoon vanilla
6–8 bananas
1 box vanilla wafer cookies

Combine milk with flour and sugar. Always remember, add your milk to your flour and sugar. If you add flour to milk, you're gonna have clumps.

Separate eggs. Beat egg yolks well and stir into milk mixture. Set aside egg whites for the meringue.

Cook the mixture of flour, milk, eggs and sugar over low heat, stirring constantly to keep it from sticking. Once it thickens, take it off the fire, add butter and vanilla. Layer pudding in a pretty bowl with bananas and vanilla wafers. Top with meringue. For those of you who don't know how to make meringue, here's my foolproof method. Take your egg whites and whip them with your blender until they begin to get stiff. Next, add your sugar slowly while still blending. (I use two tablespoons per egg white.) That's it! Once the meringue forms peaks, scoop it out and top your beautiful dessert! Now, if you like your meringue browned, all you have to do is slide it under the broiler, BRIEFLY! It can burn within a couple of minutes, so watch it carefully.

~ Jessica's Heavenly Honeybun Cake ~

SERVES 12–16

There are no actual honeybuns involved here, but stir this treat together and you'll think you're at your local bakery! My daughter's Heavenly Honeybun Cake definitely lives up to its billing. Warm a couple slices for you and your sweetie and serve with your morning coffee. Spoil yourself a little, you're worth it.

1 box yellow cake mix
4 eggs
⅔ cup vegetable oil
1 8-ounce container sour cream
1 cup brown sugar
½ cup finely chopped pecans
1½ tablespoons cinnamon
4 tablespoons milk
2 cups powdered sugar
1 tablespoon vanilla

Preheat oven to 350 degrees. Grease and flour the bottom of a 9 × 13-inch pan. Beat together cake mix, eggs, oil, and sour cream for about 2 minutes. Pour half of this mixture into the greased pan.

Combine the sugar, pecans, and cinnamon in a small bowl and spread this over batter. Top with the remaining batter and bake 45 minutes until golden brown. And now the best part—the glaze: Stir together milk, powdered sugar, and vanilla, and drizzle over the cake. Jessica says you're supposed to let it cool for an hour. I say, "Good luck"—the cooling thing never happens at this house.

~ Shellie's Plum Peachy Pie ~

SERVES 6–8

You can make this dessert with frozen fruit, but I wouldn't recommend it. This dish just begs for fresh peaches and plums! Don't skip the tapioca. It'll thicken your pudding and sweeten the whole dish.

2 cups sliced and peeled peaches
2 cups sliced and peeled plums
1 tablespoon lemon juice
¼ teaspoon almond extract
1½ cups sugar
¼ cup quick-cooking tapioca
1 teaspoon grated lemon peel
¼ teaspoon salt
2 refrigerated piecrusts
two tablespoon butter

Preheat oven to 450 degrees. Mix fruit slices with lemon juice and almond extract. Set aside.

In a small bowl combine sugar with tapioca, lemon peel, and a dash of salt. Gently stir into the fruit and let stand about 15 minutes.

Take a refrigerated piecrust, press it in pan and fill with fruit filling. Dot with pats of butter and cover with the second crust. Seal and flute the edges and cut a couple pretty slits across the top. You've done it! Cover the edges loosely with foil and cook 10 minutes, at 450 degrees before reducing the heat to 350 and cooking it another 35 or 40 minutes until it's golden brown and bubbly.

~ Meme's Signature Cake ~

SERVES 16–20

This recipe comes from my daughter-in-law's grandmother. I've found that to be one of the perks of having new blood marry into the family. They come with a whole new set of recipes. Meme's signature cake is very welcome around here. Don't let the three steps overwhelm you. It's very easy. I'll walk you through it, but be warned, you're gonna be hungry when we're done.

1 cup oatmeal (instant)
1½ cups hot water
½ cup vegetable oil
1 cup brown sugar
1 cup white sugar
1⅓ cups self-rising flour
1 teaspoon baking soda
1 teaspoon cinnamon
½ teaspoon salt
2 eggs

Frosting
1 stick butter
1 tablespoon milk
1 cup light brown sugar
1 can coconut milk
1 cup pecans, chopped

Preheat oven to 350 degrees. Mix oatmeal with hot water. While it's cooling, mix together oil and sugars. Combine oatmeal, dry ingredients, and oil, and beat together with eggs.

Pour the whole thing in a greased 9 × 13-inch pan and bake at 350 degrees for about 30 minutes or until toothpick stuck in center comes out clean. Once it's done, stir together frosting ingredients, heat until thick, and pour over the cake. Broil a minute 'til the frosting browns and enjoy!

~ Strawberry Banana Divine ~

SERVES 12–16

The combined flavor of this dessert is simply divine. One recipe makes two delicious pies. I like to share the second with a friend. They'll love you for it.

1 8-ounce cream cheese, softened

½ cup sugar

1 8-ounce tub Cool Whip

2 large graham cracker piecrusts

1 package strawberry banana Jell-O

1½ cups boiling water

2 8-ounce packages frozen strawberries, thawed

3 medium bananas, mashed

1 8-ounce can crushed pineapple, drained

In a small bowl, mix cream cheese with sugar until smooth. Gradually fold in Cool Whip. Blend well and divide mixture between two graham cracker pie shells, spreading it evenly in the bottom of each. In another bowl, completely dissolve Jell-O in boiling water. Add strawberries, mashed bananas, and pineapple. Mix well and pour this Jell-O and fruit mixture over your cream cheese base. Refrigerate until firm.

~ Mrs. Wanda's Chochoate Chip Pie ~

SERVES 6–8

My mother's good friend was the first to serve me this pie, hence its name. I've made it a hundred times over since then. Again, this is pantry cooking at its best. When you use the ingredients, just replace them on your next trip to the grocery store and you'll always be a few steps away from chocolate heaven!

1 cup sugar
½ cup flour
1 stick margarine, melted
2 eggs, well beaten
1 cup semisweet chocolate chips
¾ cup pecans (I sometimes substitute chopped macadamia nuts—Yum!)
½ cup coconut (optional)
1 teaspoon vanilla
1 ready-made piecrust

Preheat oven to 350 degrees. Blend sugar, flour, margarine, and eggs. Stir in chocolate chips, pecans, coconut, and vanilla. Pour into piecrust and bake for 30 to 35 minutes.

10

The Net Beneath Us All

Miscellaneous Pearls of Wisdom from Southern Mamas (with Lagniappe Recipes and Advice to Point You in the Right Direction)

Some of the lessons our dear Southern Mamas hand down are harder to categorize than others. This chapter is for some of the little things that fell through the cracks of the preceding pages. It seems entirely fitting, this catch-all ending, for that very notion may well be the closest description of a fine Southern Mama. She is the net beneath us all.

> My sister and I would often beg Mother to please let us do something. We'd say something like, "Mother, if you'd only let us do it this time." Her reply would be, "If a frog had wings, he wouldn't be bumping his tail all the time." With that, we knew there was no use begging. The subject was over.
>
> Carolyn Kwiterovich
> West Monroe, Louisiana

For Southern Mamas, caring for loved ones isn't optional. It's their life's mission, and heaven help anyone who gets in their way. These are women with servants' hearts and drill sergeants' tendencies.

If you're in my Southern Mama's family and you're sick of heart or body, rest assured, she will be there and you *will* be waited on. It makes little difference whether you're in desperate straits and in serious need of assistance or if you're slightly under the weather and capable of recovering on your own. Mama's thinking is, "But why should you have to? That's what family's for!" The family doctor might not make house calls any longer, but H, E, Double L will freeze over before my mama gives up the practice. She will cook, clean, and feed you until your house is spotless and your clothes are too tight.

As I have previously told y'all, my sisters and I have fondly christened our walking, talking, cooking, cleaning machine "Marshal Dillon" for her tendency not only to descend on the sick, but to organize and command any and all available troops found on the premises. Those who aren't under the weather when she arrives would do best to keep themselves busy, lest Mama draft 'em into service. Should the sick one also be the mother of the home, her dependents would do well to recognize this isn't the time to test rules the infirmed set in place before her illness. No household rules? Heaven forbid! Marshal Dillon will be glad to set up a list of her own until the entire family is fasting and praying for the recovery of the one that brought on one of Mama's household makeovers.

The Subtleties of Guilt

Do I sound ungrateful? I surely hope not. I'm just having some fun, y'all. Besides, to be unappreciative would mean facing another round of Southern Mother Guilt. Now, there's a subject I can't believe we haven't addressed in these pages. I knew something had been nagging at me.

> Mama always said, "You'll understand when you have kids of your own."
>
> Rhonda Richards
> Kingston Springs, Tennessee

My own dear mother can make me, a grown woman, change directions simply by changing tones. Let's say I had decided not to attend the funeral of my mother's aunt's daughter's cousin's husband. Should I mention this on the phone, Mama might say, "Oh, Honey, I completely understand. You only have so much time." That may sound very understanding but I wasn't born last night. It's only said to get me to lower my guard. On its heels will come something like, "Besides, I'm sure Claire will be so broken up she probably won't know who made it and who didn't, at least not until she reads the guest book, you know, later at home when she's all alone, bless her heart." Right. How hard is it to pull on a black skirt?

Southern Mama Guilt is a much discussed topic among belles. Evelyn, one of my dear Catholic friends, claims Southern Catholic Mamas have mastered the fine art of guilting. While I'm sure these church ladies are good little guilters, I wouldn't be too quick to discount the skills of the Protestant Southern Mamas. Both groups seem equally ready to make a good profession, or hear a bad confession, whatever the case might be.

My contemporaries and I have tried to learn this special skill set, and I'm sure our children would say we're coming along quite nicely, but we know the truth even if we're slow to admit it. We are Guilters-in-Waiting. There is only one Queen Bee per family. Said queen will pass the guilt torch right before she goes to meet her Maker, and not a minute before.

Not long ago a young man, who is not my son but spent enough of his growing-up years at my house to qualify, shared with me one of his Southern Mama's favorite guilt themes.

Jake said his mother spent a lot of time when he was a teenager trying to impress upon him the importance of checking in so as not to worry her unnecessarily. On the occasions when he forgot the rule and stayed out of pocket too long, he would have the devil to pay once she found him. She'd go on and on about how he had worried her to no end and then she'd light into him with her classic line: "For all I knew you could be upside-down dead in a ditch."

Jake found it amusing that being upside-down dead in a ditch always seemed a far worse fate in his dear mother's eyes than being right-side-up dead in a ditch. We laughed, but I was obligated to explain to him that she was simply honing her skills. Southern Mama Guilt may be a natural talent, but like all gifts, that special flair is perfected with time.

My Southern-born Mama liked to say, "If you can't do something about it, don't worry about it." Being a natural worrier, this didn't help me much, but Mama lived eighty-eight years practicing what she preached. I think about what she said every day of my life. Sometimes it works, sometimes not. I guess I was just born to worry.

Susie Taylor
Burton, Michigan

The Festive Flu Bug

So, let the record clearly show, I totally appreciate my mama. I can't imagine what I would've done had she not been there for those big moments: When I brought my babies home from the hospital, the first time they got sick, the first time I got sick and they were well, running around the house like wild Indians. Besides, any belle will tell you that being tended to by a military-style matriarch is always preferable to having our dearly beloved husbands take care of us. Can I hear an "amen"?

Last Christmas I got the merry flu, the festive stomach

virus, and a case of jolly infected eardrums, all at the same time. I jest. There was nothing funny about it. That evil flu bug stalked me for days before finally wrestling me down, forcing me to the doctor's, and then to the couch—where the love of my life set out to nurse me back to health. That first day he opened up canned soup, dosed out my medicine right on time, all four prescriptions, and then in true man-style looked plum disappointed that I wasn't "better yet."

He did a good job taking my phone calls too, although my messages tended to get lost in translation. The second day Mama called. She was fretting from being given sick leave when she really wanted to move in and heal the situation. "Tell her I didn't sleep a wink last night," I whispered, hoarsely. "Tell her my throat is totally raw, hurts so bad it feels like I'm swallowing crushed glass." Phil relayed: "She didn't sleep real good. I think her throat might be sore."

My stress built as the holiday chores piled up. I tried to push through the pain, but every time I thought about imposing my will, the thing threw me back to the couch and growled, "Talk to the hand 'cause the flu ain't listening."

It reminds me of a great old Southern belle story. Several years ago my cousin Jeffrey had a patient named Miss Laura come to his rehab clinic. Jeffrey had known Miss Laura as a real go-getter but she'd recently had some major health issues and she just wasn't the same. She refused to participate in therapy, even after the therapists told her that her prize hydrangeas needed her personal attention. Jeffrey finally approached Mrs. Laura as the therapist was working with her. "Now, Miss Laura," Jeffrey said, "all we're asking you to do is lift your legs." Mrs. Laura responded with no hesitation. "Son, I've been lifting my legs for eighty-nine years and I'm tired. If you want them lifted you're just gonna have to do it yourself!" Me and Miss Laura, we were sick and tired of being sick and tired.

Mama, My Biggest Fan

A Southern Mama's support isn't limited to physical ailments. From our earliest memories, my sisters and I have know that the same woman who tanned our hides always had our backs. I was barely nine years old when I wrote my first book, *Martha and Her Horse.* It had eighty-seven pages and chapter titles like "Trouble in the Pasture." Okay, it wasn't *War and Peace* but I had a story in me and I needed to tell it. My proud mother read excerpts of this literary wonder to anyone and everyone she could lasso into listening.

I'm in my forties now and as they say, the more things have changed the more they've stayed the same. I still love words and my reason for writing hasn't changed; I need to tell stories. Unfortunately, without Mama's strong-arm tactics, finding an audience in my grown-up world has proven slightly more difficult.

For years I scratched my words on the back of grocery lists and children's dentist appointment cards, or piled them next to one another in notebooks and crammed them in dresser drawers and closets before finally admitting to myself that I wanted to tell my stories to other people. And so began my odyssey into the publishing world. Remember Dorothy waking up in Oz and Alice falling down the rabbit hole? Like Dorothy's Oz and Alice's Wonderland, the publishing world is an elusive and distant land with its own time system, language, and laws. Slowly, through careful observation, I've been able to ascertain much about this alien culture. The inhabitants of Publisher Land are a hardworking group of people with a special affinity for riddles, as evidenced by their little inside joke: Show me your clips.

"Clips" are paper trophies, copies of your past glories, proof that you've been published before. You need these clips; you must have them in order to get clips. No, silly, you can't buy clips. Welcome to Publisher Land.

The laws of the land are simple. If you've been published, you can get published. If you haven't been published you need to get published, so you can be published. Your chances of getting published are much better if you have an agent. Most agents like to represent people who have already been published.

I've determined there are actually only six people running Publisher Land. *Writer's Market 2007* lists at least one-gazillion editors (a gazillion is a little more than a million), but I think most of them are the same person because their letters are suspiciously similar.

All six of these people speak publisher-ese, a second language I've been somewhat successful in learning. For example their letters might say, "We regret to inform you that after carefully reviewing your manuscript we feel it's not right for our present needs." Upon careful translation, this reads, "You haven't been published before and pigs will fly before we take the first chance."

Just as their words have different meanings, the laws of time in Publisher Land are different also. Often a letter from a publishing house will say they hope to have a firm reply concerning your manuscript in four to six weeks. You might think this is a month or two. The people in Publisher Land are laughing at you. They know it means sometime this calendar year, maybe.

It seemed the impossible dream, but I had a secret weapon: a Southern Mama who had taught me to keep on keeping on. Winners never quit and quitters never win, you know? I set my mind to play their game. I read books on writing and books about books about writing, all the while filing rejection slips alphabetically. And when my head got sore from banging it against the walls of Publisher Land, I set those goals aside, briefly, to chart my own course. I opened a website and self-published my first book to see my words in black and white.

Nothing happened overnight, but over time I found an audience willing to read my columns and listen to my television and radio segments without Mama twisting their arms. Those developments led to this book. Me and Publisher Land, together at last, which is just as well. I was very close to pulling out my ace-in-the-hole: Mama the Literary Agent. Laugh. It worked before.

Southern Mamas have your back on all the playing fields of life. My papa has never been much of a sports buff, due largely to the fact that when he was young and other kids his age were playing sports, Papa was working to help support his family. My Southern Mama, however, is a real sports fan, a high school basketball star who passed her love for the game down to her girls. She was front and center when we got old enough to shoot hoops.

Mama's high standards for our conduct were not waived when we put on our basketball uniforms. She wanted us to play the game, and play it well, but we were still expected to act like little ladies. Allow me to confess. For me and my sisters this was, at best, a delicate balance. It's a good thing we had some raising to offset our competitive natures. (Side note: I'm growing quite tired of spell check telling me *raising* is not a word. I know the rule: People raise crops and rear kids. As my Papa would say, "That dog won't hunt.") Now, as I was saying, not everyone has had the benefit of that sort of raising.

Sue me, honey, but this was way obvious at the last Winter

Olympics, the ones in Seoul, Korea, that no one watched but me and the husband. At least that's what the news reports said. Please, allow me to fill y'all in on what happened at the Ice Skating Couples competition.

The first night was awful. If folks weren't stumbling, they were dropping their partners like a bad habit. It was hard to watch, but most of 'em showed real class. That is, everyone but Miss Italy! When her partner dropped her, Miss Italy glared at the poor man right there on the ice in front of the whole world and she kept it up while they waited on their scores at the kiss and cry booth, as if to say, "Well, I'll be a suck-egg mule. I know you didn't drop me, not at the Olympics!"

I don't know what Miss Italy's Mama thought about her child being so ugly in public, but I can tell you that my Southern Mama would've been slip sliding across the ice to adjust somebody's attitude. I have a pretty good visual just thinking about it. "Girl, you best pull that lip in before you trip on it. Dry it up before these judges give you something to cry about! What's wrong with you? You act like the world owes you something!"

The incident reminds me of a basketball game my sisters and I played in years ago. As the clock wound down with us trailing by a bucket, this ten-foot-tall Amazon girl held the ball high above her head while my short sister, Cyndie, jumped and reached for it. The crowd was yelling but all Cyndie heard was Mama, and my big sister was some kind of surprised at what Mama was suggesting! Cyndie glanced Mama's way to make sure she was hearing straight. Well, alright already. Cyndie hauled off and slapped the girl right in the face!

The gym erupted. Cyndie got a technical foul. Mama was mortified. "Cynthia Darlene," she hollered, "what on earth's gotten into you?"

The crowd quieted down to hear my sister's response. This

should be good. Cyndie was shamed but defensive. "You said slap her."

"It!" Mama roared. "I said slap it! I meant the ball!"

Mama promised Cyndie something for later and then she made her apologize to the victim, her team, and all the spectators. I thought about that the second night when Miss Italy took the ice. The girl was all smiles after she and her partner had a successful performance. That was nice, but me and Mama couldn't help thinking everyone there would've rather heard an apology.

To reinforce the importance of doing the right thing, Mama would say, "Your actions speak so loud I can't hear your words!"

Regina Marsh
Daughter of Vernette Hardy
Lizella, Georgia

Once I grew up and had kids of my own, I came to fully understand why Mama had been in the stands every time we girls laced up our tennis shoes. I didn't have to go to every sporting event my children played in. And trust me, between softball, baseball, tennis, track, football, and basketball, there were a lot of events. No, indeed, I *wanted* to be there.

My Southern Mama had taught me by example just how important it was for my son and my daughter to know that there was always someone there rooting for them, someone who would love them whether they got the winning hit, or missed the winning free throw. Those were trying and exhausting days, but I wouldn't trade the memories for all the free time in all the free world.

My mother always told me to "love the person, even though you may not love what they do." Unconditional love is what my parents taught me by their actions and I hope to pass on to my children one day.

Amy Cagle
Ridgeland, Mississippi

Of all the leagues my children played in, I miss T-ball the most. T-ballers are the least-focused athletes you'll ever meet—and the most charming. I've seen first basemen distracted for entire innings by a fuzzy, wuzzy worm, and I've seen potential homers interrupted by a base runner's nature call, a call that was answered by my own dear nephew right then, right there. But I'll never forget one little girl who played by her own law of physics: A ball in motion should stay in motion.

"Get it, Sugar!" her parents would yell as the ball rolled toward her.

"Stop it, Honey," her grandparents would add as it rolled beside her.

"Fall on it!" her desperate coach would plead as it passed her by. Sweet Thing would look at every last one of them as if to say, "When it quits moving, people, and not a moment before."

T-ball turned into Little League and time marched on. I miss it. Some of it. I miss the look on a child's face when he gets a hit, brushes himself off at first base and looks for his parents in the crowd. I don't miss the special torture of pitchers' moms everywhere. To a small boy, the position of pitcher is one of honor. To his mama it's the loneliest mound of dirt on earth. Pitchers' moms get so proficient at lobbying for a larger strike zone that many go on to successful careers in Washington. (Well, they could.) I know you've heard us. I mean them, you've heard them. "What do mean ball four, Ump? That kid could've hit that pitch without taking more than three steps in any direction!" Note to pitchers' moms everywhere: "Swing, batter, batter, swing!" is a call best left to the wee ones on the field.

Mama said, "He couldn't pour pee out of a boot with directions on the heel!"

Debbie Demoss
West Monroe, Louisiana

Someone once told me that at a crucial point during a Little League game, a coach turned and questioned one of his young players. "Do you understand what cooperation is? What a team is?" The little boy nodded yes to both questions.

"Do you understand that what matters is whether we win together as a team?" The little boy nodded yes again.

"So," the coach continued, "when a strike is called, or you're out at first, you don't argue or curse or attack the umpire. Do you understand all that?" Another nod.

"Good," said the coach. "Now go over there and explain it to your mother."

There's a little bit of humor there, and a whole lot of truth.

The Realist

Truth is what a belle comes to expect from her mama. I was on the phone with my own daughter recently when I mentioned I was working on the lagniappe chapter of the Southern Mama book. Her response was immediate. "Well, if you haven't talked about her sometimes brutal honesty, make sure you get it in. I've always known not to ask for your opinion if I wasn't ready to hear the truth, the whole truth, and nothing but the truth, so help me God."

Jessica makes a valid point. Paul Harvey isn't the only one known for telling the rest of the story. Let's say the belle gets a new look, a new man, a new job offer, etc. If she wants someone to blow smoke up her dress, she'll ask anyone but her mama for an opinion. If she wants the truth, she's going to that dependable

> Mama said if he runs around with you, he'll run around on you—and that goes both ways.
>
> Susie Guimbellot
> Winnsboro, Louisiana

source she can always count on to have her best interests at heart: her Southern Mama.

It may be popular to say you can be anything you want to be, but Southern Mamas don't ascribe to that philosophy. They believe you're gonna need some amount of natural talent or inclination or you'll just be spitting in the wind. It's not that Southern Mamas aren't tactful. They may not believe in fueling their daughters' hopeless dreams, but neither do they enjoy crushing 'em. Their skill lies more in redirection.

This is one of the reasons why I don't need Simon Cowell to tell me I don't have a future in the singing business. As a kid, I bemoaned the fact that I couldn't sing and everyone else in my musically gifted family could. "Why?" I'd ask my Southern Mama, who would soothe my hurt feelings by pointing out that I had good hair. Good hair or not, I got the point. Chances were good I wouldn't be singing at the Opry anytime soon.

While Mama can be honest to a fault where it concerns her friends and family, like most of her fellow Southerners, she's been known to tell foreigners what they want to hear, if only to pull their legs a little. And only if she has deemed the situation to be harmless, like the time an honest-to-goodness movie star came to her hometown. Mama was a young girl living with her family on Pine Ridge Road in Natchez, Mississippi, the summer Elizabeth Taylor came to town to shoot a movie called *Raintree County* at a historic antebellum home up the road.

Mama said, "It's okay to know the truth, you just don't always have to tell it."

Chastity Crain
Columbia, Louisiana

Mama remembers peering down the drive and watching the filming with her sisters. She also remembers all the newspaper accounts of Liz's arrival and how intrigued the famous beauty was with the beautiful cypress trees and the graceful moss covering them. But the quote that's still retold around Natchez is what Liz said when she opened her mouth. "Why, look at this lovely moss draping the trees!" she exclaimed. "Did you people do this for me?"

Mama says she can't say for sure what the people assigned to escort Ms. Taylor said, but she and her friends were all thinking the same thing, "Yeah, Sugar, we've been out here for weeks hanging this stuff, just for you..."

When Chains Become Bonds

My daughter tells me that I have inherited Mama's knack of redirection, also known as the skill of delivering tough opinions with soft edges. There was a time when I wouldn't have liked hearing that. Like so many of my friends, during my teenage years I swore to myself that I was nothing at all like my mother and, what's more, I never would be.

Everyone has the right to be wrong. Since those days, time has worked its special charms. To paraphrase a famous quote: I have met my mother, and she is me.

Several summers ago, my sister Cyndie and I witnessed a moment not unlike the passing of the torch. The extended family was grouped up at my house celebrating the Fourth of July. This particular evening, my daughter and her cousin Hillary were on sink duty in the kitchen. As Cyndie and I carried yet another round of dirty dishes in from the dining room, we overheard our daughters discussing the latest developments in their lives. High on their list of shared woes was the realization that they could see themselves turning into us with each passing day. Hallelujah! Pay it forward, here we go again.

There are a lot of things I do for no other reason than because Mama did it that way before me. Some of these traditions are meaningful, others more trivial, but when I see them repeated in my daughter's life I realize that however insignificant, these traditions tie me to the future and to the past. And where they once seemed like chains, they've now become precious bonds.

Whenever I was leaving the house, Mama would always say, "Remember whose daughter you are."

Marylyn Mitchum Bruins
Raised "out on the mountain" in
Genery's Gap, Alabama

I once heard a story about a young girl who was about to get married. In preparation for running her own house, she was paying special attention to her mother's daily responsibilities.

"Mom," she asked, as they prepared supper together, "why do you cut the ends off of the ham before you cook it?"

Her mom was stumped. "Well, that's just how my mom did it. You can call her if you really want to know."

The young bride-to-be called her grandmother and repeated the question, getting the same answer. By now, her curiosity was getting the best of her so she called her great-grandmother. The young girl talked a minute and then repeated her question. "Mama and Granny both cut the ends off of their hams before they cook them, but they don't know why. They say it's because you did it that way. I was just wondering. Do you mind telling me why you do that?"

A smile tugged at the corners of the older lady's mouth, "Of course not, dear," she said. "It's because my pot's not big enough."

While we may question some of our mamas handed-down traditions—its human nature after all—the Southern belle is much more likely to value her roots even as she tries her wings.

Honestly, we don't mean to imply that our customs are better. We simply value their uniqueness.

Mama said, "If you don't have anything nice to say, don't say anything at all!"

Brenda Bahn-Moore
Bentonville, Arkansas

I once made that distinction for a visitor who dropped by my cyber porch with a bur under her saddle. Curious in Connecticut demanded to know why we Southerners go on and on about being Southern. It's a fair question when it's not thrown down like a gauntlet opening a duel, and while many much more talented Southern writers than I have put pen to this one, I'd be honored to take another stab at it.

To be frank, we go on about our manners because we have some. Most every time someone drops by brewing for a fight, trying to convince me how happy they are not to be from the South because of our "backward-redneck-mama-obsessed-hillbilly" ways they reveal an embarrassing lack of etiquette. You'd be hard-pressed to find a Southern child who has reached the age of accountability without being removed from the room and disciplined for making insensitive comments to the host. Once returned, said child will either discover a new fondness for whatever is being served or he might realize he isn't hungry—but he will never again abuse the gracious hospitality of the host or hostess in their own home.

My mother taught me from two books, the Bible and Emily Post. I remember her saying, "When you are dining in someone's home, don't ever say that you don't like something. Smile and eat it anyway." She also taught me not to take the last piece of food from the serving platter. She'd tell me to leave it for "Mr. Manners."

Peggy Mitchell Huggins
Daughter of Lorraine Lewis Mitchell
Mechanicsville, South Carolina

As for our food, for the life of me I don't see how anyone could blame us for going on there! With special thanks to the Good Lord, the land, and the skills of our aforementioned mamas, the list of mouthwatering Southern dishes is endless. 'Nuff said.

Let's see... We go on about our language because we're proud of taking the necessity of communication and dressing it up 'til it doubles for entertainment. We go on about our family trees because we know we're a composite of every branch. We study their faces and their stories and try to hold on to what is best and improve on what is not.

After considerable thought it seems obvious to me that we go on and on about such things because we see in our lives something worth celebrating. It's my hope, dear reader, that my simple words will inspire you to find and treasure the similar beauty in your own life, regardless of where you call home.

Lagniappe Recipes, A Little Something Extra

Our Southern Mamas have filled our lives with important values and silly little lagniappe, all woven into the fabric of our lives so subtly that it takes a discerning eye and a determined focus to bring them to light. Like a sentimental add-a-pearl necklace, each gem symbolizing an important event or a milestone, these mother-daughter jewels all have a unique value. It is up to each of us, the daughters of the South, to take the time to thread them into beautiful heirlooms worthy of bequeathing to the next generation. Here are a few extra little recipes from my kitchen to yours.

~ Extra-Special Spice Tea ~

SERVES 60–70

Mama taught me to always have something to offer to guests in my home. I enjoy keeping this tea on hand during the winter months for those who don't drink coffee. There are special teas in the grocery store, but this recipe is easy to mix up at just a fraction of the cost. It's nice sitting in a pretty glass jar on your counter and it makes a great gift for a friend.

½ cup instant tea
2 cups Tang
1 teaspoon cloves
2½ cups sugar
2 envelops of unsweetened lemonade mix
2 teaspoons ground cinnamon

Combine all ingredients in a large freezer bag. Shake it together well and store it in a tightly closed container to keep the spices fresh. When you're ready to share a cup with a friend add 2 heaping teaspoons to a cup of boiling water and enjoy.

~ Homemade Caramel Corn ~

SERVES 10–15

Once a year, a magical thing happens in the South. We call it football season. My homemade caramel corn is just right for taking to that tailgating party or after-game get-together.

- 16 cups freshly popped corn (you can use a hot air popper or microwave popcorn)
- 2 cups dry roasted nuts, or your favorite roasted nut
- ⅔ cup butter
- ⅔ cup dark corn syrup
- 1¼ cups sugar
- 1½ teaspoons vanilla

Prehead oven to 250 degrees. Pour popcorn in a 9 × 13-inch metal pan, toss with two cups of your favorite roasted nuts, and set aside.

In a medium-size saucepan combine butter, syrup, sugar, and vanilla and bring to a boil over a medium heat until it reaches 260 degrees on a candy thermometer. Pour over popcorn and nuts and slide the whole pan in a 250 degree oven for about an hour. Stir occasionally to keep from sticking. Let cool, break apart, and store in an airtight container. Good luck to your home team (unless they're playing mine).

~ Grandma Stone's Potato Candy ~

SERVES 40–50

This recipe has been in my family since the days when store-bought candy was a rare treat and sweets were made with staples. My grandma Stone always served her potato candy at Christmastime. Several years ago, I hunted this recipe down from one of my cousins, Jeffrey. There were treats to spare around our house during the holidays, but something was missing. I found it when I added Grandma Stone's Potato Candy to the offerings.

1 small white potato, peeled
1 teaspoon vanilla flavoring
1½ boxes of sifted powdered sugar (confectioners)
1 16-ounce jar of peanut butter

Boil a small white potato (about the size of a large egg) until it is about to turn into mush and a fork will easily go through it and back out. Drain and put in a large bowl. Add vanilla and continue to mash with fork until it looks like a thick liquid. Begin to add powdered sugar a small amount at a time, stirring into the potato mix. You'll be surprised to see that you'll use a box or more of sugar before it reaches the desired "confection-like" consistency. Dust your work area with more powdered sugar and roll this lump of claylike dough out into a thin sheet. Trim edges to a rectangular shape and spread peanut butter over the entire area. Taking your time, gently roll the peanut butter–covered dough into a "log." Wrap with Reynolds wrap and chill in freezer for about two hours before moving it to the fridge.

To serve, cut into thin slices. They'll look like a pretty white confection with a swirl of peanut butter. This is very sweet, so the thinner the slices are the better it'll be. It's best served with strong cappuccino or coffee.

~ Christmas Snacking Crackers ~

SERVES 25–30

Move back, Houdini. This recipe takes regular old saltine crackers and transforms 'em into delicious snacking crackers. They're great to have on hand for the holidays. Making 'em is simple; keeping 'em hid from the family long enough to soak up the seasonings is where the real challenge lies. But you'll find that out soon enough. Right now, let's get cookin'!

2 cups canola oil
1 package ranch dressing mix
1 tablespoon red pepper
1 tablespoon garlic powder
1 large box of saltine crackers (with four sleeves)

Put canola oil into a small mixing bowl. Add in ranch dressing mix, pepper, and garlic powder. Stir together well and pour over a whole carton of regular saltine crackers that you've placed in a good-size plastic bowl. With your hands or a large spoon, turn the crackers several times to help make sure that the coating reaches them all. Cover the bowl with a snug lid because you'll need to turn it occasionally while the crackers are absorbing the seasoned oil. This also works well with a plastic bag, just be careful not to break the crackers. It takes about a day to a day and a half for the complete absorption of the liquid. When they begin to look "dried" out, they're ready.

~ Bodacious Bayou Olive Spread ~

SERVES 10–12

This recipe gets a head start with pecans and cream cheese. How can it go wrong? Spread it on hot French bread and serve it with your meal, or enjoy it as a topping on your favorite party cracker. Either way, it's an extra little touch that pays off with big flavor.

1 8-ounce cream cheese, softened
1 4.5-ounce can chopped black olives
1 teaspoon Worcestershire sauce
dash of seasoned salt (I use a Cajun seasoning)
½ teaspoon lemon juice
½ cup pecans, finely chopped (optional)
dash of All Things Southern hot sauce

Combine cream cheese with black olives. Stir in Worcestershire sauce, seasoned salt, and lemon juice. Add finely chopped pecans, and the hot sauce. When you're ready to serve, split open a loaf of French bread, top it with Bodacious Bayou Olive Spread, and toast it lightly under the broiler for 10 to 15 minutes.

Mama's been gone for a few years now but I still miss her so much. She was more than my mom, she was my best friend. We liked the same things: flower gardening, sewing, cooking, and collecting antiques. We shared everything. I'm not sorry for one minute of it. Even though she's not here, the things we shared keep me going. Here's a little ditty my mama sang to me every morning when I was a little girl. Later, I sang it to my daughter. How wonderful to wake up to a song sung just for you!

"Good morning, Mary Sunshine,
How did you wake so soon?
You frightened all the stars away,
And chased away the moon!"

Susan Fairchild
Transylvania, Louisiana